PARDON MY
HEARSE

A **COLORFUL** PORTRAIT OF
WHERE THE **FUNERAL** AND
ENTERTAINMENT INDUSTRIES
MET IN **HOLLYWOOD**

PARDON MY HEARSE

A *COLORFUL* PORTRAIT OF WHERE THE *FUNERAL* AND *ENTERTAINMENT* INDUSTRIES MET IN *HOLLYWOOD*

ALLAN ABBOTT & **GREG ABBOTT**

CRAVEN STREET BOOKS

Fresno, California

In memory of Kathy, the love of my life.
My deepest appreciation to Greg, whose expertise and countless hours of
dedication made this book possible.

Marilyn Monroe back cover image by Macfadden Publications.
All images copyright by the authors unless otherwise noted.

Published by Craven Street Books
An imprint of Linden Publishing
2006 South Mary Street, Fresno, California 93721
(559) 233-6633 / (800) 345-4447
CravenStreetBooks.com

Craven Street Books and Colophon are trademarks of
Linden Publishing, Inc.

ISBN 978-1-61035-248-2

135798642

Printed in the United States of America
on acid-free paper.

Library of Congress Cataloging-in-Publication Data on file.

Contents

Foreword

Enter the mysterious world few have known in this candid, true story of two young men's lives in the funeral industry. Beginning in their late teens, Allan Abbott and Ronald Hast formed a lifelong friendship and business partnership as they hurtled through unusual challenges in an unlikely venture—the funeral and limousine business. You will be captivated by their inspiring, humorous, intriguing, graphic, and occasionally irreverent stories, spanning forty years of business in the Los Angeles area. These two young entrepreneurs took on the arduous challenge of breaking the monopoly held by three licensed limousine providers in Los Angeles, which opened the door for the numerous limousine services currently operating there today.

This book documents tragic and surreal disasters, including earthquakes, riots, and airline catastrophes. The book also demonstrates the vast differences between varied segments of our society in religious rites, the correlation of these practices and traditions, and how diverse cultures care for their dead.

Abbott personally transported some of Hollywood's brightest stars, like Elizabeth Taylor, Richard Burton, Sophia Loren, Connie Stevens (and her actor husband James Stacy), Robert Taylor, and Robert Vaughn. The book includes fascinating stories about overheard conversations, including one concerning actress Inger Stevens's secret interracial marriage, which ended with that beautiful and talented Hollywood star's tragic suicide.

Abbott & Hast Company provided funeral cars and overland transportation of human remains throughout California, Nevada, Oregon, and Arizona. The company provided support to over 100 funeral establishments in Southern California, where it assisted in conducting services for dozens of celebrities, including Marilyn Monroe, Natalie Wood, Clark Gable, Gary Cooper, Ernie Kovacs, Jeffrey Hunter, Jack Benny, Jack Warner, Jimmy Durante, Mario Lanza, Karen Carpenter, Fernando Lamas, film director John Farrow, Los Angeles Chief of Police William H.

Parker, and the wife of former CIA director John McCone. Allan has been interviewed by magazines in Germany, Japan, and England, and has done on-camera interviews spread over the last forty-plus years regarding his participation in every aspect of Marilyn Monroe's funeral.

The book will also take you behind the scenes to learn intimate details surrounding macabre newspaper headlines, such as two friends whose deaths became cold-case homicides that would take years to solve. It also delves into the strange circumstances surrounding the death one of America's wealthiest and most well known businessmen, Howard Hughes. This uniquely vivid portrait of the mysterious funeral industry proves that in life as well as in death, truth is indeed stranger than fiction.

—Karen Reider, former editor of *Four Corners Magazine*

1

Humble Beginnings

My mother's plans to spend the holiday at home got bombed by my own sneak attack, four years before the bombs dropped on Pearl Harbor. Her anticipated delivery date of December 7, 1937, had come and gone with nary a peep out of me until the 28th of the month, in a beautiful downtown Burbank maternity hospital. This procrastination on my part saved me from having to celebrate my birthday each year on the anniversary of December 7, 1941—"A date which will live in infamy."

My parents, brother, and I lived humbly in a middle-class Los Angeles neighborhood. When World War II started I was only 2, but as it progressed I couldn't help but hear about it continually and experience its effects on the population. The sights and sounds of the war were everywhere. For a young boy, it was an exciting time.

We practiced for blackouts by going into our windowless hallway with our gas masks and closing all the doors. We could see barrage balloons in the skies from our backyard, and almost any night you could go outside and see searchlights combing the sky. There was great speculation that LA may be a strategic target because of its many industries supplying war-related materials, including a great deal of aircraft manufacturing.

We would witness numerous types of aircraft in the sky. There would often be groups of single-engine fighter planes heading east that made an unforgettable sound. The P-38s, with their double hulls, were one of the first twin-engine fighters seen in the skies over LA. These aircraft carved out their own place in history when a small squadron of them intercepted and destroyed Admiral Isoroku Yamamoto's aircraft during an inspection tour in the Solomon Islands.

The most surprising thing we ever saw in the sky was the Lockheed prototype of the famous flying wing propeller-driven aircraft, which was never produced in quantity because it needed a jet engine and jet technology was still in its infancy. However, it did serve as the inspiration for the B-2 stealth bomber five decades later.

Every kid in the neighborhood spent a great deal of time on scrap drives collecting prodigious amounts of anything made of metal, cotton, and newspapers. My dad even turned bacon grease in to the butcher each week because it was used in the production of explosives. Meanwhile, he used ration stamps for difficult-to-acquire items like sugar, meat, and coffee. Many things, such as leather goods or anything made of rubber, were in short supply or completely unavailable. Even some new expressions were born, like "kicking the tires" when you were about to purchase a used car, because all of the natural rubber went toward the war effort. Tires and other rubber products were produced using synthetics of substandard quality. You were lucky if your new shoes lasted two months.

My father had received $2,000 mustering-out pay when he returned at the end of World War I, which he used to buy the house in which I grew up. When the *Los Angeles Times* ran a photo during my elementary school years, in commemoration of the Great War's end, my father submitted an image of himself. As he sat in his easy chair, with my brother and me on either side, he pointed his pipe to a famous *Times* front page headlined with the armistice signing. He won the contest.

Allan (left) with his father and brother in a 1942 contest-winning photo that commemorated the end of World War I.

Allan (left) and his brother John in a backyard foxhole, with machine guns handmade by their father.

Every Saturday we would walk to one of the movie theaters in our neighborhood. There were two films, a cartoon, and the Movietone News, which kept you up on the progress of the war effort. All this excitement cost us ten cents each. There were constant reminders of the war through newspaper cartoons and numerous patriotic songs. My recollections were mostly of songs like "It's a Long Way to Tipperary [Ireland]" and "Over There." Those patriotic and occasionally sentimental songs still take me back to that time, especially songs by French singer Edith Piaf, who engendered a real sense of that tragic, heroic era with her lilting voice.

My only negative recollection of the time was the indignity of having to eat Spam. It was supposed to be similar to ham, but in my opinion it tasted terrible. It attained a sort of mythical status because of the manufacturer's secrecy in divulging precisely what meat was used in it. Some critics even went so far as to imply that Spam was an acronym for "something posing as meat."

At age 11 I became the youngest boy ever to work for the *Los Angeles Examiner*, delivering newspapers at 5:30 each morning. Their policy was to never hire a paperboy under the age of 13, but my brother John had been working there for a number of months and he went to bat for me, explaining that anything he could do, I could do as well.

Our best friend, Jerry McMillan, lived across the street from us. He told us about a fellow student at Audubon Junior High named Hampton

Fancher, who had built an elaborate house of horrors in his backyard. We went to see it and it was even better than Jerry had described. There was a small cemetery with headstones behind the structure. When one of the headstones was tilted forward, it revealed a small tunnel that came up to a room in the haunted house. Hamp was a remarkable artist. In later years I always wondered what he was doing, so I was not surprised when the credits for the movie *Blade Runner* revealed that he had written the screenplay and been an executive producer of the film.

When I was 16, my dad took me to buy my first car, which was a metallic purple 1941 Ford Coupe with a hopped-up engine. It cost me $320, which was most of my paper route savings. With my new mobility came the freedom and desire to explore. After trips to San Diego and then Santa Barbara, I continued north, up coastal Highway 1. I saw a California Highway Patrol car parked on the roadside so I asked him about a place to stay. He directed me to turn left just ahead, to a town called Carmel, which was unfamiliar to me. The area made a significant impression on me. Instead of leaving the next morning, I spent two more days to see much of the Monterey Peninsula. When I returned home I told my mom that someday I was going to live there. She brushed it off with wave of her hand, saying, "Yeah, sure."

In my second year at Dorsey High School I met a fellow student, Ron Hast, and we became good friends. We both had the same teacher, Geraldine Howard, but we didn't attend her class together, so our meetings were chance at best. Her classes were in a bungalow, where she would let students come in and eat their lunch. Some of us would play chess, but Ron didn't play, so he would just sit and have conversations with Mrs. Howard. If the chessboard was already in use, I would sit and chat with them. Neither of us could have ever predicted that we would soon start a business together that would last over forty-five years, and that Mrs. Howard would be our bookkeeper for the first four of those years.

The following year Ron and I took as many classes as we could together and did our homework after school at his house. His parents were pleased that he raised his grade point average that year, but on almost every other level they didn't approve of me. My hair was too long, touching my collar, and my jacket was black leather. By their reactions, you would have thought it said "Hells Angels" on the back.

We would often talk about starting some kind of business together. After discussing some possible ventures, we finally decided on one. Some of the stores in Hollywood were selling property deeds to one square inch on the moon. This seemed ridiculous, since there was no basis for such ownership, but it did give us an idea.

We enjoyed spending time in Hollywood and discussed the possibility of creating a deed for one square inch of the Hollywood Hills. We felt that this deed should represent part of an actual piece of real estate, so we made a trip downtown to the Hall of Records. After sifting through many tax records, we found a vacant lot just off of famous Laurel Canyon where the street hadn't been paved yet. The owner of the lot was willing to sell us his property because he had purchased a number of lots in a row hoping the city would eventually pave the street, making them much more valuable. The man found out that the city was not going to pave the street, so we were able to purchase the small lot for $200.

The next order of business was to take out a DBA (doing business as) for a venture we called Hollywood Investment Company. We found an attorney named Louis Sackin, who had an office in Hollywood. He didn't quite know what to make of us on our first visit, but after we explained the purchase of the property and showed him our concept for the deed I had designed, he agreed to represent us and formalize the necessary paperwork. When we inquired about his fee, he told us that it would be pro bono because he felt that we had shown a modicum of ingenuity to start this venture on our own, while still in school.

After that, we needed to get the deed printed and do our marketing. We paid a fellow student to take pictures of points of interest in Hollywood, which included the Brown Derby restaurant, Grauman's Chinese Theatre, where a Marilyn Monroe movie happened to be showing, and the newly constructed Capitol Records Building. The faux deed included the photos, along with a map of the property's location and other information. The next task was to market the deeds, which we were totally unqualified for. We went from store to store down Hollywood Boulevard without making a single sale, so the deeds ended up in a closet as our focus returned to school.

Since I had graduated half a year ahead of Ron, I decided to work for six months so we could both start college at the same time. After Ron graduated we decided to take advantage of the break and go on a long trip before starting college. We headed north up the coast of California by Greyhound Bus until we reached Seattle, Washington. Since we could get off the bus anytime, even if it was not a designated stop, we took full advantage of this option and often found ourselves standing on Highway 1 flagging down another Greyhound the following morning.

From Seattle, we boarded a ferry to Victoria, British Columbia, then on to Vancouver. The Canadians operated a train that went from Vancouver to the Great Lakes, and we got on and off the train at different towns. On the way back we left the train and decided to hitchhike into Yellowstone National Park. Our last stop was Las Vegas, and in those days the casinos on the strip were about a half a mile apart with nothing in between.

The real significance of the trip was that for over a month we were together twenty-four hours a day. Many times we didn't agree about where to stop or what to see, which demonstrated that even when we had different interests, we could compromise and still get along well. At summer's end I started my first semester at El Camino College majoring in geology. Science was my favorite subject, with some of the influence coming from my uncle Lyle, who had been the science editor for the *Los Angeles Examiner* for almost twenty years. Lyle was my father's older brother, and he had interviewed some of the world's top scientists, including Albert Einstein and J. Robert Oppenheimer.

Lyle had one of the largest privately owned telescopes in the country at his Silver Lake home, and I loved to go to his house and look into the heavens. When the decision was made to construct the world's largest telescope on Mount Palomar near San Diego, Lyle was chosen to be on the panel of scientists who coordinated the effort. He told me that when they poured the first casting for the telescope's lens, the molten glass was so hot it melted the iron bolts that were to be used to mount it, so they tried again with carbon steel bolts. The 200-inch lens made Palomar the largest telescope in the world for decades. Someone standing in front of the lens would only come up to a little over a third of its height. Today, the lens is hooked up to the largest digital camera ever built, which is capable of tracking a star more than 10 billion light-years away.

I didn't know a great deal about my uncle until he died and the *Examiner* printed a half-page memorial about him. Along with being noted for his work at Palomar, he was credited for coining the word "motorcade," a term he used while writing an article about a visit to California by the president.

2

Our First Hearse

My first semester studying geology proved to be extremely interesting, and all my spare time was consumed with prospecting for rocks and fossils. Ron would always accompany me, and the first few times we ended up in remote areas, which made it necessary for us to sleep in the car. One weekend, we were driving through Culver City and spotted something interesting. It was an old hearse with a For Sale sign. We reasoned that we could stretch out in comfort with a car like that, so we stopped to check it out.

It was a big, black, morbid-looking 1941 Packard hearse, consigned to a hearse salesman named Bob Blake by Gutierrez and Weber Mortuary in downtown Los Angeles. Bob told us that the owner was asking $200 for it, which was well beyond our means, so he offered to call Mrs. Gutierrez and see if she would consider reducing the price.

We sat there as he made the call, and he explained to her that in the six months he had stored and tried to sell the hearse, we two young college

Ron, John, and Allan in 1957, in front of their first hearse used for funerals, a 1948 Packard.

kids were the only ones to show any interest. Mrs. Gutierrez argued that she had recently spent $40 just for the license fee. Irritated that she was being stubborn, he finally told her that she should send someone over and get the car out of his lot. She finally gave in, and we purchased it for just the $40 that the license had cost her. Had we not spotted it, we would have never purchased such a unique and seemingly single-purpose vehicle. Without knowing it, Mrs. Gutierrez had done us all an enormous favor, because that move would launch our careers and allow us to be of service to her and her son Rick for many years.

We weren't sure what our parents would think about our "black elephant." Not only did my parents think it was quite novel, they said we could park it in front of our house. We learned that this was called a three-way-side-loader hearse, as opposed to the end-loaders being used in most of the other states.

Unlike my parents, Ron's parents had a big problem with the hearse. They made him park it a block away from their house and the tension between them grew each day. When I stopped at Ron's house one afternoon, he came running out and said that he and his parents were involved in their worst argument ever. As we sat in the car he told me that they had given him an ultimatum, which was to disassociate from me and get rid of the hearse or else move out of their house. My parents were aware of his family situation, so I suggested the latter option, knowing full well that they would agree to let him come live with us. He went back into the house to get some clothing and then left with me, never to reside there again.

We began using our camping car on a regular basis and it worked perfectly, with a mattress fitting right between the wheel wells. We also put a chest in it for food storage and cooking gear. So does that mean, since Al Gore claimed to have created the Internet, that we had just created the first motor home? I guess not, since most people wouldn't want to be caught dead in a car like that. Even for us, it took awhile to get used to seeing people make the sign of the cross or remove their hats as we drove by.

Back at school, my geology professor announced that any interested students could participate in a field trip to an area known for abundant trilobites, which have been described as one of the oldest-known extinct creatures to ever inhabit the earth. As we gathered on the campus parking lot, we suggested that it might be a good idea for us to lead the motorcade with our hearse, because there were about twelve cars full of students and our destination was over 100 miles away. The students who didn't have a car would pair up with someone who did and help pay for the gasoline, but for some reason only one male student offered to go with us in the hearse. To further enhance our little procession, we suggested that all the drivers turn their headlights on, and like magic, other cars on the highway couldn't get out of our way fast enough.

My teacher also told me about a place that sounded particularly interesting. It was a town that had an extinct volcano featuring a breach cinder cone, meaning one side of it had a large V-shaped opening. A few years earlier, some of the local kids had dragged a number of old tires into the breach and set them ablaze. Everyone in the small desert town panicked because the smoke made them think the volcano had come back to life and was about to erupt. The townsfolk didn't appreciate the students' brand of humor, including that of one wit who remarked that if it had been a real eruption, it would just be the mountain getting its rocks off.

During our next school break we drove to Death Valley, a rather apropos place for our vehicle. This was the first time we used my portable black light. After dark we set out to try to locate some fluorescent rocks. When I saw the first object that fluoresced, rather than picking it up, I had Ron run to the hearse for a flashlight. My geology professor had told me something that caused me to hesitate. He said that some snakes and scorpions also fluoresce. Sure enough, it was a scorpion with its stinger up and ready.

The place that fascinated me most in Death Valley was an area called the Devil's Golf Course in Badwater, the lowest point in North America at almost 300 feet below sea level. We walked toward an area with salt pools and jagged salt spires coming up from the ground.

From my studies in geology, it occurred to me that these ultra-briny salt pools should have salt crystals growing just under the edge of the pools. These crystals took the shape of hundreds of perfect little cubes of transparent salt, all stuck to one another. Ron held my ankles as I dangled over the edge and put my entire arm in the water, up to my shoulder, to pry some loose with a tire iron. A local rock shop owner said that they were the nicest sample of halite crystals that he had ever seen since most crystals are opaque, but these were clear and transparent. The sale of some of these exceptional crystals paid for our entire trip.

Ron was happy to let me do most of the driving. Since our return trip was going to be about a seven-hour drive, he got into the back of the hearse and went to sleep. At one point, my devilish side kicked in, because this was a perfect opportunity to pull a devious stunt on him and liven up the boring trip home. We were on a desolate stretch of highway, so I slid across into the passenger's seat carefully, while keeping my left foot on the gas pedal. Then, to keep the car driving straight, it was just a matter of resting my arm on the center console and using my thumb and finger at the very bottom of the steering wheel. Because of the darkened interior, I knew he would not be able to see my grip on the steering wheel. When I began yelling his name, he woke up and looked forward to see that we were traveling down the highway with no one in the driver's seat. He let out a scream but soon realized what was going on because I was laughing so hard. After that, he decided to do the driving the rest of the way home.

After just a few months, the car's muffler needed to be replaced. Many people, including the muffler shop's owner, were curious why two kids would be driving around in an old hearse. We explained our camping car concept, and he became very interested. He asked if we would be willing to sell it, so we discussed it and came up with a price of $400. Amazingly, he went for it. With our nice profit in hand, we went to the central servicing garage at Pierce Brothers Mortuary, which was the largest chain operator in Los Angeles. The downtown branch operated a service facility storing a fleet of about thirty funeral cars. They had just bought two new hearses to replace their two oldest ones, so with the $400 we purchased both of them. Now we each had our own personal hearse so we could go places independently of each other.

3

Our Career Begins

My mom and dad welcomed Ron into our family, but we needed to find a place for him to sleep. My parents had some extra furniture in the backyard shed left over from our move from Los Angeles to Inglewood, and one of the things my dad didn't want anymore was a butcher's block table. We drove to a used-furniture store and tried to sell or trade it for a rollaway bed. The salesman followed us out to the hearse parked in front of the store. When we opened the large side doors, he looked at the butcher's table and said, "Exactly what kind of business are you guys in?" The trade worked out great, because Ron would roll the bed into my room each night and back out to the shed the next morning.

When school let out, we needed to get some type of employment. Ron had worked the previous summer for a florist delivering flowers to funeral homes so he came up with an idea. We could use our hearses to deliver flowers from mortuaries to cemeteries, even though he admitted that when he had to place flowers next to the casket, his legs would start to shake.

Our first stop was at McGlynn's Mortuary in Inglewood where the manager, Bob Johnson, was very receptive to the idea. He told us that most of the local funeral homes were using Johnson's Transfer if they had to hire someone to deliver flowers. Johnson's Transfer was a furniture moving company that used large canvas-covered trucks. They charged $12 and their employees wore coveralls, so we agreed to charge $7.50 and dress appropriately.

We called our new venture Abbott & Hast Mortuary Accommodation Company and had business cards printed up. That was a real mouthful, so we later shortened it to just Abbott & Hast Company. Within a few months we had talked to almost every mortuary owner in greater Los Angeles, and were getting so many calls that we had to buy a third hearse and talk my father and brother into driving for us on busy days.

We were conducting all of this business from my parents' home. Soon, our neighbors were leaving nasty notes on our cars, asking us not to park near their houses. So many complaints came in that the police department started leaving notices on our hearses, warning us that it was illegal to leave a vehicle on the streets for over two days without moving it. We started putting 3" x 5" cards in the windows of each hearse stating the day and time they were moved. As a result of neighbors' continuing complaints, the Inglewood City Council passed a local ordinance that no car could be left on the street overnight. The newspaper printed an article that was headlined, "Inglewood Passes Law to Get Hearses off the Streets." Of course, they never enforced the law except in our case.

The next giant leap came when McGlynn's called to ask if we would be interested in picking up a body in Sacramento. We readily agreed but didn't have the slightest idea what to charge. The manager at the mortuary, Bob Johnson, was apparently talking to us in the presence of the mortuary owner. When we were hesitant to quote a price, he said, "Ninety-five dollars? That sounds very reasonable."

Now we were faced with another predicament because we didn't have any stretchers. There were some old ambulance cots in a storage room of the hearse lot, so we called Bob Blake and asked if they might be for sale. He stated that they were very old and dirty, but if we wanted one we could take our pick for $20. We polished it with steel wool and made a trip to the dime store to buy the largest fat man's belts they sold, because the cot straps on it were stained and worn. That same afternoon, we took it into our living room and practiced picking my mother up off the floor and placing her on the cot.

As we took off the next morning, we marveled at how great it felt to be earning that much money just driving. Sacramento was about 450 miles away, but in those days gasoline was only 19¢ a gallon, so we figured we would net about $75. There was never any thought about the eighteen hours we would be on the road. As we drove we discussed how we would react when actually confronted with a deceased person to pick up, so we were a little apprehensive.

Everything went well at the mortuary, so we headed back to Los Angeles. I had driven all the way up and part of the way back, so just before dawn I woke Ron and told him that he needed to take over so I could get some sleep. I didn't realize it at the time, but this was the beginning of many years of burning the midnight oil. The hearse had a divider just behind the front bench seat that pretty much isolated us from the rear compartment. We specifically chose our only end-loading hearse for this job because we really didn't want to be in an open-interior hearse with the deceased. The divider was solid except for a window through which you could see out with the rearview mirror.

Ron immediately started watching his rear view mirror very intently, but not to check traffic. He wanted to keep an eye on the dead guy in the back. Soon he had gained a reasonable amount of assurance that the body wasn't going anywhere. In fact, he had gotten relaxed enough to start steering the car with only his wrist at the top of the steering wheel. All of a sudden the hearse started to swerve and Ron was screaming, "Allan, Allan." He quickly pulled over to the shoulder and stopped the car. Needless to say, it was pretty scary being woken up like that. Ron was breathing fast and holding his hand over his heart, and for a few moments it seemed like he might be having a heart attack. He finally calmed down enough to blurt out what had happened.

As the morning sunlight slowly started coming through the windshield, the reflection of his own hand appeared on the glass divider behind his head. When he glanced in the rearview mirror, he thought the guy on the cot was trying to slide the divider glass open to get him. His story was so funny that it was impossible for me not to bust out laughing. Now the time had come for us to decide if we were really prepared to be in such a predictably disquieting line of work, and we needed to know if we were mentally resolved to deal with what was sure to come.

The common term for picking up human remains is "making a removal," but in the jargon used by mortuary personnel it was "making a first call." Usually, the first contact with a family member comes when the mortuary is notified by phone that a death has occurred. Some mortuaries preferred using a vehicle that wasn't easily identified, especially on house calls. In fairly short order, we became aware that there were mortuary vehicles that appeared to be nothing more than a limousine.

Before the mid-'50s, many American cars had standard front doors, but the rear doors opened in the opposite direction. The only thing separating the front and rear doors was a five-inch post from the roof to the rocker panel below. Some companies in the East were modifying early Cadillac limousines that had this door configuration. They would cut this post at top and bottom and attach it to the rear door, so when both doors were opened, it would give unobstructed access for a stretcher to be placed inside.

Groman Mortuary in Los Angeles had a modified 1949 Cadillac limousine first-call car for sale, so we went to see it. We met the embalmer, Tony Martini, who showed us the car. Inside were two bucket seats on the driver's side and a void on the right side for the cot. Tony suggested that we follow him into the embalming room, where he would relate more details about the car.

The public rarely has any reason to enter an embalming room, and the law in California requires that the door to the "prep room," as it is called, must have a warning sign stating this restriction. I'm sure it never occurred to Tony that we had never been in a prep room before. After all, we were there to see about buying a first-call car. He proceeded to unwrap a sheet containing the body of an elderly woman they had picked up at a local hospital. They had performed what is known as a "full post." Post stands for postmortem, and this type of autopsy is referred to as a full post because it includes opening not only the chest cavity, but the skull as well.

By this time, we had picked up only one body, and it had been in a body bag. Now this was the real deal and a journey into uncharted territory, because we still weren't sure that this was something that we wanted to pursue to the next level. As we watched, Tony proceeded to cut the sutures from the head and pull the scalp back over the face in order to remove the skullcap, or calvarium, which had been cut with a Stryker vibrating bone-saw. The brain had been removed and we found ourselves standing there, peering into an empty brain cavity.

In cases where an autopsy has been performed and the vascular loop has been interrupted in many places by the post, it becomes necessary to inject embalming fluid at different points, a procedure called six-point

John and Allan in front of a 1948 Cadillac Limousine first-call car used for picking up bodies.

injection. Not really knowing what to expect, we just remained standing at the head end of the table, showing no sign of anxiety about what was unfolding in front of us.

Suddenly a gush of embalming fluid squirted from the brain cavity, catching us totally by surprise as we jumped back to avoid getting our faces full of formaldehyde. It happened so fast that we didn't really have time to think about the bizarre circumstances. Somehow, we were still able to maintain our composure, but inside we were probably both thinking, "Please pass the barf bag." We tried to act like this was just another typical embalming, which may have been the case for Tony, but was memorable for us because we had just seen our first "no-brainer."

As we drove home after witnessing this unsettling event, we hardly talked until we got off the freeway. Unexpectedly, Ron pulled into an ice cream parlor and suggested we each get a banana split with all the trimmings. After what we had just experienced, he wanted to see if we had the fortitude to keep them down.

At this point in our careers, we were flying by the seats of our pants. We had no formal training and we would experience situations that left us with more questions than answers. Quite often on house calls, a family member would ask us to pronounce the person dead, realizing that they might just be in a moribund state. There was no one we could turn to, so we just learned by trial and error. If the body was lying with its mouth or eyes open and cold to the touch, we would assure the family that their loved one was in fact dead. It was not as if we had any medical training, and we certainly didn't have stethoscopes hanging from our necks.

One of our first embarrassing incidents occurred when we were given a removal order from one of Los Angeles' many infirmaries, where we had already made some first calls. The nurse walked with us to the room where a female patient had died; then she simply pointed toward the open door and left. The dead woman must have been about 90, because she couldn't have weighed over eighty pounds. We pulled the sheet off her. Ron grabbed her feet while I grabbed her by the shoulders, with my fingers firmly under her arms. Just as we started to lift her up, her eyes popped open and she let out a muffled moan. We were more startled than she was.

The only thing that came to mind as we set her down was to say we were just making sure she was comfortable. As we started to back away, we noticed a second bed in the room with a portable screen around it where the actual deceased was lying.

4

Life in the Fast Lane

Because of Inglewood's new regulation aimed directly at our hearses, our next step was to rent some office space above Bob Walker's Harley-Davidson motorcycle shop in Inglewood. The rent was cheap because it was a noisy place, but this first office was a key factor in our first year of operation because of our proximity to the motorcycle dealership.

We began visiting every mortuary in Los Angeles to inform them of our service. One of these visits was to Malloy Mortuary. David Malloy and his wife lived in the upstairs of the mortuary, which was quite common in the business. Dave invited us into his beautiful private office, which was richly decorated with antique furniture. He said, "You can sit in those chairs, they're paid for." He was quite dignified and charming. Little did we know at the time that Dave would become one of our most ardent supporters, and through his intervention, we would make a giant leap forward.

In less than a year we were approached by the general manager of Utter-McKinley Mortuary, which had seventeen branches scattered all over Los Angeles County. Utter-McKinley had been using us for flower deliveries and trusted us enough to offer a contract to get all their death certificates (or DCs) signed by doctors, file them at the Los Angeles County Health Department, obtain a human remains disposition permit in return, and deliver it to the main branch downtown. The mortuary offered us $2.50 for every permit we delivered by the end of each day. We saw this as a great way to guarantee a certain level of continual revenue, which meant we could hire additional personnel.

Getting a disposition permit required a signed death certificate. A family doctor could sign the certificate, or the medical examiner's office would simply do a sign-out based on age and lack of suspicious conditions. However, the medical examiner's office became involved if the person had died from anything other than natural causes. Then it would be their responsibility to investigate the cause of death through an autopsy and toxicological blood testing.

The major challenge was trying to figure out how to get an average of ten certificates a day signed by doctors who were spread out all over Los Angeles, particularly during the afternoon rush hour. The last stop each day would be at the Los Angeles County Health Department. It turned out to be more difficult than we had anticipated, especially when the health department closed at 5 P.M. It seemed that the only answer was to do it on a motorcycle, so I went downstairs to purchase a new Harley-Davidson.

I knew nothing about motorcycles and relied on the shop owner to suggest which bike would be the best one, after explaining the grind it would be subjected to each day. He recommended a small bike with a two-stroke engine that they were promoting. The terminology was not familiar to me, but it did seem strange that you had to mix motor oil with the gasoline.

It soon became apparent that this small motor could not stand up to the strain of the job, because it had to be worked on multiple times during the first year. One afternoon I kick-started it to head back to the office, but as I engaged the clutch the motorcycle started to go backward. *Jumpin'*

Allan on his Harley in 1958, prepared to transport death certificates.

Jehoshaphat, this can't be happening! Motorcycles don't have a reverse gear, so I realized that something was radically wrong. It turned out that a small part in the distributor had broken and the engine was actually running backward.

It was time to have a showdown with Bob Walker, who'd recommended this disaster. He stubbornly refused to take it back, so I reminded him that he carried the insurance on the bike and that it might catch fire or be stolen. He said, "You wouldn't really do that, would you?" and my answer was an unequivocal "Yes, I would." He finally reconsidered and took it back.

The bike had about 10,000 miles on it after only ten months of use. Since the stairway leading up to our office was adjacent to the Harley shop's work area, I saw the bike on a stand near the door. A red shop towel was over the gas tank, which housed the speedometer. My suspicion aroused, I stepped inside and looked under the towel. Lo and behold, a miracle! Now the bike had only 5,000 miles on it.

I had seen an article in a movie magazine stating that James Dean had purchased a Triumph motorcycle from Ted Evans Motorcycles in nearby Santa Monica. It must have been a good choice, because he could surely afford the best. I went to the store and purchased a two-year-old British Triumph. It was a screaming machine and sure to get me into a lot of trouble.

When the bike needed service at Ted Evans, I would chat with other customers in the waiting area. On several occasions, there was another rider waiting for his bike who looked very familiar. He seemed to think he was very talented and didn't mind telling everyone. It finally occurred to me that it was the up-and-coming film star Lee Marvin. This was early in his career, but the swagger in his character was already evident. After his successful TV show *M Squad*, he began getting better roles until he eventually got on Hollywood's A-list. Unfortunately, he is probably remembered just as much for the precedent-setting court case he was involved in with his live-in girlfriend, Michelle Triola. She sued him for "palimony" and tried to make him pony up some big bucks for years of companionship, but lost.

I was often riding over 100 miles some days and got into two accidents the first year. One was fairly minor, but the second one was pretty serious. While speeding along a very curvy road along the side of the Silver Lake

Reservoir, I was really tempting fate because it was impossible to know what was waiting for me around the next curve. Someone had left on lawn sprinklers, and water was flowing down onto the street from a hillside. Applying hard brakes would be the worst thing to do, but the next sharp turn was coming up fast, and I was still doing about thirty miles per hour. Lying the bike down on its right side seemed like the only option, but when my right foot peg came in contact with the pavement, the bike went airborne. My uniform was ruined, and there was about $400 in damage to the bike. Situations like these are one reason motorcycles got their bad reputation, but that hasn't stopped me from riding to this day.

Going to the Los Angeles County Coroner's Office to pick up DCs became a daily task. I overheard the deputies talking about one of the pathologists who worked there. They called him a "working fool," but not in a pejorative sense. He was just very dedicated and worked long hours. His name was Thomas Noguchi, and he eventually became head of the office. It was no surprise because he was by far the best candidate for this position, in great contrast to his boss, Dr. Theodore Curphey, who never spent much time in the lab as Noguchi did.

The coroner's office, commonly known as the morgue, was downtown on the ground floor of the Hall of Justice building, made famous during the Charles Manson trial when his clan of groupie female followers occupied the adjacent corner for weeks. The building's seventh floor housed the Los Angeles City Jail. The entire bank of north-facing windows of the coroner's office gave them a panoramic view of the large parking lot where every day the county sheriff's black-and-white buses, with bars on their windows, would park and unload prisoners. These men were all handcuffed and connected to each other by a long chain. Uniformed officers would herd them into the elevator at one corner of the lot and take them upstairs to get booked.

The deputies always let me use their phone, and late one afternoon I called the doctor at my final stop that day to confirm my arrival. The doctor's office was about twenty miles away in Huntington Park, and his receptionist told me that he would be leaving in thirty minutes. After I exited the freeway, the street traffic slowed me down considerably. Within a few blocks of his office I slowed down for an upcoming red light, but it turned green as I entered the crosswalk. Since my motorcycle was still in motion, I cranked it and shot a fast left turn before the oncoming cars had time to start moving. To my dismay, two California Highway Patrol

(CHP) motorcycle officers were parked near the corner. This bonehead stunt was going to cost me, because oncoming traffic always has the right of way. To stop and get ticketed would surely make me miss the doctor, so I pulled out all the stops and blasted off.

Getting ticketed wouldn't have been anything more than part of the cost of doing business, but my impulse to run was brought on by the fact that only five minutes were left. Still, it occurred to me that the consequence of my reckless behavior might end up causing me to take up temporary residency on a cold slab, in the company of my friends at the morgue.

The sound of the pursuing motorcycles was barely audible, but looking back would be too obvious, so some high-speed hijinks were in order. Come on, Allan, you can outrun these guys with some fast moves! At that time, all police officers were riding big Harley-Davidsons referred to as "hogs." I was riding a TR3, which was much faster and more nimble. It was getting dark, so I turned off my lights and made a rapid series of turns. Amazingly, I then noticed a house with a large bush halfway up the driveway behind which I could hide.

Well, so much for my grand scheme, because ten seconds later the first CHP officer came around the corner and pulled into the driveway. He got on his radio and called his partner with the street address. Three minutes later his fellow officer arrived and approached me, drawing his fist back to clean my clock. Luckily, his partner grabbed his hand and said, "Come on, he's just a kid"—probably because I looked about 15 at the time. The angry officer replied, "This guy almost got me killed." It was clear that this was a terrible mistake, and I feared what would be coming next.

The second officer commented about my turning off my lights. The light switch had actually been having problems, which required me to flip it a few times to get them to work. With that in mind, I ever so gently flipped the switch into the on position, while praying that it wouldn't function. The plan worked. I demonstrated to the officers that it was in the on position but not working. After I flipped it a few times, it finally came on, making me look a little less guilty.

Now it was time to face the music. They called a tow truck for the bike, handcuffed me, and made a radio call for a transport vehicle. They drove me to the CHP's Firestone Substation until it was time to do a prisoner transfer to the Hall of Justice. Yes, that's right, the same Hall of Justice where my phone call had originated half an hour earlier.

The really pressing issue now would be to contact the office and apprise them of my plight, but the jailer said that no one got to use the phone until after booking. One of the officers seemed friendly, so it was worth a shot. After asking his name, I took the opportunity to explain the importance of the contents of my briefcase. If he were to keep me from informing the office about the whereabouts of the DCs, then he would have to deal with the consequences. These were legal documents, so it was imperative to let someone know where they could be recovered. He pondered for a few minutes and finally decided to make the call himself.

Ron immediately called the coroner's office and talked to one of the senior deputies, who assured him that he would call the CHP and ask them to simply write me a traffic citation. The officer came over to the bus, where I was still handcuffed and told me that a deputy coroner had called in, but explained that once someone has been placed on the bus, nothing could be done until it reached the city jail.

On the longest twenty-mile ride of my life, one thing was driving me bananas. How in hell did that CHP officer know I was hiding behind that stupid bush? I had pulled into the driveway well before he had turned the corner. But then it finally came to me, in a moment of clarity. It was almost dark, and I had failed to take my foot off the brake pedal. As he rounded the corner, he saw my rear brake light shining like a beacon in the night. Was that stupid or what?

When we arrived at the city jail parking lot, all the deputy coroners on duty were looking out the windows to see me. There I was, chained to all these other prisoners as we departed the bus. It's one thing to have news cameras record your "perp walk," but much worse when your friends are watching you in the flesh. I'm not sure what was more embarrassing, being seen like that or taking a shower with the prisoners and getting dusted for lice. They fingerprinted me and took my mug shot. Unfortunately, my hair is extremely fine, and without any Brylcreem my hair looked worse than Nick Nolte's did in his mug shot.

My incarceration in the city jail began in 1958 and ended in 1959. Well, actually, it was New Year's Eve and totaled only about four hours. When I appeared in court, the charges against me were reckless driving and evading arrest. My explanation emphasized the importance of the documents and the fact that I was self-employed at the age of 18 and had a great deal of responsibility. After I explained the circumstances with the faulty headlight switch, the judge let me slide on the evading arrest charge, but the reckless driving charge was upheld. Whew! Thank goodness my grandparents had enough cash to make my bail.

Following that incident, the senior deputy at the coroner's office, Phil Schwartzberg, called me "jailbird" for a while. It wasn't so funny at the time, but a few years later he made up for it. He dropped off a broken stretcher for repair, expecting to leave it with me for a few days, but it was going to take me only about fifteen minutes to fix. I repaired it on the spot and he said, "It's always a pleasure to watch an expert at work." By this time I had already repaired many broken cots for the coroner's office, so they didn't have to send the cots back to the manufacturer in Ohio.

We hired my brother full-time to take phone calls and transcribe vital statistics onto blank DCs. Every morning I would plan my schedule using a map and the information attached to each DC stating the doctor's name, address, and his hours for that day. The most frustrating thing was sitting in a doctor's office, waiting for him to get around to signing it. It amazed me that some doctors even asked me into their office to explain the procedure. After their years of medical training, they wanted an 18-year-old kid to tell them how to do it properly. At other times, the problem was reversed when a doctor used medical terminology unfamiliar to me. In those cases, it was necessary to wait until the county health department reviewed the diagnosis to determine whether I could file it, or whether it would be referred to the coroner's office for a ruling.

A death certificate is a matter of public record that serves many purposes. It's a legal certification declaring a person dead. The listed cause of death provides information for public health statistics. But the most important function of a DC is to obtain a permit, without which you can't bury, cremate, or ship the remains to another state. Another common necessity is the basic requirement that legal proceedings depend on proof of death in order to close estates and proceed with financial activities. Over the years, DCs have been used to fake a death to collect insurance benefits or evade law enforcement investigations. According to Dr. Kenneth Iserson's book *Death to Dust*, in the mid-'90s people could purchase an "official-looking" Los Angeles County DC for a fee ranging from $500 to $1,000.

As forensic science improved greatly over the years, it became much more difficult to cover up the actual cause of one's death. With the invention of the gas chromatograph-mass spectrometer, it is possible to detect minute amounts of chemicals in blood. Although it was developed during the '50s, these devices were fragile, bulky, and expensive, so only the largest medical examiner's offices could afford one. This machine allegedly found as many as sixteen different drugs—in minuscule quantities—in Elvis Presley's body after his death.

The expression "deep six" refers to the disposal of something in a way that makes its reappearance unlikely, the "six" representing the depth in feet at which graves are dug. With today's sophisticated forensic tools, it is no longer an applicable expression. Law enforcement officials have often obtained court orders to exhume bodies for further examination in cases where new facts have come to light. Exhumations are now performed even years later, after newly discovered information has aroused suspicions.

When we began getting requests to transport flowers for the rich and famous, we decided to get a high-capacity flower truck. From then on, we always maintained a large flower truck in our fleet of vehicles. Over the years, we used it for the funerals of Mario Lanza, Jack Warner of Warner Brothers, and Jimmy Durante. Mario Lanza was entombed in the mausoleum at Calvary Cemetery, which didn't allow flowers to be placed inside the hall of their mausoleum, so we placed them on both sides of the stairs leading up to the mausoleum entrance. So many flowers were there that in today's dollars they would probably have cost about $40,000.

5

All in the Family

For a year Ron and I were still living with my parents. We had hired my brother full-time, so it was just the three of us and a few students. Most of our mortuary customers were in downtown Los Angeles. It was convenient to have our office close to where we lived, but it wasn't very practical. That became painfully clear one afternoon when we got a call from Utter-McKinley. Someone from its central dispatching office had forgotten to order a flower truck for its Glendale branch, which was twenty-five miles from our office in Inglewood.

Upon my arrival, the funeral had already concluded and the flowers were in the parking lot. Since I had never been to this branch, I opened the rear door, which was unlocked, and started opening doors to alert someone. The second door happened to be the embalming room. A body was on the table, which wasn't covered with a sheet. The embalmer must have been called away quickly, because a large chrome-plated sword was sticking out of the body's stomach. I had no idea what this was or its function, and my reaction was probably comparable to a person discovering the body of someone who had been brutally murdered. In other words, it startled the crap out of me. I hightailed it out of there so fast nobody even saw me.

I found out later that this instrument is called a "trocar," which is about two-and-a-half feet long and used in the embalming process. It's basically a hollow metal tube with a very sharp point on one end and a handle on the other end. The opening in the handle is connected to rubber tubing, which in turn is connected to a device called a hydro-aspirator. As soon as the embalmer turns the aspirator on, water begins flowing through it into a sink drain and the sheer flow of water creates a vacuum that is transferred to the tubing and trocar. The function of this instrument is to remove any fluids and gasses from the vital organs. On this occasion, the hose wasn't attached to the handle of the trocar, so it appeared as though something had harpooned the corpse. It never occurred to me that we would soon be knee-deep in the minutiae of this unfamiliar technology.

The funeral director from Utter-McKinley was very displeased that his dispatcher had forgotten the flower truck order. That was one of those moments when you realize that much of your future business may depend on your ability to respond quickly, so back at the office we started discussing the possibility of moving our office closer to the highest concentration of potential customers.

Each evening at home, the whole family would sit around the dinner table discussing the day's events. From out of the blue my mom and dad asked us if we would consider taking my brother, John, in as a full partner. One reason this seemed like a bad idea was that we had already invested a year into our business, and there had been many occasions when even the two of us had a hard time deciding something.

Another indicator of potential problems with my brother came from the teachers whom John had before me. They had a bad opinion about me by proxy, before they even got to know me. The most significant reaction came from my Spanish teacher during roll call the first day, asking me in front of all the other students if John was my brother. When she got her answer it was clear that it didn't sit well with her because her exact words were "Not another Abbott." That evening, when I talked to my brother, it became evident why she was so upset. She had scolded John on a number of occasions for talking during class. Once, when he didn't stop, in total frustration she blurted out, "John, John, John," and in response he hollered back, "Marsha, Marsha, Marsha."

In 1951 an aspiring comic named Stan Freberg recorded an extremely funny skit called "John and Marsha." The only dialogue involved the couple repeating each other's names. At first it was "Oh John" and "Oh Marsha" in anger, but eventually they started mellowing out and lowering their voices. Marsha's next utterances were more lovey-dovey, followed by something sounding naughty, with him responding in kind. In the ensuing sexual tryst, it was easy for the listener to imagine what was going on. The skit was not censored because the only dialogue was their names, although the inflection in their voices said it all. Capitol Records sold a quarter-million copies of this brilliant spoof, and it began Stan Freberg's long career.

Having seen the clues, I didn't want my brother's role to deteriorate into a family problem. Ron and I decided that it was the right time for us to move, which meant that we could end the discussion and simultaneously find a more centralized location for our business.

6

Death Row

Our new base of operations turned out to be an old abandoned two-story Victorian funeral home, located right in the center of what was referred to by many in the industry as "Death Row." During the '30s and '40s, only two streets were zoned for mortuary operations in Los Angeles and they were two blocks apart, running parallel to each other. Washington and Venice were main business streets, and between them there were approximately thirty mortuaries. They were mom-and-pop operations, and this old building was right in the middle of all these firms.

It was built around 1900 and had operated for many years as the Ivy Overholser Funeral Home. Since it had been closed for three or four years, the estate was anxious to get it rented. We negotiated a monthly rate of $300, which wasn't very expensive considering it was a large building with multiple offices, a spacious kitchen, and a garage large enough to accommodate seven cars. It also had some amenities that we didn't need, including a chapel and an embalming room. The one feature of this old Victorian structure that stood out the most was the old cast-iron bathtub that sat in the center of the kitchen. It was intended to be covered during meals with a dining table top and uncovered when someone needed to take a bath. Now we were able to live in an apartment inside our large building.

In the cellar we found a large quantity of old mortuary paraphernalia, including artificial arms, legs, and hundreds of old dentures. Many family members would bring in granny's false teeth after she was already embalmed, so it was too late to use them, but they were always accepted without explanation. We also discovered one adult and two infant wicker caskets. There was a strange funnel-shaped glass container with a large opening at the top that slowly tapered toward the bottom. Before the invention of the embalming machine, mortuaries used this bottle, which had a metal stand that kept the glass about six feet off the floor, so that pressure would be generated from gravity. This apparatus was eventually supplanted by the much more efficient use of an electric pump known as a Porti-Boy Embalming Machine.

We soon found out that these different-size wicker caskets were taken to private residences and used as temporary caskets because many people, even after the turn of the century, were still being embalmed in their home. In the Victorian era, many people had a room in their home called the "parlor," where the deceased would often be laid out in state so the family could invite guests to stop and pay their respects. This gave rise to mortuaries using the words "funeral parlor" in their title. The only mortuary in Los Angeles that was still using this somewhat outdated nomenclature was the Culver City Funeral Parlor, whose only competitor was Smith and Salsbury, who had the distinction of being the one that had the word "Undertaking" on their sign.

The funeral practices of the Victorian era produced expressions that are still used today, though not always in their original context. For instance, the term "graveyard shift" was coined as a result of someone being paid by a family to stay up all night with the body, in case the person might awaken from a misdiagnosed death. This is also where the word "wake" came from, which designates a gathering held the night before the funeral. Today, a graveyard shift refers to an all-night job in any line of work.

Because of the lack of sophisticated diagnostic equipment in the Victorian era, such as electrocardiograms and encephalograms that detect heart and brain activity, people in a coma were sometimes mistaken as being dead. The fear of someone being buried alive gave rise to the invention of a coffin with a small bell aboveground, tethered to the deceased's hand through a small tunnel from the casket, which they could ring upon regaining consciousness and finding themselves "six feet under." This led to the expression "dead ringer," used to describe someone who looks just like another, implying that they really are one and the same, having come back to life after being assumed dead. What's most interesting about these expressions, many of which have become clichés, is that when you examine their origins, the original meanings were literal.

After the death of her husband, Prince Albert, Queen Victoria wore only black clothing, thus beginning the tradition of wearing black to funerals. Many of our funeral traditions were direct carryovers from the

British Isles. In almost every respect we have adopted British funeral traditions, while changing only some of the terminology. In the United States, the word "casket" has been used for generations, while "coffin" is still used exclusively throughout England. In addition, we refer to "cemeteries," while the British refer to them as "graveyards." The British will still use the terms "undertaker" and "mortician," while "funeral director" is a much more commonly used expression in the Unites States. George Bernard Shaw may have stated it best when he said, "England and America are two countries separated by a common language."

Ron and I frequently dined at a favorite restaurant from our school days at Dorsey High. They had excellent food for a drive-in. One day, we happened to meet the assistant chef, Bill Carnes. We started talking about what we did for a living and how we provided our employees with free rent and payment for each call they made. He seemed very interested in this arrangement and said he would like to participate after his shift was over at the restaurant. By furnishing our own in-house chef in exchange for a room, we found the perfect solution for the crew's meal breaks

Our first-call men ranged in age from about 17 to 20, while Bill was at least 50 and was missing four teeth. We never envisioned the possibility that he would ever assist on any calls. Our most complex manpower issue the first few years wasn't finding enough students willing to do this type of work, but rather a recurring phenomenon of timing. We wouldn't get any calls for three or four hours, and then two or three might come in within thirty minutes of each other.

One busy evening our biggest customer, Utter-McKinley, phoned in a house call while our other two crews were already out. This was one of those times we needed to resort to some pretty drastic solutions. I asked Bill if he had a suit and if he would be willing to go on a call with me. When he got dressed, it was obvious that his suit was too big and looked very old.

We had a first-call car but were down to our last cot and no more cot covers. Knowing that it would look terrible to make a house call without a cot cover, I thought, "What would Scarlett O'Hara do?" I went into the chapel that had been sitting unused and took down a maroon velvet drape. The only problem was that it had brass rings sewed along the top seam about a foot apart. After that, my biggest concern was to tell Bill to keep his mouth shut just before we entered the mortuary prep room.

When the night attendant heard us come in, he came downstairs from his apartment to give us a hand. The cots we had were old and only eleven inches in height, whereas the prep table was waist-high. The revolutionary Ferno-Washington Model #22 cot hadn't been invented yet, which was the first truly one-man cot. It was engineered so it could be lifted up and locked in place, level with the embalming table. We lifted the cot while the night man pulled the deceased onto the table. The velvet drape that I had so carefully folded just before we entered the prep room slipped off the foot end of the cot. Out flopped the end with the brass rings. If that wasn't bad enough, Bill must have seen the humor in my feeble attempt to disguise it and broke out in a big toothless grin, once again proving that Murphy's Law never fails.

We purchased our first new vehicle, which was a 1958 Chevy Sedan Delivery. It was readily apparent that a good source of revenue would be statewide body transportation and graveside services, to areas as far as 400 miles away. Early in our entry into making these calls, we got an order from the manager of Utter-McKinley's Highland Park branch, requesting a special favor. He wanted to know if it would be possible to also take the son of the deceased in the hearse with his mother's casket for a graveside service in Cambria, California. In a sympathetic gesture I agreed, deciding to make the drive myself.

It took over four hours to get there, so we had plenty of time to talk. He asked me if we would be furnishing one of "them gadgets" to lower the casket into the grave, and I explained that the cemeteries always provide these. When we arrived in Cambria, the two gravediggers had just finished spending four hours opening the grave by hand because they had no backhoe. More significantly, they had no lowering device, either. The picturesque town's slogan was "Where the Pines Meet the Sea," but it felt like a more appropriate description would have been "Where the Sea Meets the Stone Age." After driving into the downtown area and purchasing some rope, we finally got the casket lowered into the ground.

For long trips we were using an old van because it had always been an iffy proposition transporting caskets in old hearses up and down the state. I was returning to LA on California's notorious grade called the "Grapevine," which ran from the San Fernando Valley to the bottom of the San Joaquin Valley, just short of Bakersfield. This grade was so steep that it had escarpment ramps for trucks to use in case their brakes failed from overheating. I was just starting up the grade from the north end, heading back to Los Angeles, when the motor froze. Not wanting to call an expensive tow truck, we decided to use one of our old Packard hearses to see if we could push the van up the grade.

The Grapevine, a mountainous section of the I-5, is one of very few highways in the state that gets closed during snowstorms in the dead of winter, but snowplows had cleared it earlier that day. Because the van was blocking the flow of air to the radiator of the hearse, it overheated—even though it was very cold at that altitude. As we pushed it along, we could go only so far and then we would have to stop and let the engine cool, which took about thirty minutes. It was the middle of the night, so we climbed into the back of the hearse and tried to get some sleep. This time, we didn't have the comfort of a mattress but instead were lying on a table covered with metal rollers. Between the cold temperature and uncomfortable table, it was a very long night.

There were few opportunities to ever watch TV or do any reading, unless you counted the Burma-Shave signs on the state highways. Without a doubt, the single most difficult problem we encountered was never getting enough sleep. We felt lucky just to get a few extra nods here and there. The most humorous description of this working condition is in Loretta Lynn's hit record, *Coal Miner's Daughter*. In one verse she recounts, "The work we done was hard, at night we'd sleep 'cause we were tarred." Well, at least it rhymes.

A year or so after we had leased our Victorian mortuary, a man from the Los Angeles City Planning Commission came for a visit. He informed me that the Grand Avenue off-ramp of the soon-to-be-built Santa Monica Freeway would be coming right through this parcel of land. After all the restoration we had done, it was time to find another place. We got two months of free rent before we had to leave, but the water heater started leaking when we still had five weeks to go. Installing a new one was out of the question, but we all needed the use of the shower. After purchasing two bottles of radiator stop-leak fluid, I disconnected the water supply to the water heater and poured it into the storage tank. After I reconnected the water supply twelve hours later, the leak had stopped. The downside was that we all smelled like a leaky radiator.

7

Reluctant Hearse Driver

W e were beginning to threaten our only competitor in the funeral car livery business, California Hearse Service, which had been in business for about twenty-five years and had an extensive fleet of Cadillac hearses. They would be a formidable competitor if we were to ever try to take away any of their business. I remember wondering at the time, who came up with the term "livery service"? The word "livery" is indicative of a stable, where you pay someone for housing and feeding your horse. Well, I guess horse and hearse sound alike.

At this point we were like David, while the owner of Cal Hearse was the Goliath of the funeral car business. We were about to become the burr under his saddle. The owner's name was Art Simpson, but considering his attitude, it should have been Bart Simpson. When anyone called him with a complaint he would pretty much blow it off, knowing he was the only game in town. He employed a full-time mechanic, who knew all the eccentricities with hearses and their foibles, of which there were many.

Unlike cars, hearses had hydraulic or mechanical electric tables that were capable of bringing a casket out either side of the hearse or out the back end. These hearses also had hydraulic levelizers, which are different from anything you would ordinarily deal with on an automobile. The levelizer was used to raise one side of the hearse at the curb in front of a church to compensate for the slant in the gutters. Without a levelizer, the two four-foot-wide doors would strike the curb.

McGlynn's Mortuary called and proposed that we purchase some newer hearses, so they could rent them from us instead of using Cal Hearse. At that time their hearse was a 1948 Packard, and many other firms in town had this same year and model. Forest Lawn, who owned (and owns) the most famous cemeteries in the United States, had two '48 Packard hearses for sale at its Hollywood Hills facility, so we purchased both of them.

Word always got around very quickly and before long some of the drivers for Cal Hearse switched over to us, which was great because they brought with them years of experience. Art must have seen the writing on the wall, because we kept expanding while his business declined. The three biggest mortuary chain operators in Los Angeles County all had full-time mechanics maintaining their fleets. Eventually, this became one of my most important functions because the five major hearse-manufacturing companies all had different methods of powering the tables in their hearses.

Now that we had these two newer hearses, we still had to use them occasionally just to deliver flowers on busy days. On one such morning, I made a flower delivery and headed back across town for a funeral at McGlynn's. One of our older drivers would be meeting me there and continue on with the hearse so I could return to the office and start my DC signings. The service that morning was just a short blessing at the mortuary for a 2-year-old child. The priest had already finished by the time of my arrival, so he said that he would meet us at Holy Cross Cemetery for the interment.

Because the blessing was so brief, our older driver hadn't arrived there yet, and they were ready to form the procession. I immediately started brushing the flower petals from the hearse when the manager, Bob Johnson, informed me that it was time to leave and expected me to drive the hearse. Having never done this before, I was very reluctant to even attempt it without some rudimentary training. It didn't seem to matter to Bob, the person who encouraged us to start our flower delivery service. Informing him of my lack of experience, he responded: "This will be a good opportunity for you to get some practice."

Rather than being dressed in formal attire, I was wearing my motorcycle uniform. The motorcycle escort that day was Lyle Chown, and he gave me a "crash course"— no, that's not a good choice of words—so, let's say, a very quick dissertation on the do's and don'ts of funeral procession etiquette. We pulled out of the mortuary parking lot with about twelve cars.

Being very nervous wasn't helping my concentration, so as we approached the first main intersection my eyes were focused on the side-view mirror, trying to see where Lyle was. I forgot that he had instructed me to turn right on Century Boulevard. Just about then he came up alongside the procession, flashing his lights at me and screaming, "Right! Right!" The hearse was well into the intersection, but luckily we were moving slowly enough to all make a very wide right-hand turn. We arrived without incident. From that time on, Lyle took credit for teaching me the ropes, as he continued escorting all of our hearse drivers and me for the next twenty-five years.

Escorts were all required to wear slate-gray uniforms, so as not to be confused with the Los Angeles Police Department's dark blues or the California Highway Patrol's tans. They all rode Harley "hogs," just as all the police departments did. The "hogs" were cumbersome and lacked the precision of English motorcycles. Later, many of the escorts started to buy the new Kawasaki 750-cubic-centimeter bikes. All escorts' motors had to be painted the traditional black and white and have two amber (not red) lights on either side of the headlights in order to pass inspection by the CHP.

Very quickly, we got to know every funeral escort in Los Angeles and considered them good friends. When my father died, the escorts contacted each other and we ended up with almost as many of them on their motorcycles as cars in the procession.

8

Medical Examiner Misadventures

In no time, we were making first calls and flower deliveries for almost every mortuary in Los Angeles and the surrounding counties. After a funeral arrangement counselor completed gathering the vital statistics for the DC and noted the type of service the family had chosen, he would then call a vehicle order in to "the kids," as we were known the first few years. We were very pleased when we got a call from the county coroner's office offering us a verbal contract to do all their overflow calls, which were numerous.

In the late '50s, the coroner's office was relatively small and didn't have enough employees to cover all of the calls, so they came up with a program they called "Coroner of the Month." The mortuaries participating in this program were always located in the outlying communities, which were farthest from downtown and would have taken the greatest time for the investigators to reach, so many of them used us to make their death calls. These designated mortuaries liked the program, because they always did more business during their assigned coroner's month.

On these calls our employees would interview the families and fill out a Mortuary Death Report, which would describe the family's observations of any symptoms or conditions noted just prior to the person's death. Each of our first-call cars was supplied with all the necessary paperwork that had been provided by the coroner's office. In a city the size of Los Angeles, the coroner's office should have been much larger to cover an area that ran from the northwest boundary of the San Fernando Valley to the port area, which are approximately sixty miles apart. The coroner's office would send a pathologist to whichever mortuary had picked up a case, and would review the death report to help him determine whether he would do an autopsy or a sign-out on the DC.

Culver City had two firms that rotated each month as acting coroner. One of them called and directed us to a small cottage on our first suicide call. During the '30s and '40s, LA had many bungalow courts—multiple small structures having only one bedroom. Anyone looking at old movies from that era can see them in abundance, especially in Old Hollywood, where these bungalows were often occupied by starving artists trying to break into the motion picture industry. A uniformed police officer was already there waiting outside, which told you one of two things. It was going to be bloody, or worse, it might have been a decomposed body, in which case the officer always stayed outside. During our early years, Ron and I were almost always together because we had only two additional employees at the time doing first calls.

We opened the door, paused for a few seconds, and just looked at each other in shock. In the center of the room sat a man wearing shorts and an undershirt, with a high-powered hunting rifle resting on his chest and his big toe inside the rifle's trigger guard. The muzzle blast took off most of his head, so here was a guy just sitting there with a chin on his neck and nothing more. Skull fragments and brain matter were all over the walls, and a large pool of blood was on the floor. We spent about forty-five minutes cleaning up the place. Yuck! Later, we learned that wasn't part of our responsibility.

Another bad coroner's case we were given was also in Culver City. A man was in his car where he had committed suicide by carbon monoxide poisoning about eight days earlier. The bloating squeezed him between the steering wheel and the seat. Ron kept running outside for some fresh air, leaving me alone to try to pull him out. He said that the smell was really making him sick. My response was, "No shit, Sherlock, now get back in here and let's get this guy out."

The Los Angeles County Health Department declined to accept one DC on which the doctor had written the cause of death (COD) as silicosis, which is better known by its common name, "black lung" or "coal miner's disease." The department instructed me to take the DC to the coroner's office, because it was considered an industrial disease and the department wished to confirm the diagnosis. UCLA had already done an autopsy, but when the coroner's doctor undid the sutures and opened him up, he discovered the man had been totally eviscerated.

When an embalmer prepares a posted case, he places the internal organs in plastic viscera bags and then returns them to the stomach cavity. The only thing the coroner's doctor found inside this individual was a couple of bloody paper towels. That was when the proverbial you-know-what hit the fan. The coroner went ballistic and demanded a full investigation. UCLA was required to return all the organs they had removed, and the story made all the newspapers. At least we finally found out what the term "visceral" meant when describing a gut feeling.

By the time we arrived on some of these calls, the coroner's investigator had already gone. There was usually a coroner's seal on the door, so we had to break it in order to gain entrance. In those days, they had very meager technology in forensic pathology and the lab could do only limited toxicology and microscopic examinations. Many times it took weeks to run these tests, so the coroner would sign a temporary DC that had no cause of death but simply said "Pending Tox and Cajal," meaning toxicological evaluation of the blood and microscopic examination of tissue. Everyone just referred to these DCs as pending certificates, which could be filed at the health department to obtain permits. These certified copies enabled families to settle a person's affairs that were not dependent on a cause of death being given. Usually they issued what was called the final DC after the test results became available.

The coroner's office was often criticized for not bringing every case into their facility and only performing an autopsy if the deceased was younger. An older person rated a more scrutinized investigation only if the remains had a gunshot wound, a protruding knife, or ligature marks on the throat. In all other cases the pathologist would do a sign-out, which meant no autopsy or any further investigation. That was because of the vast resources that would be required to determine the exact cause of death for every person in which foul play was not suspected. As a result, the coroner would make an educated guess about the cause of death based on the person's age and other easily ascertainable evidence. Because of the arbitrary nature of that policy, some even joked that if the coroner's doctor showed up at your mortuary on a Wednesday, the diagnosis du jour would be arteriosclerotic heart disease, representing hardening of the arteries with plaque caused by cholesterol.

The five basic categories of death were murder, suicide, accidental, natural, and undetermined. If the death occurred in another state, the out-of-state permit for disposition had to be refiled at the county health department for a funeral service in California. It has been estimated that only one in five doctors receives any training on how to complete a death certificate properly. According to Dr. Kenneth Iserson's *Death to Dust*, only 70 percent of them do it correctly.

In one sensational case, Dr. Peter Veger listed Los Angeles smog as a contributing cause of death on a DC. The health department wanted him to sign another one and leave out this part of his diagnosis, but he refused, so it became necessary to take up the issue with the coroner's office. If a DC is signed by an attending physician, it's the responsibility of the health department to determine the allowable causes of death that can appear on the DC. In cases where the circumstances of death occur by any means other than natural causes, the coroner must "rule on it" (make a determination on the cause of death). His purview includes suicides, homicides, auto accidents, industrial accidents, or any other circumstance when death is the result of an external force.

In the case of Dr. Veger's DC, the coroner didn't want any part of going on the record saying Los Angeles smog had contributed to the deceased's death, so they instructed the health department to let it be filed "as is." The newspapers soon had bold headlines reading "Smog Kills LA Resident." In today's litigious society, people would probably be suing Los Angeles for allowing it to be smoggy.

In Los Angeles, the problem wasn't just carbon monoxide emissions from motor vehicles, but also a lack of sufficient airflow. When Native Americans first inhabited the area, they called it the "Valley of Smoke" because the soot from their campfires kept hovering in the sky afterward.

9

Levity Rules

In 1959, we leased what had been Los Angeles' first Automobile Club of Southern California building. It was a brick, two-story structure, and we figured the upstairs offices could be turned into individual dormitory rooms, while the downstairs would be our offices. It also had a fifteen-car garage connected to the rear of the building. Each employee would have use of the kitchen, shower, and recreation room.

Most people assume that the funeral business is a depressing one to work in, but it can also be interesting and full of surprises. As compensation for being somber so much of the time, we shared a lot of goofy inside jokes among ourselves. There was great camaraderie among all of us because everyone lived in the building. It was like living in a frat house, and every evening we would all gather in the recreation room and have wrestling matches or play pool. We pulled pranks on one another, the likes of which could have been portrayed in John Belushi's *Animal House*, except in our case there was no alcohol.

Ron and I were about the same age as our crew, and they never felt subservient to us because we went on calls with them regularly. When a call came in the middle of the night, we had to decide whose turn it was to make the call. This wasn't always easy, so we set up a system. Every student making a night call got one dollar extra for each call he made. Like everything else, the guys came up with a term for this policy, calling it "a buck a bod." A first-call man could augment his income by as much as $40 on this system. The only client who ever gave our employees a gratuity was David Malloy. At that time you could go to a bank and request $2 bills, so Dave would give each of our men a tip using these bills.

We would often have lighthearted discussions in the recreation room. On one occasion the conversation turned to everyone's favorite radio station, KFWB. It was the most popular station for young people because it played the current favorites, but everyone also agreed that the best and funniest disc jockey on the air was Gary Owens, who worked there. We got to play a joke on him. One day Gary gave a traffic report that a cattle truck had turned over on the Pasadena Freeway, requiring the California Highway Patrol to respond and round up the cows wandering about. Because of the freeway's tight turns, the same thing happened again a short time later, so Gary named his traffic update the "Moo Cow Report."

One of our first-call staff, Frankie Bonnet, lived in Glendale, where the Altadena Dairy had a full-size fiberglass cow in front of their facility. We had a large flower truck that was big enough to hold the cow. A couple of our guys asked permission to use the truck to "borrow" the cow, with the proviso that if they got caught, we would disavow any knowledge of their actions. Our boys returned about 11 P.M. with the cow, which looked so lifelike that Frankie got down on his haunches and pretended to milk it.

The next morning Frankie and I went to the station on Hollywood Boulevard, where they did the broadcast from the second-floor studio. We pushed the visitor button and said we needed to talk to Gary about his Moo Cow Report. KFWB continuously broadcasted from a speaker above the stairway entrance, so anyone walking down Hollywood Boulevard could hear the broadcast. Just before playing the next song, Gary said on the air that a Moo Cow Delegation was waiting downstairs.

When he saw the cow, he couldn't believe it. He was very cordial and even gave us some free records, including "Tom Dooley," which began the career of the Kingston Trio. We requested that when he was done with the borrowed heifer that he would have someone return it to the dairy, and he agreed. A few days later he mailed me a picture of himself, sitting backward on the cow. He was wearing his trademark Earl C. Festoon 1941 wide necktie. We were surprised when we first met him because this man with the golden voice looked like a hippie, with his long hair in a ponytail.

One night, a first call came in after midnight. After writing up the work order, Ron went to awaken two of our students. He came back into the apartment with a blank look on his face and informed me that every room was empty. Even the guys who were not on duty and usually in their rooms were also gone. The whole building seemed to be totally empty, but suddenly there was a great roar of laughter coming from the kitchen, where the crew had hidden themselves. Our employee Drake Jasso called in the fake order because it was April 1 and this was their big April fool's gag on us. Everyone thought it was a riot seeing their boss running up and down the hallway in his briefs and T-shirt, knocking on all the doors and calling people's names but not finding a single person.

Our crew always had many jokes about us. They called our company "Grab It and Fast" to play on the sound of Abbott and Hast, and would say that our slogan was "You stab 'em, we slab 'em," or "We don't want you to die, but if you die we want you." They called me the worker and Ron the schmoozer, because I was always working on cars and he would spend most of his time on the phone doing PR work. They'd also joked that our business was "Half-Hast."

Utter-McKinley Mortuary also had a joke about their name. One of their employees would say, "If you are about to kick the bucket, your dying breath should be used to utter McKinley." But if you believe that a name can be indicative of one's profession, then there were a number of people destined to be in the funeral business. There was the Amigone Funeral Home (am I gone?) and other ironic names like Bury and Roberts, Dunaway (done away), and Farwell (farewell). One of the funniest was Goodbody Funeral Home. How's that for branding?

Allan and Ron with their fleet of vehicles, in front of their downtown Los Angeles office.

10

Driving Myself Crazy

By this time, we were giving Cal Hearse a run for their money. I had to go to their facility every Saturday on my Triumph, since you could only file DCs at the Los Angeles County Health Department during the workweek. The county had an arrangement with them to do these filings on weekends and Cal Hearse's manager, Jimmy Houston, would glower at me with an adversarial look every time I rode into their fleet garage. We had been renting our two '48 Packards to their old customers for a lot less, so he obviously resented us.

One day we got a call from our friend Dave Malloy, a well-respected funeral director who originated the Hollywood Christmas Parade down Hollywood Boulevard. Dave had been using Cal Hearse for years, but had also started using us for some of his funeral car rentals and all of his first calls. He phoned us to ask if we had heard that Jimmy had quit Cal Hearse after being their manager for many years.

Jimmy had quit for ethical reasons. Woods' Glendale Mortuary had been using Cal Hearse's services for years. Late one night, one of Art Simpson's employees dropped a case (the coroners office's term for each body they handled) off there. The owner's wife just happened to look out their apartment window and saw the man stealing bricks from their parking lot. When Jimmy Woods called Cal Hearse and reported what had happened, Art Simpson wouldn't do anything about it, so Jimmy Houston quit.

We told Dave that we hadn't heard, but asked him what it had to do with us. He said he would like to set up a meeting with the four of us at his mortuary. We told Dave that we doubted that Jimmy would agree to such a meeting, because it was obvious he didn't like us one bit. Dave assured us that he had encouraged him to meet with us and he was willing. Jimmy agreed to become our manager at a cut in salary. This was a fortuitous event because he brought with him years of practical experience that would prove to be providential, all thanks to Dave.

That very day in October 1959, Jimmy proclaimed that our first order of business would be to buy three brand-new hearses. We never thought that we could qualify for a loan to finance a $25,000 purchase at our ages, so he and Dave got together and, along with one other mortuary owner, raised enough money for the down payments. We went to the bank with hat in hand to try to secure financing. The bank manager wanted to know our credit history, and all we could report was eighteen consecutive payments of $13.11 made to Bank of America a year and a half earlier for a typewriter we had purchased to type DCs. Remarkably, the bank gave us the loan, and we were even able to pay everyone back in one year.

Two of our new hearses were already in Los Angeles, but the third one still had to be built at the Superior Coach factory in Lima, Ohio. It was scheduled to be ready in December, so the hearse salesman agreed to let us use their demo hearse, but only until the day that the new one was ready to be picked up. I flew to Chicago to catch another flight to Dayton, but the airport was closed just after landing because of snow. The trains were still running, so I took a taxi from the airport to the train station. On the way there, the cab got caught in a snowdrift, so it was necessary for me to get out and push it until it broke free. No seats were left on the train because everyone traveling by air had been diverted to rail travel, so I stood the entire trip.

After I left the factory with the new hearse, all went well until my first gas stop. For some reason the battery had died, so they gave me a jump-start. After I reached the outskirts of the town, the dash lights dimmed and the engine started to miss. There was one lonely house off to the left, but as I started to cut across the highway the engine went dead, leaving me on the wrong side of the highway in a black car at night, with no lights and a fast-approaching truck. I flagged him down, and he helped me push the hearse off the highway. The man in the house let me call for a tow truck.

Great. Here I was, on the outskirts of a little Podunk town in my California summer suit, with the temperature hovering around twenty degrees, waiting for the cavalry to arrive. There were no mechanics facilities open at this time, so an all-night service station was my only option. On closer inspection, I realized that the bracket that held tension on the generator belt was missing, and that was why the battery wasn't getting any charge. There were some tailpipe brackets in the station garage that looked strong enough to make my own bracket with some bending and drilling. The attendant agreed to let me use some of the shop tools if I purchased a bracket. In about twenty minutes, it was finished and it actually worked.

We had ordered a side-loading hearse, which required the installation of a hydraulic reservoir and pulley system to operate the levelizer. In these cases the generator had to be moved to the left side of the engine, which then needed a tension-adjusting bracket not produced by Cadillac. The factory's representative was surprised by my phone call about this blunder. He offered to pay all of my expenses and ship me a new custom bracket by special delivery. I informed him that there was no big rush, because my homemade bracket had already survived 2,000 miles of driving.

The Cadillac division of General Motors produced a hearse in the 1920s, but eventually some dedicated coachbuilders sprang up to build the bodies of hearses. Cadillac would ship the five Ohio hearse manufacturers a commercial chassis, which had a windshield, a complete front end, drivetrain, and wheels. The windshields were about ten inches higher than those on a normal car. The hearse's roof had to be taller to get a casket into the side or rear doors without having to remove the flowers from the top of the casket.

It was extremely interesting to go to the national funeral directors convention and see five new hearses that were all built using the same Cadillac commercial chassis. They all looked different from one another except for the same Cadillac front end and taillights of that year's model. The main difference between models was the rooflines, the number and shape of the windows, and the landau bars. The bars were a carryover from turn-of-the-century buggies with folding convertible tops. They were hinged in the middle and enabled the top of the buggy to have support in either the up or down position. Landau bars somehow made the transition to funeral cars in a decorative capacity only and have been used on them ever since.

One of the biggest changes in hearses came when Cadillac incorporated a significant engineering development for their commercial chassis: an x-frame with hollow tubing instead of the solid steel ones. For a normal automobile this hollow tubing worked fine, but for a side-loading coach, which most California firms used, it was sort of a disaster. The three new hearses we purchased could not have the side doors opened if the levelizer was on. Being less rigid, the body of the hearses would twist when the levelizer was activated.

I called Superior Coach Company and said they should bevel the closing latches, but they responded that it wouldn't cure the problem. After two hours of grinding away, I successfully beveled the latches. I sent the company a film of the modification, so they finally sent two of their engineers to look at it. The factory responded that side-loading hearses accounted for only about 20 percent of their sales, and it would be too costly to make these changes. However, the next year, they had a new side-loading hearse at the funeral convention and it had beveled latches. I sent them a letter asking for a rebate of $500 for each hearse and promptly received a check for $1,500, which we used for a trip to Hawaii.

The year after my first hearse pickup, we ordered another new Superior hearse. I was hoping this trip would not be as eventful as the last one. One day before my departure, one of our drivers, who was an ex-fighter pilot, got smashed in his six o'clock by a truck during a rainstorm. This left us one hearse short of the four we had in service, and we had been getting busier by the month. I called Superior Coach to order a replacement quarter panel for our wrecked '59 and requested that they place it in the back of the new coach I would be picking up two days later. A new quarter panel wasn't available anywhere else, because all the hearse builders fabricate the body, with no two being exactly alike.

After leaving the factory, I stopped for some breakfast and wondered about the possibility of driving straight back to Los Angeles without stopping. Like most guys my age, I had a feeling of invincibility; otherwise something that hare-brained would never have occurred to me. Nevertheless, this would solve the problem of fixing the wrecked hearse faster and getting this new hearse in service sooner. To borrow a line from poet Robert Frost, "I had promises to keep and miles to go before I sleep"—and that happened to be a whopping 2,450 miles.

Some of the southwestern states still didn't have any speed limits, so 100 miles per hour seemed like a nice round number. Cadillac hearses weighed 6,200 pounds at the time and rode really smoothly at high speeds. When I reached New Mexico, it was time to get the oil changed for the second time and get a lube job. Albuquerque had a large Cadillac dealership and they informed me it would be ready in about two hours. If only I could have curled up in the hearse for some much needed shut-eye.

Later that day, the highway had become straight and flat—ideal for cruising at about 110. It was dusk, and both sides of the highway were lined with hundreds of birds. Because of my high speed, they must have heard me coming a long way off. They started to fly, but they all seemed to fly across the highway instead of away from it. By this time I hadn't slept for well over thirty hours and the highway was extremely monotonous, but when a bird hit my windshield it was like getting a slap in the face. My mind couldn't process exactly what had happened, but I instinctively looked in the rearview mirror, witnessing a scene almost like something you might expect to see in a cartoon. In the turbulence behind me, the air was completely full of flying feathers. A second later, the limp bird dropped through them and hit the highway. I rapidly dropped my speed to avoid having any more birds fall victim to my insane speeding.

My diet on the road consisted of candy bars, coffee, and a popular diet pill that contained ephedrine. The only trouble was that the combination of this chemical and lack of sleep would play tricks on my mind. A herd of sheep crossing the highway would suddenly vanish, or a hitchhiker became a signpost as it got closer.

The most bizarre thing I saw was the shadow of a giant hand on the road ahead. A ruby ring appeared to be on the finger that turned out to be the taillights of a car about a mile ahead of me. Seeing these strange things should have been a clear message that I should stop and smell the coffee. There were only a few hundred miles to go, so I just rolled down the driver's window and let in some nice cool air to help me stay awake.

Just before dawn I could see some lights off in the distance that appeared to have halos around them, so it looked like the glass in the windshield was defective. Soon there were more lights and more halos, as if all the windows had defective glass. Suddenly, it dawned on me that the driver's window was down and the glass was not the problem. After all those hours of driving my eyes were giving out, but Los Angeles was now only about six hours away, so stopping was not an option. Who said Capricorns are stubborn?

I finally arrived home. In a little more than forty-five hours, I had racked up over 2,400 miles. Even with all the gas stops, two oil changes, and a two-hour layover in New Mexico, I had still averaged fifty miles per hour over the entire trip. I slept for twenty-four hours and woke up four pounds lighter. The new hearse went out on its first service on Monday morning.

Six months later it was time for another twenty-four-hour drive, with some new twists. There were three bodies to either pick up or deliver up and down the state. My last drop would be in Yreka, California, just shy of the Oregon border. After driving all day and night, I arrived there about six in the morning and took a short nap until the mortuary opened at 8 A.M. Then it was time to head back to Los Angeles, but for no apparent reason a California Highway Patrol officer flagged me down. He approached my window and asked if I worked for Abbott & Hast Company. He explained that the owner of the mortuary in Yreka contacted them to intercept me with a message to call the office. Ron had just missed me by ten minutes, so the funeral home owner had offered to call his buddies at the local CHP office. Ron was assured that they would spot the vehicle as it passed through the little town of Weed. The only question running through my mind was, who the hell named the town Weed?

When I phoned Ron, he said we had been given a first call at a hospital in San Francisco, easy to reach on my way back. We always carried an extra fold-up stretcher in the storage compartment, so it would be easy to pull the body off the one-man cot onto the folding model and use the more versatile version to make the call.

Shortly after that next pickup I drove through the town of Merced. On the outskirts of town was farmland, with a very large, freshly plowed field on the right side of Highway 99. There was an old '40s sedan ahead of me in the slow lane doing about thirty miles per hour. At the same time, a pickup truck on a dirt road was coming from the plowed field. It was approaching the highway at a high rate of speed, trailing a huge cloud of dust.

The man in the right lane must have been startled by the pickup, because without any warning he swerved into the fast lane and slammed on his brakes. I headed for the median strip in the center of the highway, but he just kept coming left. At the last second I cranked the steering wheel to the right with all my strength to avoid him, but back he came to the right lane. It was as if he was tracking my movement. Everywhere I went, there he was. My tires were screeching as I tightened my grip on the steering wheel. Just before I slammed into him there was enough time to think: "This is really going to hurt."

The crash was loud enough to wake the dead. Fortunately, it didn't. The impact was so great that the bolts holding the bench seat to the floor of my station wagon sheared off. The steering wheel collapsed on both sides, and my face struck one of the broken ends, punching a crescent-shaped hole above my upper lip. I was completely bent over the collapsed steering wheel because the seat had moved about a foot and a half forward, while the stretcher behind me had become airborne, coming to rest on my neck and shoulders.

My first thought was wondering what part of my body had been most injured. The answer came quickly, with the feeling of warm blood soaking my white dress shirt. The driver's door wouldn't budge, but I was able to push the cot on my shoulders back far enough to roll down the window and crawl out of the crumpled wreck. My next task was to drag both cots back into the rear of the car. Since I was bleeding profusely, blood got all over the white sheets covering the bodies.

About this time, the man from the pickup truck stuck his head in the open tailgate and inquired about my condition. When he saw the bodies and the blood, he said, "My God, is them folks dead?" I assured him they were dead before the accident. Obviously quite shaken, he went to check on the occupants of the other car, a family of six on their Sunday drive to the local church.

Ambulances arrived and transported some of us to Merced General Hospital. A nurse sterilized my wound and covered my face with a cloth that had a hole in it so the emergency room doctor could access the gash. After the first few stitches, the doctor said "Oops," which sounded pretty ominous. My immediate response was to tell him, "Please do not use that word while you're sewing up my face, okay?" He never did explain himself.

Ron came from Los Angeles and picked me up at the hospital along with the two bodies, which were in the hospital's morgue. Wasn't that smart of me to crash near a place that had a refrigerated morgue? Months later, a plastic surgeon reopened the wound and removed the scar tissue that had formed. After the surgery, they rolled me into a room occupied by another patient. The next morning, after I woke up and was getting dressed to leave, my roommate asked me: "Are you all right to be getting up? I thought you were seriously injured because the minute they rolled you into the room yesterday afternoon, you never opened your eyes until just now." "Not to worry," I explained. "This was just my first full night's sleep in over two weeks."

When I appeared in court before a judge to determine responsibility for the accident, the only eyewitness was the man driving the pickup truck. He explained, "Ah was leavin' the farm and headin' fur the highway at a pretty good clip, and Ah guess this old guy thought Ah wasn't gunna stop, so he swerved in front of this here station wagon. After the crash, Ah got out ta see if the guy in the wagon was okay, and he was a-draggin' these dead bodies inta the back of his wagon, and he was bleedin' all over 'em. He said it was okay 'cause they was already dead, so Ah just went back to ma truck, sat down, and got sick until the powlice showed up." His testimony got a good laugh out everyone in the courtroom, including the judge. Thanks in part to his hilarious testimony, the opposing attorney decided to settle in my favor.

On another trip to Ohio to pick up two new hearses, one of our employees, Duane Graham, accompanied me. Duane knew what I'd done the previous years, so he suggested we also do a banzai run this time as well. He must not have realized that this was a bit more difficult than it sounded. When we crossed into Arizona, he flashed his lights at me and asked for a short nap. An hour later, I woke him so we could continue. After several minutes talking to him, he finally said, "I need some coffee." When we made a coffee stop, he said he didn't know where we were or what was going on for the first few minutes. That's what happens when you drive yourself crazy.

11

Breaking New Ground

We continued getting busier by the week while Cal Hearse was declining. We realized that the addition of Jimmy, with his superlative guidance, put us on a fast track to success because he was able to augment our expansion with his knowledge and experience.

When Utter-McKinley opened a mortuary inside Inglewood Park Cemetery, the public was very receptive. This meant that it was no longer necessary to escort a large procession of cars across town. The cemetery had three chapels. Chapel of the Chimes was the busiest and also housed the crematorium in the basement. During hundreds of services there, the only place you could sit down was about eight steps down a staircase into the room that housed the furnace, called a retort, used for cremations. The thing that was always eerie was that you would be in a room that had these furnaces going constantly. There was a ten-inch window in the door of each retort that a worker peered into to check the status of a cremation in progress. That room could give some people the creeps, but it was a great place to sit while waiting, especially on cold days.

On many occasions, we were requested to furnish six pallbearers, as we did for the funeral of retired CIA director John McCone's wife, Rosemary. John McCone was the acting head of the CIA during the White House meetings when President John F. Kennedy implemented the blockade of Cuba. It was going to be a very formal service, and we had been instructed to rent funeral director "stripes," which consisted of slacks with black, gray, and white stripes, and a formal black jacket. Most funeral directors had pretty much stopped wearing this attire, except for the two big Catholic firms, Callanan and Cunningham and O'Connor.

Another tradition that seemed to fade away with time was a practice followed by both the Catholic and Episcopal Churches. The altar boys would place a large fabric covering over the casket called a pall. This was the origin of the word "pallbearer," denoting the people who carry the casket.

Movie studios would call mortuaries to rent hearses, and they started referring them to me. Our first rental was a '48 Packard to be used in a horror film called *The House on Haunted Hill,* starring Vincent Price. The opening shot showed our hearse being followed by about five cars, arriving at a home that had been designed by Frank Lloyd Wright in the Hollywood Hills. Soon every studio in town was calling us for funeral cars.

After three years of doing calls for the coroner's office, we inquired if it might be possible to get some type of official identification or some kind of badges for our employees to carry, because they did not wear the tan uniform and shoulder patches that identified them as deputy coroners. We got absolutely no response to our inquiry, so I finally decided, "We don't need no stinking badges." As I look back, we had become de facto deputy coroners, with all the powers and authority of the fully trained and uniformed deputies. In our case, the only training our young crew members received was what we taught them.

In 1960, many mortuaries began inquiring if we would be willing to add limousine service to our fleet. The city required us to buy one permit for each limo we wanted to put into service in LA. We were hoping to start with four new limos, but at $5,000 per permit that was out of the question. The California Public Utilities Commission (PUC) was the agency that issued these permits, so we decided to make an appeal to them. We explained that our intention was not to compete with the three existing limousine services in Los Angeles, but to make our cars available exclusively to mortuaries. They said that we still needed to buy permits and that if we wanted to pursue the issue further we would need to appear before a PUC hearing board. Yikes.

Five members were on the board and one of them, Morton Silverman, happened to be a partner at Malinow and Silverman Mortuary. They had been renting cars and drivers from us for over two years and urged us to add this service, so they wouldn't have to use the three existing limo services. Morton assured us that we would get his full support. In addition, one of the brothers who owned Callanan Mortuary in Hollywood was an attorney and offered to assist us.

We contacted numerous funeral directors who appeared with us at the hearing. Each had horror stories to tell about the untrained and disinterested services being provided by the limo drivers who were employed by the three companies. There was a great deal of live testimony from mortuary owners who supported the premise that Los Angeles needed a limo service that specialized in funeral work. After about thirty minutes of testimony, we were a little surprised when Morton said we had made a good case, and he placed a motion to do away with the permit system. He asked if anyone would second the motion, and another board member said, "I do." After a quick vote, the gavel hit the bench and Morton announced that the motion had passed.

We never dreamed that our efforts would result in a discontinuance of all limo permits. In a town the size of Los Angeles, there had to be a good reason for having only three limousine services and the permit system was that reason. Now there were going to be four providers, and without realizing it at the time, we had opened the door for at least fifty future limousine companies to start renting limos. In an ironic twist, the three existing limo services eventually began calling us to do backup drives for them.

Our limos were busy during the day on funerals, but at night they were idle, except for Catholic rosaries and Japanese funerals. From that time forward, we sent all ten of our limos out for the Academy Awards, Grammy Awards, Emmy Awards, the Rose Parade, and the Rose Bowl football game on New Year's Day. When *Playboy* magazine started their own limo service we helped them cover their drives for many years, although I never got to meet a Playboy Bunny.

One of the most notable orders was from the Democratic National Committee. Two of our new limos were kept busy for about a week taking nominee John F. Kennedy and his entourage all over Los Angeles during the 1960 Democratic Convention. Unfortunately, it took months for them to pay us for our services. They must have been deficit spending.

Even UCLA and two chiropractic colleges contracted with us to pick up willed bodies that had been donated to them for medical research. The donor cards that were given out didn't even have UCLA's phone number on it, only ours. We couldn't help but observe UCLA Medical Center's rather unique way of storing cadavers.

In the '40s, many people still had an icebox, which was nothing more than a tin-lined wooden box with insulation to keep in the cold. People would put an Ice sign in their window to get a delivery, and a truck would drive down residential streets and stop whenever the driver saw the sign. The driver would get out large ice tongs, grab a large chunk of ice, throw it over his leather-covered shoulder, and carry it to your front door.

The UCLA Medical Center used a device that looked very similar to these ice tongs in their large walk-in refrigerator. The only thing distasteful about this method was that cadavers were suspended in place by having the tongs placed in the ear canal. This was done because storing cadavers for long periods of time creates unique problems. If a cadaver is kept too long on a slab, mold grows where the body rests, but this is lessened if the entire body is kept in a cold, dry environment. It was rather upsetting the first time we observed all these bodies hanging in this fashion, covered with transparent plastic bags.

In a book called *Lenin's Embalmers*, the author discusses the scientists who kept the body of Russia's most well-known citizen from getting moldy in his tomb. They had to bathe him in a special solution they developed, and it had to be reapplied quite often so the people walking by him wouldn't be aware of the inevitability of his condition worsening with time. After all, nobody wants to look at a moldy national icon.

The Secret Service arranged for us to provide limousines when Prime Minister Miki Takeo of Japan visited LA. They sent agents to thoroughly search each limo and run background checks on all our drivers. The Dalai Lama also availed himself of our services on his visit to Los Angeles. When we drove the Rolling Stones, fans mobbed our two limos and they sustained a great deal of damage. When the Beatles came for their first American tour in San Diego, we decided that it would be much wiser to take them in a vehicle that no one would suspect. Ron contacted an associate of ours, Eldon Gabor, who agreed to have them stay at his home in the Beverly Hills area. Eldon also owned a motor home, which we used, knowing that it would be much more discreet.

When we returned the Beatles to Eldon's residence after the concert, to everyone's surprise, a whole group of girls was waiting outside for their return. Ron was astounded when the Fab Four didn't invite any of the young ladies to party with them that night. Instead, they just wanted to go into Eldon's game room to shoot pool. Some years later, the Beatles rented a limo from us for over a month while producing the Sgt. Pepper's Lonely Hearts Club Band album, but they provided their own driver.

Soon after that we got a drive for the revered actor Robert Young, of the *Marcus Welby, M.D.* TV show. I wanted to make a great impression, but at the first main intersection from Young's Beverly Hills home, I made a right turn that cut too sharp and the rear tire jumped the corner of the curb. Kerplop! *That's right, Allan, demonstrate your professional driving skills.* Thankfully, the rest of the drive went smoothly.

12

What a Way to Go

Over the years we responded to a great variety of suicide calls, which included death by hanging, shooting, wrist slashing, and carbon monoxide poisoning. We once made a call in a very secluded part of Baldwin Hills, with spectacular views of the city lights at night. All the high school kids called this area "Pecker's Point," because this was where all the guys parked to make out with their girlfriends. A man had consumed an entire bottle of whiskey, written a suicide note, and done the deed. We wondered why the body looked like an overripe tomato, with red blotches all over his face. We found out later that this was the body's reaction to carbon monoxide poisoning.

Some people get quite creative in choosing a method of suicide. One person we picked up had swallowed a pint of fluid used in Ditto machines, which were the forerunner of photocopiers. This must have been an agonizing way of saying "good-bye cruel world," so I wouldn't advise anyone to copy that. We also discovered that people who commit suicide often try one strategy unsuccessfully, or with painful results, and then switch to another method. This concept was depicted in Arthur Miller's play *Death of a Salesman*, when Willy Loman makes a couple of attempts before he is successful.

Some of the most unusual calls that mortuaries got were the result of industrial accidents. One of these involved an electrical worker who was high up on a power pole, along the side of a dirt road used only by the utility company to service their equipment. Being in such a remote area, when he had to urinate, he didn't bother climbing down. Big mistake. A surge of electricity traveled up the stream and electrocuted him.

One of America's claims to fame comes from its early Wild West history, when our heroes were gun-toting lawmen with their lightning-speed fast draws. This was the inspiration for the successful cartoon series *Quick Draw McGraw*, a favorite of thousands of boys. It got to a point where young men across the country began entering quick draw contests. One casualty of this craze was a boy practicing in front of his mirror. He drew so fast that when he fumbled the draw, his revolver discharged and shot him through the eye. His hysterical mother explained to us that he always practiced with live ammunition in the weapon, so its weight would be the same as it would be in a contest.

A body that remains in an open environment, as opposed to one in a house or car, is much more likely to be subjected to all variety of insects. Anyone who has ever watched *CSI* knows that insects, particularly blowflies, can be used to determine the approximate date of death. This is done by examining a fly larva, which transforms from a maggot to a fly at a known rate. Picking up a body thoroughly infested with maggots is disgusting. You can hear the sound of them feasting on the body from ten feet away. Maggots are very hard to kill because they seem to be unaffected by embalming fluid, but someone did discover that ordinary gasoline could be used to exterminate them. We never did find out how many maggots you can get to a gallon of gas.

Our relationship with the coroner's office was always a love-hate one. We loved the money but hated the work—the very worst being the "decomps." When a body is well into this stage, we referred to it as being "ripe." At a later stage of decomposition, the body undergoes a condition called "skin slip." It is very much like what happens to a tomato's skin that has been left in the refrigerator too long.

One of my earliest coroner calls was to pick up a deputy at the down-town morgue and assist him on a suicide call. We went in one of our first-call cars, and he directed me to the Yucca Motel in Hollywood. The deceased was a weekly renter and when the maid went into the room to bring fresh linen, she discovered him dead. The decomposition was so far along that the body had many fluid-filled blisters. Without saying anything to me, the deputy went into the kitchenette and brought back a sharp pointed can opener. He calmly walked over to the bed and started using it to pop the blisters. He must have seen the expression on my face because he said, "Do you want these to break while we're moving him and get this stuff on us?" You really have to have a strong stomach to do this kind of work. We referred to it as the infamous "Yucca Motel Call," but it should have been the "Yucky Motel Call."

Some of the more unusual places we have made first calls were business facilities like the Procter & Gamble factory. We also made a number of removals from famous San Quentin State Prison during the times they were holding executions. We were even called to make a removal at a candy factory after an employee had fallen into a chocolate mixing vat and drowned. Some devout chocolate lovers out there probably dream of meeting their end that way.

One common place where many people die is in the bathroom, still sitting on the toilet. Apparently, many people become ill with symptoms like nausea, chest pain, light-headedness, perspiration, shortness of breath, and stomach cramping. These may be symptoms of common conditions, like high blood pressure or congested arteries, but many people mistakenly equate them with gastrointestinal problems, which make them feel that they need to get to the bathroom. That's an insight that will give readers something new to ponder each time they visit the restroom.

Almost everyone has seen images of the famous Hollywood sign, but no one I've spoken to remembers the small building with a forty-foot antenna next to it just to the right of the sign. This was owned by one of TV's first broadcasters in Los Angeles, Don Lee. Everyone living in Southern California in the '50s had heard an announcer saying, "This program has been brought to you by Don Lee Broadcasting Company." One of our earliest death calls from somewhere other than a hospital, sanitarium, or residence came from this location. Ron and I arrived there in the dead of night to pick up the night watchman, who had died on his shift.

One night there was a call from my office to inform me that one of our drivers had called in requesting assistance. He had picked up an extremely overweight woman at the hospital with the help of personnel there, but he needed someone to meet him at Forest Lawn Hollywood Hills for delivery. After I arrived, we removed the covers. It was clear that the only thing keeping her in the middle of the stretcher was the nylon strapping.

When we attempted to transfer her to the embalming table, her stomach was so large that it wouldn't stay in place. If we moved the body in one direction, her massive stomach would start to roll her off the table on one side, and the same thing happened on the other side in the opposite direction. We finally borrowed a roll of duct tape, and with help from the night attendant we were able to stabilize the moving mass. I've heard of many practical uses of duct tape, but this was one for the books.

One call I'm glad I missed was from a mortuary in Long Beach. Ron and one of our employees responded to a coroner's case at a residence. The deceased man had been extremely thoughtful of his family by going into his backyard before shooting himself with a shotgun, thus avoiding a very messy cleanup. He had placed the barrel at his temple and somehow reached the trigger with his right hand. As they placed what was left of him in a disaster pouch, there was a blood-curdling scream from the next yard. They looked over the fence and saw the neighbor lady standing in front of her barbecue grill, which had a large piece of the man's brain sitting on it.

There came a time when we realized that our linen costs were getting out of hand. On each removal we would use two sheets, one to cover the cot mattress and the other to cover the remains. Keeping my eyes out for an alternative, I noticed on the new homes being built that each exterior wall was covered with a white synthetic material as a moisture barrier. It was a strong sheet-like material that said "Tyvek" on it. We found out where it could be purchased in large rolls that weighed about 100 pounds. It would have been impractical to have someone cut seven-foot sheets from the roll, one at a time, so we had a carpenter build a roller apparatus out of wood and we purchased a professional fabric-cutting tool. As soon as we deployed our Tyvek sheets we began getting requests from many mortuaries to sell them quantities of the material as well.

David Malloy called us for a removal in the town of Lancaster, fifty miles north of Los Angeles. He directed us to deliver the remains to the Los Angeles County Coroner's Office. I arrived at the private residence and noticed that the air was thick with the odor of death. After entering the house, which was unlocked, I realized that some assistance was going to be needed to complete this call. There was a local funeral home owner in town who owed me a favor because he was in Los Angeles one night on business and ran short on money—so I loaned him some. Now it was payback time. After a quick phone call, he agreed to have me pick him up at his mortuary, along with one of his employees to assist us on this difficult call.

The deceased was lying in his bed, his body totally black and twice its normal size. Fluid had saturated the carpeting, so we rolled out a large sheet of plastic that we planned to wrap him up in before placing the body in a cremation box. The area was relatively rural at that time, and there weren't any fences between the properties. The couple who lived next door was standing in their backyard observing our activities and finally the husband's curiosity got the best of him. He walked over and started to talk to me as the plastic was being unrolled in the yard. He didn't seem surprised that the old man had died, but nothing was brought up about the condition of the remains.

When I reentered the house, he followed me toward the bedroom. Because he was doing all the talking, he hadn't taken a breath until we reached the bedroom. He stopped dead in his tracks, grabbed his throat with his hands, let out a gagging sound, and ran for the backdoor. A few minutes later it was necessary to go back to the car. The man's wife came running over screaming, "What did you do to my husband? I'm going to have to take him to the hospital." You know what they say about curiosity being a killer.

Dave had instructed me to be sure to get the deceased's Social Security card, which was on the dresser. As the three of us drove back to the mortuary, something unforgettable happened. We were sitting three abreast on the station wagon's bench seat, and Dave's helper was seated next to the passenger door. He quietly rolled down the passenger's window and, without saying a word, took off his damp shoes and threw them out the window.

I dropped the body off at the coroner's office, went home, took a shower, and went to bed, because the call had kept me out until 1:00 in the morning. The next morning, I went to drop off the Social Security card and noticed a terrible smell. I was in my own personal car. Where was it coming from? Then it struck me. Even though the wallet was many feet away from the body, it had absorbed the smell and was sitting in my shirt pocket.

13

Man Does Not Live on Bread Alone

For the first few years in business, we hadn't taken a single day or night off and had no social life whatsoever. We were on call twenty-four hours a day, and when we ate out we would always tell the person answering our phones where we could be reached. My only evening off was on Wednesdays, when I would drive to my parents' house for dinner.

One night my brother brought a beautiful girl named Kathy to our house. He had just started dating her, and all I could think of was, "Where in the world had he found this gorgeous blue-eyed blonde?" It turned out that he met her through our mother, who managed the basement of the J.J. Newberry dime store in Inglewood, where Kathy was employed as a part-time worker.

During high school, Kathy was working to supplement her family's income. At that time, many schools allowed students to participate in a program that enabled them to go to school for half a day and work the other half. There were four girls working at the store from Washington High, but Kathy was definitely our mom's favorite, and it was obvious that she would have liked to have Kathy as a daughter-in-law. My brother and Kathy dated for about five months, at which time he had proposed to her. She was still in high school and declined. Mom wasn't about to give up so easily, so she asked Kathy if she would accompany her to see our newly refurbished Auto Club building. At the end of our visit I asked Kathy if I could call her sometime, and she agreed.

John was now serving in the Marine Corps, so I wrote him a letter and asked if he had any objection to my dating Kathy. He didn't seem to care, so we started spending time together, and it was great to be dating after a three-year drought. Although it was difficult to take time off, it was very important to finally get some semblance of a personal life back. I had no car and Kathy didn't even have a driver's license, so if we wanted to go somewhere we would go in a company car. Imagine picking up your date in a first-call car that looked like a small hearse!

After we had dated for about four months, Kathy told me that the first few times she saw me at my parents' house, arriving on my motorcycle, wearing my gray uniform and leather jacket, she thought that I must have been the black sheep of the family.

When Kathy graduated from high school, I taught her how to drive and had a private phone installed in her bedroom. I purchased a five-year-old Buick from my brother and gave it to her. The only thing that was weird about the situation was that we were now dating in the same car that she and John had been going out in. Talk about hand-me-downs.

When we got engaged, our business was still straining to expand and Kathy was still in high school, so we set our wedding date for the following June. A year later, her parents were not well-off financially, even though Paul, her Russian immigrant father, was an excellent engineer. He worked for another Russian man who owned an engineering firm, but received a fairly low salary because he hadn't yet mastered the English language.

Paul would later get a good job with the City of Los Angeles in their streetlighting department, but at the time he could not afford the kind of wedding Kathy had always wanted. In the ensuing year, she hoped to earn enough money for a traditional Russian Orthodox wedding. Kathy got a job working for the United States Air Force as a secretary. Once she received a security clearance, she was given a job at their Space Systems Division in Inglewood, working on the Gemini and similar projects in the early years of the space program.

Kathy and Allan at her high school prom in 1960.

I wrote a letter to John again, but this time I was requesting that he be best man at our wedding. He wrote me a letter back that simply said, "Go to hell," so Ron volunteered. The choir from Holy Virgin Mary Russian Orthodox Church in Silver Lake that performed the traditional singing for our wedding later sang the background music for the film *Cinerama Goes to Russia*. That church was quite small, so we rented Saint Sophia's Greek Orthodox Cathedral for the ceremony. It is probably the largest cathedral in Southern California and had been built largely from contributions by Spyros Skouras, who had been the president of 20th Century Fox Studios since 1942.

We went to Hawaii for our honeymoon, which was the first real break I had taken in four years. It was time for some connubial bliss. Our plane was delayed, so we arrived late on the night of June 11, 1961. We finally got to sleep about 2 A.M., awoke around 9:00 the next morning, and were doing what newlyweds do on their honeymoon. The front desk called to tell us that the King Kamehameha Day Parade was going to pass down the main street in case we wanted to come down and watch. I thought, "On our honeymoon, are you serious?"

Ron had given us an 8-mm movie camera as a wedding present, which was perfect for recording our wonderful time there. They were building an eleven-story hotel on the main street called the Princess Kaiulani Hotel. It was the only high-rise hotel in Oahu, and it towered over everything. We snuck up the stairs to the top floor, even though it was still under construction, and from an observation deck we filmed the whole coastline.

14

Lessons on Freedom from Kathy's Family

On the numerous occasions we had dinner at Kathy's parents' house, the only language spoken was Russian. Most of the time, I had no idea what they were talking about. After dinner, we would sometimes watch TV. When we changed channels, a war movie would sometimes come on the screen and Kathy's mother, Vera, would immediately get up and go to another room, mumbling something in Russian. Paul eventually explained that Vera reacted that way because of their terrifying experiences fleeing Yugoslavia during the war. Vera had lost her mother and four-month-old baby during the war, and she didn't want any reminders.

Paul was 17 when he joined the White Russian Army, fighting against the Bolshevik Red Army in the Russian Civil War that followed the 1917 revolution. After one battle, he found himself the sole surviving soldier in a town surrounded by the Bolsheviks. His only escape was to swim out to a freighter anchored in the port. He was permitted on board after he told the ship's crew that if captured he would have been executed immediately.

He was subsequently asked to get off the ship at the first port they reached, located on the island of Malta, which has been described by historians as one of the most bombed locations during World War II. He then made his way to Zagreb, Yugoslavia, where he attended a university. Four years later, he received an engineering degree and met Vera, his future wife. After they were married, Kathy was born in Skopje, Yugoslavia. They became quite well-off. Every morning, a driver would pick Paul up and take him to the government engineering office, where he would oversee all the other civil engineers.

In 1944, the Red Army invaded Yugoslavia, driving out the occupying Germans. Paul and Vera were told they had twenty minutes to evacuate because White Russian expatriates and their families would be imprisoned or killed. They grabbed two suitcases and filled them with some of their possessions and valuables that could be traded for food, like jewelry and gold coins. When they got to the Skopje train station, the only passage available was a train heading in the direction of Germany, because all the other trains were already filled with people fleeing the country.

At the end of the railroad line, the family came upon a group of German army trucks being loaded with troops fleeing back to Germany. Paul could speak several languages, so he approached a German officer and asked if he and his family could get asylum in Germany. He was told that it was totally against regulations to transport civilians in these troop trucks, but Paul pleaded that he had a wife,

Kathy at age 3, in Europe during World War II in 1944.

two daughters, and Vera's mother, who were all trying to escape imprisonment or death. Kathy was 4 and her baby sister, Tatiana, was only four months old. The officer compassionately agreed and proceeded to put Paul, Kathy, and her grandmother in the first truck, while Vera and the baby were loaded into the second one.

The troop truck's headlights were taped over with just small slits to let light out to make them more difficult for the enemy to observe. On a winding road in the mountains of Yugoslavia they came to a sharp curve that the driver couldn't see and his truck plunged off the steep grade, rolling over. A large gun crushed Kathy's grandmother and broke Paul's leg. The survivors were subsequently loaded into other trucks and they continued on to Germany, without anyone even attending to the dead.

Paul ended up in a hospital in Berlin, while Kathy, her baby sister, and Vera were interned in a displaced persons (DP) camp in Munich. They were transferred to additional locations, under very tenuous circumstances, because it was not known who was going to win the war in Europe. After two months they were finally reunited.

Kathy clearly recalled the many times sirens wailed as they were herded into a train tunnel serving as a bomb shelter. Paul said that the Americans bombed during the day and the British bombed at night. Even though Kathy was barely 4 at the time, she could clearly recall the many hours spent underground until the all-clear siren would sound, and they would come out and see the death and destruction from the bombings.

In wartime Germany, disease was rampant. During my childhood you would often hear the expression, "Good night, sleep tight, and don't let the bed bugs bite." In the DP camp, biting bugs were not the only problem. Along with malnutrition, there were a number of deadly diseases, so crews would go through the housing quarters spraying disinfectant. As a result of this spraying, Kathy's sister, Tatiana, died.

German measles was by far one of the worst diseases in the camps. Any children running a temperature were immediately taken from their parents and usually never seen again. One day, Kathy started getting sick and showing signs of a fever. The camp nurse told Vera that she was going to have to take her away, but Vera pleaded with her to wait at least until the following morning. She promised that if Kathy still had a temperature the following day, she would let her go. Vera stayed up the entire night praying that if Kathy's temperature would just go down, she could get the measles at any other time, just not here and now. Vera kept repeating this prayer over and over, all night long. When the nurse came in the following morning, her daughter's fever was gone. Kathy did come down with the measles two years later, but by then she was in America.

When the war ended, the DP camps were taken over by American forces that were much more lenient. Kathy and Vera would stand in line day after day, trying to get permission to immigrate to another country. The World Church Organization eventually sponsored the family for passage on a ship to the last place still accepting immigrants, which was America. Kathy was seasick the entire trip, but when they sailed into New York Harbor and got their first look at the Statue of Liberty, it was one of her life's greatest rewards.

Paul, Vera, and Kathy were processed on Ellis Island. When asked their family name, Paul said "Tzarenko," from the root word "tsar" or "czar," the recognized title of Russian emperors who ruled before 1917. (The word "tsar," in turn, came from the word "caesar.") Spelling being what it was during this mass influx of foreigners, they were tagged as the Zarenko family. Kathy was only 6 when they arrived in New York, but she had a vivid recollection of something they had eaten there, which was Lipton's instant chicken soup. She remembered that it was the best thing she had tasted for years, except for the chocolate given to her by American soldiers at the camp.

When Kathy entered Catholic school, she was held back one year because she couldn't speak English. This school had Dominican nuns as teachers who, fortunately for Kathy, spoke German, which she had picked up in the camps. Kathy met a nice classmate in school, and they became friends. In spite of knowing very little English, Kathy and Sandra Gehl seemed to communicate without much talking, as kids often do. On the first day of school Sandy took Kathy by the hand, got on the school bus, and took Kathy home with her. Sandy's mother had to call the school to find out where Kathy's family lived so she could get her safely home. Sandy was eventually one of Kathy's bridesmaids.

In 1976, we took Kathy's parents to Yugoslavia and Greece with us. Although many years had passed since the war, you could still feel the tension between the Serbians and the Croatians. Our guide pointed out the large number of old women walking on the streets and highways, dressed all in black. These were the widows of soldiers who had died in the war, thirty years earlier.

As we were traveling down the Yugoslavian coast, our tour guide made a significant announcement. Because of tour bus robberies in Albania, we were going to have to take a 200-mile detour. During a conversation with the regional guide in Yugoslavia, it came to light that he was originally from Skopje, where Kathy was born, and that our new route would take us within fifteen miles of that town. It was as if fate had intervened. A passenger on the bus suggested that it would be nice to drive through town, so Kathy could see where she was born. He was quick to explain that it would not be proper to divert the other passengers just for her sake, but everyone in the group chimed in and said, "We all want to go there!"

Skopje was beautiful, but it had been mostly rebuilt after a terrible 1963 earthquake had destroyed much of the town. However, a single brick structure was purposely left standing. It was one wall of the very same train station Kathy's family had gone to in their attempt to escape from Yugoslavia decades before. The section of a wall still standing had a large clock that was frozen at 5:17, the exact time the earthquake had struck, so the people of Skopje decided to leave it as a permanent memorial. I photographed the wall so that Kathy could have a picture of the train station where her family's long and desperate journey to freedom had begun.

15

Secrets of the Stars

The last movie that Clark Gable appeared in was *The Misfits*, which was written by Marilyn Monroe's third husband, Arthur Miller. Gable died a few days after it was completed, and it turned out to be Marilyn's last film as well. It was an odd coincidence for me to have been involved in both of their funerals. I drove a family car for Gable's funeral at Forest Lawn Glendale in 1960 and would also be very involved in Marilyn's service two years later.

It took many years before enough limousine services were operating in Los Angeles to cover the high demand in a city that had more celebrities per capita than anywhere else in the world. We started doing backup orders for some of the existing limo services, like Tanner Gray Line and Playboy Limo Service.

Tanner Gray Line offered travel services in many large cities and was one of the three limousine companies that tried to keep us from entering the limousine business. They had a contract with Matson Lines, which had a large cruise ship called the *Lurline* that ran from Los Angeles Harbor to Hawaii and other ports. There were numerous occasions when we would meet the ship arriving back in Long Beach to pick up the corpse of someone who had died while on a Matson Lines cruise. They simply placed the deceased in one of their large refrigerators until the ship arrived back in LA. I hope it was not the same refrigerator they used for food storage, as William Petersen's character Gil Grissom did in *CSI*.

Years later, in the '80s, an entrepreneurial young man started a service in Hollywood taking tourists around in a limousine-style hearse that had windows all around, much like a station wagon. He toured people from one cemetery to another, showing them where famous people were buried. He called his new venture Grave Line Tours, a takeoff on the Gray Line limos and buses that had been known throughout the area.

Doing backup work for the high-profile limousine services gave me an opportunity to drive celebrities we would have never gotten on our own unless they happened to be dead. As I look back, it seems a little strange that they trusted us enough to give us these celebrity drives and not worry about the possibility that we might start soliciting them ourselves. Had the movie studios given us these drives directly, there are many that I would never have farmed out to another limo service. No matter how busy we were, I would have taken these drives myself.

A good example of this was an order from another limousine service in the early 1960s to pick up television and film star Inger Stevens and take her to LAX to fly to Chicago for a meeting with her production company. At the time, Inger Stevens had a popular television show called *The Farmer's Daughter*, which we watched. Her studio apartment was just off Hollywood Boulevard, and her unit was on the corner as you enter the complex and it had the bedroom on the second floor upstairs. After I knocked on the door, a man spoke to me from behind it and asked, "What is it?" I told him that the limo had arrived to take Miss Stevens to the airport, but he informed me that she had already gone in her own car.

Ready for cruising through Hollywood on Allan's Triumph motorcycle in 1964.

Kathy and I drove from our apartment in Inglewood to Hollywood almost every weekend. This was a time when it was a magical place. People would cruise back and forth on Hollywood Boulevard. The high-powered searchlights used during World War II did not go to waste after the war, because movie theaters purchased them to light up the sky whenever they were showing a big movie premiere. People would get in their car and drive to where the lights were just to see what was being shown there. Big premieres were always taking place in the numerous famous theaters in Hollywood, and it was very exciting to see the latest epic film.

After we saw a movie in Hollywood, Kathy asked me to show her Inger Stevens's apartment, which was only a couple of blocks away. As we turned onto Martel Avenue, we could see the lights were on in her apartment. There were no available parking spaces on the street, so we pulled into the driveway of the house next door. It was an exceptionally balmy August night, and the apartment windows were open. The only thing separating us from her front door was a six-foot hedge.

We could clearly hear a man's voice talking on the telephone, and it was the same voice from behind the door a week earlier. He was attempting to get a date for that night, but these ladies all turned him down because it was already after 10 P.M. His next call was to some male friend. During this phone conversation he repeatedly mentioned Inger by name and started to talk about her sexual preferences. He concluded by saying that he was going to go to the Ash Grove to see if he could "get lucky." While the cat's away . . . .

This seemed like a good time to leave, but as we were backing up, he exited the apartment very quickly. Before we had time to turn left toward home, he passed in front of our car and was illuminated by the headlights. We were caught a little off-guard for a second, because he was a black man. He drove away in a new Chevy Impala, and Kathy wanted to see where he was going so we followed him. When he parked near the front of the tavern, I got out and looked into the open window and there was a box of business cards, which read: "Isaac Jones, President of Kell-Cole Productions."

A month later, we got another order to pick up Miss Stevens at the same apartment for

Inger Stevens in 1961.

another airport run. Here was the same voice on the other side of the same door, telling me the same thing about her taking her own car again. It was like that Yogi Berra line about déjà vu all over again.

A week later, we went to another movie in Hollywood, so we visited her apartment again. We parked in the same neighbor's driveway. The living room windows were open, and we could clearly hear the occupants having an argument. As they were yelling back and forth, we heard Isaac say that Martin Luther King was a "jerk" and an "opportunist." She was infuriated by his remarks and said that he should be ashamed of himself, because King had done great things by using a nonviolent approach to attain civil rights for his people. Then she started asking Isaac where he had spent the previous night and when he finally screamed, "It's none of your goddamned business!" She yelled back, "I have a right to know, I am your wife."

We just sat there in stunned silence, but what happened next really knocked our socks off. There were sounds of some kind of altercation. Then it clearly sounded like he had picked her up and went stomping upstairs. Their subsequent roll in the hay sounded much more graphic than the adventures of "John and Marsha." It may have been hard to believe they were married, but we had just heard it straight from the horse's mouth.

Now it all made sense. The studio probably didn't have a clue about her relationship with Isaac. Had Inger used the limo, the driver might have told someone at the studio he had observed a man at her apartment. Taking her own car assured them that there would be no witnesses, and when the studio got the limo bill, they paid it, assuming she had used it. Those were the bad old days, when the studios had almost total control over an actor's life.

Ironically, Inger had starred in a film called *The World, the Flesh and the Devil* that touched upon the issue of interracial relationships. The story was about the last three people in the world surviving a nuclear exchange. Along with Inger, it starred Harry Belafonte and Mel Ferrer. The subject matter was so controversial at that time the studio shot three endings to the film: one where she chooses Mel Ferrer, another where she goes off with Harry Belafonte, and the third where she convinces the two male rivals that they can all live in peace and harmony as they walk off into the sunset. After test showings of the film during which each of the possible endings was judged, the studio chose the third kiss-and-make-up ending.

Kathy started paying particular attention to the articles about Inger in the movie magazines. She had told many of her girlfriends about what we had heard, and their reactions were dubious. Even my mother asked me how this could possibly be true after so much was being written about Inger and Burt Reynolds dating. Hey, if your own mother doesn't believe you, you're in big trouble.

After dating Burt for about a year, they had a knock-down, drag-out fight one night, and Burt allegedly told her he would never marry her. A close girlfriend of hers told a reporter that he had gotten physically abusive with her, and the next day her body was discovered on her kitchen floor. According to one of her closest friends, Inger had called her immediately after the fight. She was crying and telling her friend how hopeless things had gotten. The cause of death was listed as a suicide from ingesting a combination of sleeping pills and alcohol.

In 1990, there was an article in a book club newsletter about a writer working on a book to be called *Everything You Ever Wanted to Know about Inger Stevens*. He was asking anyone who knew anything about her to contact him by phone in nearby Studio City. During our phone conversation, he wanted to know if he could interview me. This was about twenty years after she had died, and by this time he had already interviewed nearly a hundred people. He confirmed the accuracy of all my facts and later gave me a manuscript of his book, along with a beautiful studio photo of her.

Because of the paparazzi, it was very difficult to have to a private funeral and maintain any kind of security. The mortuary that directed Gary Cooper's funeral in 1961 called us for cars and drivers. The mortuary went to great lengths to keep the funeral as private as possible and did a good job weeding out spectators. The interment was at Holy Cross Cemetery in "The Grotto," the most prodigious section of the cemetery where Bing Crosby and Béla Lugosi are buried. The graves in this area are quite expensive because they went to great lengths to bring in rocks and form a shallow cave, with exotic flowers growing between the rocks and many bonsai trees, cut in the traditional Japanese fashion, on each side of the opening.

Just across the street from the cemetery was Fox Hills County Club, so one journalist hired a limo and had it wait there until the funeral cars entered the cemetery. Then the limo driver was instructed to fall in at the rear of the procession. No one questioned the extra limo, so at the graveside service, he lowered his window and started shooting photos of everyone present.

We also furnished limos for the wedding of Ricky Nelson to Kristin Harmon, whom he had met at Hollywood High School. We were instructed to report to the very exclusive Beverly Hills estate of the famous sportsman turned sports radio announcer, Tom Harmon. Kristin and other family members had gathered there to be taken to the church in four limos.

Sports never interested me, but everyone knew who Tom Harmon was. Ron even agreed to drive one of the cars, in spite of his total lack of interest in the entertainment industry. We were lined up in the long driveway of the Harmon estate. The grounds were quite large, even for this affluent part of town. The backyard looked to be about half the size of a football field, replete with a tennis court. Their wedding was held at Saint Martin of Tours Catholic Church on Sunset Boulevard. *Life* magazine named it "The Wedding of the Year."

Years later, while doing a shoot at Hollywood Cemetery, we were asked to provide a hearse for the TV show *Reasonable Doubt* with Mark Harmon, Kristin's brother, and Marlee Matlin. The baseball bug must have bitten Mark like his father because every time they would yell "cut," he would walk off camera, pick up his glove and baseball, and start throwing a few balls with one of the crew members. There is often more downtime than actual filming.

Tom Harmon was married to film star Elyse Knox, who played Jane in some of the Tarzan movies. Ricky and Kristin eventually had a daughter, Tracy Nelson, who had her own TV show and made some movies, including *Down and Out in Beverly Hills*. Ricky Nelson's song "Travelin' Man" is still played on some of the oldies stations, which brings me great pleasure as it was the number one hit while Kathy and I were on our honeymoon in Hawaii in 1961.

Kathy approached me one month with a celebrity magazine that had a beautiful layout featuring Kim Novak at her home in Big Sur, twenty miles south of Carmel. One photograph was taken of her in a bubble bath, with an ocean view from the window above her bathtub. We were planning a trip to nearby Monterey, so Kathy asked me if it would be possible to locate her home. She received my absolute assurances that it would be easy to do. When we drove to Big Sur from our motel, it was simply a matter of looking at homes along the shore of Highway 1. We kept working our way up the coast until we reached Carmel Highlands, just south of Carmel.

We turned onto Spindrift Road, where there was only one spot from which you could not see the ocean. The only access to this property was down a narrow dirt road posted Private Property—No Trespassing. The shoreline in the area was all sheer cliffs about twenty-five feet above the water, exactly what you would expect to see when looking out the window shown in the magazine. A quarter-mile north of these cliffs, Spindrift went downhill until the road was only about eight feet above the shoreline, but it was extremely rocky. The only way to see what was at the end of the road without crossing private property would be to backtrack along these rocks.

Kathy wasn't sure if she wanted to take this circuitous route just on my hunch that it had to be the right place, but after about ten minutes of somewhat risky climbing, we were standing at the bottom of a huge cliff well below what had to be her home. We started climbing up the cliff face just far enough to get to a fairly flat part of the rocks, about eight feet above the waterline. Then, all of a sudden, we were accosted by her attack dog. Well, it wasn't exactly a dog, but her pet billy goat, which put us in great peril as we clung precariously to the rocky face of the cliff. The goat was taking great pleasure in butting us, and although Kathy was laughing nervously, she was using her purse like a shield while yelling at it to go away.

The commotion finally drew Kim's attention as she was standing in her living room, painting at her easel. She spotted us just as we were starting our descent. Her young companion came out onto the balcony and threatened to call the sheriff on us. I informed him that we were on tideland and not private property. At that point Kim joined him on the balcony and they stood arm in arm, watching us climb down. I paused just long enough to point my movie camera at them and record the moment, at which time Kim gave us a nice friendly wave. Cameras often have that effect on movie stars.

16

Marilyn Monroe

In December 1961 we purchased three brand-new 1962 funeral coaches. When a funeral home had a service for someone famous, they wouldn't use their own funeral cars because many were ten to fifteen years old. The reason was that hearses only had to be replaced after many years of service because they get limited use. They're not the kind of cars you drive when dropping your kids off at school or doing your grocery shopping. *Wait a minute, that's exactly what I did.* Well, at least normal people don't do that.

In the early hours of August 5, 1962, the night watch commander of the West Los Angeles Police Station, Sergeant Jack Clemmons, received a call from a man identifying himself as Dr. Hyman Engelberg. He said Dr. Ralph Greenson had informed him of the death of Marilyn Monroe from an overdose of Nembutal, a suicide. Clemmons immediately assigned another officer to take over from him, jumped into a squad car, and set off for 1230 Fifth Helena Drive in Brentwood, one of twenty-five short cul-de-sacs in the neighborhood.

Westwood Village Memorial Cemetery received a call from the Los Angeles County Coroner's Office, instructing them to make the removal from her home. Manager Guy Hockett arrived on the call, noticed immediately that her body was in the early stages of rigor mortis, and discussed his observation with the policeman.

This condition can set in as soon as six to eight hours after death, depending on many outside factors, but it seemed suspicious since he was told death had occurred only about three hours prior to his arrival. Guy made the removal and returned to the mortuary. Deputies were later sent to the mortuary to bring her body downtown instead.

The news of Marilyn's death spread like wildfire. Many of the reporters in Los Angeles had even showed up at the morgue to no avail, because it was off-limits to reporters. Only one very clever photographer formulated

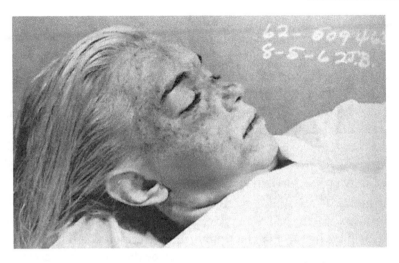

Marilyn Monroe body at the Los Angeles County Medical Examiner's Office. *Photo originally appeared in* Goddess: The Secret Lives of Marilyn Monroe *by Anthony Summers.*

a plan to get some limited access to the morgue. It was more than thirty years later that this photographer shared his story with me at a book signing. Meanwhile, the coroner's office, realizing the magnitude of her death, instructed their staff to give no interviews.

Westwood Village did not own any hearses or limos, so it rented from us for all services. Two brothers, James and Clarence Pierce, owned the Westwood Village operation and were also part owners of a downtown facility called Pierce-Hamrock. We had been assisting these two mortuaries for years. When Westwood Village finally got the call to go to the coroner's office and pick up Marilyn's remains, one of our employees, Leonard "Chris" Kreminski, assisted Clarence Pierce in making the removal.

Because of the tremendous implications of this case, it took much longer for Coroner Theodore Curphey to finally make some statements. His best and most dedicated pathologist, Thomas Noguchi, known to some as "The Knife," spent about three times as much time as it usually took him to do a full postmortem. The deputies at the coroner's office informed me that Dr. Noguchi had been extremely thorough with his examination of her body. He spent a great deal of time looking for hypodermic needle marks, which he did discover in her arm pit, but this area is often used by doctors when treating female movie stars. He continued to search in unusual places like inside her nose, between her toes and fingers, under her tongue, and in her genitals, but was unable to discover any additional injection points.

Marilyn's death caused Dr. Curphey to initiate a new procedure, a "psychological autopsy," or an examination of a person's mental state. Coroner's inquests were not new, but this examination delved into areas that were not usually considered at a coroner's inquest, which is very similar to a grand jury inquest. Grand juries are composed of people who do not know the person involved, but in this case, almost everyone questioned were people Marilyn knew.

The mortuary received numerous phone calls from everywhere. 20th Century Fox Studios had even relayed a message to Westwood that they would help in any way possible with their many resources. It became apparent immediately that this was going to be the funeral of the century and was going to involve a great deal of contingency planning on their part. The following day, Clarence Pierce called and asked me to go to Westwood and assist on every aspect of the planning for her service. I called Kathy and told her about the order. She loved Marilyn and instructed me to watch and listen very carefully to everything that was said and done so that I could share all the details with her.

The cemetery grounds were crawling with photographers, journalists, and fans. Some of them were even checking the doors and windows of the building that housed the embalming room. There were three structures at this facility: an office, an A-frame chapel, and a utility building with the embalming room inside it.

It was clear that some precautions needed to be taken, or this was going to become a disaster. I informed Mrs. Hockett that a serious security problem was developing on the grounds. Her husband was at the coroner's office taking care of the paperwork, so she asked me what should be done. I told her to contact a security company right away and get some guards. She said she didn't have the authority to place such a call, and the two owners were directing a service at their downtown mortuary. I recommended she call the Los Angeles branch and talk to them to get their permission. She made the call, and Clarence told her that this was exactly why he had asked me to oversee everything and do whatever I suggested.

The only name in my mind that stood out was Pinkerton, which had been providing security services for over a hundred years. My rationale was that someone was needed to take control of the situation in the following few days, particularly to dissuade any opportunists from breaching the security of the utility building housing the prep room. Already a rumor was floating around that $30,000 was being offered for a picture of Marilyn in the prep room or in her casket. I immediately called them and requested six uniformed officers. When they asked if I wanted them to wear side arms, my answer was "Absolutely!" Half an hour later, a gray Chevy station wagon showed up with six uniformed guards. Simultaneously, the embalmer arrived from the Los Angeles branch, and we went to the embalming room.

The staff called the embalmer by his nickname, "Frenchie," so no one at our office ever knew his real name, but he was French as champagne and had the accent to prove it. He unlocked the embalming room and we entered together. When we removed the sheet covering her, it was almost impossible to believe this was the body of Marilyn Monroe. She looked like a very average, aging woman who had not been taking very good care of herself. Obviously, the circumstances surrounding her death had greatly exacerbated her poor appearance and she was unrecognizable.

When someone dies, gravity causes the blood to settle to the lowest point of the body. This condition is called lividity, and considering that many people die lying on their backs, the discoloration that occurs is seldom visible. In Marilyn's case, she died face down, so there were purple blotches on her face, and her neck was very swollen. They had bathed her at the coroner's office, and her hair was frizzy and fairly short. You could tell she had not bleached it for some time, because the roots were darker and had grown out about half an inch. Her natural hair color was a light brown, not blonde. Her legs hadn't been shaved for at least a week, and her lips were badly chapped. She was also in need of a manicure and pedicure.

We began discussing the terrible swelling in her neck, and Frenchie decided that a surgical procedure was needed. This was out of my area of expertise, so I deferred to his decision. Frenchie knew how to correct the problem, but it wasn't going to be pretty. He instructed me to hold her on her side so he could make an incision in the back of her neck in the shape of a marquis diamond and remove about two square inches of skin. He then pulled the sides together and stitched it up. It wasn't pleasant to watch, but it was quite effective in reducing the swelling.

In all the years we were involved with the coroner's office, we saw hundreds of nude bodies. Whenever a body was released to a mortuary, it was always without any clothing. In Marilyn's case, someone at the coroner's office had very thoughtfully taken the extra effort to fashion a diaper of sorts for her by cutting up a white sheet. Marilyn's executrix had just brought in her clothing, so Mrs. Hockett rang me to come up to the office and pick up the package. She also informed me that the lady said Marilyn didn't wear panties, and she couldn't find any among her clothing. I also noticed that among the items was a small pair of false breasts. I had seen falsies before, but these were much smaller than any I'd seen.

The dress was a beautiful chartreuse puce design with a Florence, Italy, label. If it weren't for Kathy's encouragement, some of these details would probably have slipped by me, but she wanted me to make a mental note of everything. Just as we finished dressing her, Mary Hamrock came into the embalming room. She had driven to Westwood from the downtown facility that she and the two Pierce brothers co-owned.

As she stood there for a few long moments, she finally voiced her opinion: "That doesn't look like Marilyn Monroe." Mrs. Hamrock was a seasoned businesswoman who didn't pull any punches. Her next comment was "What happened to her boobs?" In his own defense, Frenchie told her that the cutting of the ribs during the autopsy had caused this condition. He further stated that he had even used the falsies that were brought in with her clothing, but they had been much too small to enhance her physique.

Mrs. Hamrock reached down and pulled at the neck of the dress, which was a very springy material. She reached in with her other hand to remove the falsies and threw them into the trash can. She then pulled some clumps of cotton off a roll and formed much larger breasts by stuffing her bra. At this point she stepped back and proudly exclaimed, "Now that looks like Marilyn Monroe!"

After she exited the prep room, I found myself with a dilemma: Should I retrieve the falsies for Kathy? If the embalmer saw me do that, it would have been very embarrassing, so while he was washing up, I kept my eyes on him while reaching into the trash can, retrieving them, and stuffing them into my suit coat pocket. Later, to my surprise, I discovered a lock of her hair sandwiched between them. This was some of the hair that was cut from her neck to access the area for the surgical procedure.

Frenchie didn't feel qualified to prepare Marilyn's makeup and hair, so Fox sent her hairdresser, Sydney Guilaroff, and her makeup man, Allan "Whitey" Snyder, to the mortuary to prepare her. Sydney brought with him a hatbox containing the wig that she wore during the filming of *Something's Got to Give*, which was never completed because of her tardiness and lack of preparation.

It was fascinating watching as Whitey applied her makeup and Sydney combed and sprayed the wig. I got up enough nerve to ask Whitey about the falsies, and he told me that Marilyn was 36 and beginning to show the effects of gravity on her breasts. He said she would wear a bra for support and then place the falsies between her sweater and bra to make it appear that she was unsupported, which was more provocative. When these professionals finished, Marilyn had gone through a remarkable transformation and looked beautiful.

Kathy asked me to take her to Westwood the night before the funeral so she could see Marilyn herself. She had never made such a request in the past, even though there were other celebrities whose visitation would have been accessible to me. Marilyn's visitation was scheduled to end at 9 P.M. Her former husband, Joe DiMaggio, had arrived at the mortuary earlier in the afternoon, stepping up to the plate to take over final plan-

Marilyn Monroe with President John F. Kennedy (right) and Attorney General Robert F. Kennedy, at the occasion of President Kennedy's 45th birthday celebration on May 19, 1962, less than three months before her death. *Photo by Cecil Stoughton. John F. Kennedy Presidential Library and Museum.*

ning of her funeral. He had given Guy Hockett a list of about thirty-one people permitted to attend the funeral.

Lee Strasberg, Marilyn's acting coach from New York's famous Actors Studio, was chosen to give the eulogy at her service. No other Hollywood personalities were allowed to attend the visitation or the funeral. Joe disliked the motion picture industry and hated the things she was asked to do in certain films. The famous scene of her standing over the subway ventilation grate, with the wind blowing her dress up to her waist, was particularly disturbing to him. Marilyn herself seemed to enjoy the attention. She didn't seem the least bit bashful about the accentuation of her cleavage and curves through skin-tight dresses, such as the one she wore at President Kennedy's birthday celebration on May 19, 1962.

Joe and his entourage were at the mortuary when we arrived at 8:45 P.M. He would go up to Marilyn's casket for a while, then leave the chapel and walk outside into the small cemetery to cry. He repeated this pattern until about 10:45, but the night manager, Pat Spinelli, was not about to tell Joe DiMaggio that the visitation was over. I informed Kathy that we would have to leave, because there was much for me to do in preparation for the service the next morning. Just as we started to drive away we saw Joe and his people leave, so we parked and went in.

Pat told us that she had placed a rollaway bed next to Marilyn's casket and slept next to her the previous night to make sure no one could get in and photograph her. As soon as Kathy saw Marilyn, she started to cry. When she finally stopped, we both stood there in silence. After a long moment, Kathy made an interesting observation. Marilyn's eyes were very wide. In retrospect, perhaps that's why no other actress has ever really looked like Marilyn.

Ron and I drove the next morning to Westwood in one of our newly acquired 1962 Eureka hearses. They had me stand at the front door of the chapel, checking invitations and passing out memorial folders. The Los Angeles Police Department had cordoned off large parts of the cemetery with yellow tape. Most of the well-known gossip columnists like Walter Winchell, Hedda Hopper, and Louella Parsons showed up for the funeral, but they had also been present on that first day, when the Pinkerton officers were ordered to control the crowd.

The service in the chapel was recorded. A musical selection of "Somewhere Over the Rainbow" was played, with the casket open so that

Marilyn Monroe's 1962 funeral procession, with Allan and Ron behind their hearse. *Photo by Leigh Wiener. Reprint permission granted by Devik Wiener.*

friends and family could pass by and pay their final respects. After that, James and Clarence Pierce closed the casket and brought it to the back of the chapel. They asked me to direct Sydney and Whitey to prepare for placing it in the hearse. Ron and I were pallbearers.

It was quiet as I opened the chapel door, but the moment we started through the door, with the casket resting on a church truck, all hell broke loose. In an instant, the silence exploded with the sound of a thousand camera shutters clicking simultaneously, and the sky lit up as if lightning struck. Soon, the clamor of hundreds of people screaming from the cordoned-off areas became so loud you could hardly hear the sound of the cameras.

Ron and Allan stand next to Marilyn Monroe's casket as it is positioned just prior to her cryptside service. *Photo by Leigh Wiener. Reprint permission granted by Devik Wiener.*

It was a short drive from the chapel to the lawn crypt as we walked behind the hearse, flanked on either side by the Pinkerton guards. I could see that Sydney was crying, using his handkerchief to wipe tears from his eyes. The hearse stopped slightly past the wall crypt, leaving us enough space to remove the casket from the hearse and carry it about ten feet to the crypt, assisted by Clarence Pierce and Chris Kreminski as the last two pallbearers. We then placed it on a second church truck, where it remained throughout the short cryptside service.

Joe and his son, who was wearing his military attire, were seated on folding chairs with friends seated behind them. A curtain was covering the open end of the vault so that no one could see into the crypt. By now, the crowd was so loud that throughout the service you could hardly hear the minister. James Pierce tried to get the fans to stop all the noise to no avail.

In the end, Marilyn's service had the largest number of fans and press of any funeral on which we ever assisted. According to Clarence Pierce, Marilyn was a frequent visitor at Westwood Cemetery in the late '50s, where she would sit on the grass and read a book while eating her lunch. It seems fitting that she now rests in a place where she sought peace and solace.

Kathy kept the items I had given her in our safe and would get them out only to show some of her girlfriends. She ended up with the falsies, a lock of hair, and two memorial folders left over after all the invited guests were seated. She even kept the white carnation boutonniere that I wore at her service. She kept all of the items inside a gift box, with the falsies protected in a plastic bag. For a number of years, when the plastic bag was opened, you could still smell Marilyn's perfume emanating from them. Of all these remembrances, the one Kathy most treasured was the falsies, because Marilyn had probably stitched the little round pieces of cloth on their backs, which helped keep them in place. Kathy was extremely happy that she could have something so personal of Marilyn's.

Ron and Allan standing near Joe DiMaggio and Joe DiMaggio, Jr.
Photo by Leigh Wiener. Reprint permission granted by Devik Wiener.

17

Growing Needs in the Industry

After their introduction, we started using the Chevy Sedan Delivery and Ford Courier to make death calls, but the automakers produced these types of cars for only a few years. The main difference between these vehicles and a station wagon is that they don't have side windows in the storage area, only passenger and rear windows. The body above the beltline is solid metal.

Immediately, we got great resistance from some mortuaries in using this type of vehicle because the cot could be loaded only through the rear of the car. Some firms used their rear-loading hearse to make death calls, so it seemed like our service cars fit in well. However, many other mortuaries would only do first calls using a specially built, side-loading Cadillac limousine conversion. These vehicles were very expensive because first you had to purchase the limousine, then you had to pay a company to do the necessary modifications so that a cot would fit inside.

There were no car modification companies in California doing this kind of work, which presented a big problem. In order to serve every mortuary in Southern California, we would need at least six removal cars to start. We really had to put on our thinking caps and figure out the financial ramifications and efficacy of solving our diverse customers' needs. Eventually, Ron's PR work established the mortuaries' objection to these vehicles. Some of the funeral directors were equating this new vehicle with the proverbial "meat wagon," which was a police or morgue vehicle used to transport the dead after disasters or terrible accidents.

This was the inspiration that led us to produce our first conversions from station wagons to mini-hearses. Wagons were reasonably priced, and by covering the large rear side windows with sheet metal, placing chrome landau bars on the panels, drapes in the passenger windows, and sandblasted palm leaves in the rear window, everyone was at last satisfied.

Now, there was only one small but important problem left to solve: where to get a pair of thirty-eight-inch landau bars. The ones on the hearses were much too long to use on the smaller wagons, so I drew a scale model pattern and submitted it to a carpentry company that made right- and left-side wooden bars from my drawing. These were then given to a bronze foundry that started casting pairs of bars and chrome-plating them. In the ensuing years our conversions went through a number of permutations, from painted metal panels and landau bars to covering two-thirds of our crown model's roof, to a complete black vinyl roof covering.

Before drapes could be made up, it was necessary for me to fabricate a curtain frame out of welding rod material to match the exact shape of the passenger door windows. There was a large fabric warehouse in downtown Los Angeles, so it was possible to find the perfect material: a black fabric with silver metallic thread running through it. The great thing about this material was that it had a loose-enough weave that the driver could see out, but no one could see inside the interior of the wagon. Unfortunately, after we lost our initial resource for drapery fabrication we weren't able to find anyone to do the sewing, so it was up to me to do it myself.

We made these conversions solely for our own use to have service cars that were new, fairly inexpensive, and acceptable to the firms we were serving. However, these Ford wagons were mechanical disasters and deserved their "FORD" acronym, "Fix Or Repair Daily." We switched to Dodge wagons that were far superior. After our drivers started showing up in our new conversions, the mortuaries would call and ask where we had gotten them. When they found we made them, they began asking if we would consider making conversions for them as well. By now, over half of my workday was devoted to working on our fleet, which was growing rapidly. Converting wagons, mounting and balancing tires, and customizing vans to enable them to carry four stretchers with electric lift tables were all part of the routine.

As soon as we rented floor space to demonstrate our first station wagon conversions at the mid-'60s California Funeral Directors Association Convention, we began receiving orders immediately. By a sheer stroke of luck, the booth next to us was occupied by the owner of a company called Ferno-Washington that produced mortuary equipment. When we didn't have any attendees looking at our conversions, we would speak with the gentleman in that booth, whose name was Elroy Bourgraf. In his booth, El was featuring the newly created one-man cot. He had hired an attractive young model to lie on the cot as he demonstrated the ease with which it would collapse when pushed into a rear-loading vehicle.

We struck a deal with El to become a dealer for Ferno Washington's products. El had purchased the company from Dick Ferneau (pronounced "Ferno") just one year after we started our business. He kept Dick on staff as head engineer, which was the best business decision he ever made. A funeral director in Cincinnati, Ohio, had approached El and Dick about developing and manufacturing a new cot that would do exactly what this new model now did. Some of the people in the industry said it was "the best thing to come along since sliced bread."

After we replaced all of our old cots with Ferno equipment, we began prototype-testing for Dick, because we could put as much use on a cot in one month as an average mortuary would in a year. Every time we came up with some new brainstorm, I would send Dick some drawings and he would figure out a way to build it. They also started producing and selling the identical pairs of landau bars from my pattern.

Most mortuaries had a station wagon that they used for flower deliveries, first calls, and general utility. Some of these firms didn't want a car that was obviously made just for doing death calls. We asked Dick to make a large rectangular-shaped cart on wheels covered with vinyl that could be placed in an unconverted station wagon. From the outside, no one could see a cot or casket being transported. After completing a transport, the mortuary would simply remove it from the wagon. This became the "cover-up," and Ferno-Washington built and sold them for years.

Over the years, the one-man cot was improved on. For years it was rated at 400-pound capacity, but more recently Ferno-Washington have added a new model rated at 1,000 pounds, because of more frequently encountered morbid obesity. Incredibly, the incidence of adult-onset diabetes is now rampant among teenagers. (It sounds rather simplistic to remind your kids about the importance of healthy eating. My mother advised me to stop consuming soft drinks because of the large amount of sugar in them, or else I would get fat and my teeth would be rotten by the time I was 50. It was good advice, because I still weigh 160 pounds and have all my teeth.)

Ford was the first to come out with a tailgate that could be opened like a door. The problem was that it only opened out forty-five degrees, making it almost impossible to get two Ferno cots in if they had bodies on them. After I scrutinized the hinges, it appeared that the doorstop post could be cut, allowing the door to open ninety degrees, but the spring pressure was lost. Some careful modifications of mine restored the pressure to hold the wider-opening door. Ford found out about it and sent an engineer from Detroit to see my work. They didn't use the idea because there were only about 20,000 mortuaries in the United States, and they replaced their service vehicles only about every ten years.

The conversions that we built served as removal cars and inexpensive mini-hearses for long-distance graveside services. After the word got out about these conversions, we started getting inquiries from Mexico. Since the Mexican government would not allow its funeral homes to have a vehicle that was not built in Mexico, Cadillac hearses and station wagons were not permitted. However, Chrysler and Ford both had assembly plants in Mexico, so the cars we converted for the Mexican funeral homes were the only hearses that they owned.

The well-known entertainer Danny Thomas had seen one of our conversions on a visit to Dick Cunningham's mortuary. As a result, he asked us to build him a wagon conversion to hold a traveling wardrobe, with no landau bars, curtains, or frosted glass in the tailgate. We covered the entire roof and rear side windows with vinyl, and then we had Ferno build two custom-made metal clothing cabinets attached to multilevel cot frames.

In addition to serving all of Los Angeles County for local and long-distance removal, we were regularly serving adjoining counties. We even began interstate work, with frequent trips to Nevada, Arizona, and Oregon. Los Angeles County alone is nearly 5,000 square miles, and there were never any times that we didn't have someone on the road or making local calls. On rainy days or when the traffic was particularly congested with accidents, it could take a driver over an hour to get to the San Fernando Valley. The problem was that from downtown, the only way to get there was through the Cahuenga Pass, which could be a real bottleneck. We had more than enough business in the valley to warrant getting a facility there for some of our vehicles.

As luck would have it, we found the perfect location in the valley to set up an office and garages. We purchased a property called The

Cedars Motel, a long one-story structure with many individual garages, which was unique because no other motels furnished garages for their customers. It was to our advantage to continue to run it as a working motel, but we always wondered what the customers thought when they looked out the windows and saw our funeral cars pulling out of the garages each morning. We operated this as a working motel for twenty years, and only sold it when we got out of the funeral car livery business many years later. After we sold it, they added X-rated in-house TV programming. Now why didn't we think of that?

Meanwhile, we switched to a different hearse builder whose cars were more reasonably priced. Almost immediately we began having problems with the electric tables, which were powered by a worm gear like those used on electric garage doors. The motor that powered the table was connected to the gear by a rubber coupling that would sometimes break. I soon found a coupler that wouldn't break. I sent one to the company, but they said they couldn't use it. At the next convention, its new hearse had this coupler. Another letter went out and another $1,500 was paid to us, which funded another vacation in Hawaii.

18

Behind the Scenes of the Rich and Famous

Every day brought new surprises, and some of them were very good. After the scandal brought on by the filming of *Cleopatra*, the most expensive film ever made up until that time at $44 million (the equivalent of $330 million now), Richard Burton and Elizabeth Taylor had the entertainment media going berserk. Their very public affair during the filming made them front-page news all over the country, particularly because of its open and salacious nature, which seemed to titillate everyone at home and abroad. This was made even more so by the fact that Burton was still married. When they arrived at LAX shortly after the film's premiere, a crowd in the hundreds was there to greet them. While pushing through the mob of fans, they were accosted and even had their clothing and hair pulled.

Sometime later, they returned to California from their East Coast residence because Elizabeth wanted to spend time with her two boys. Hoping to avoid a repeat of the unruly reception on their earlier trip, they arrived by train. They didn't even want to risk coming into the main Los Angeles terminal, so they arrived in San Bernardino, sixty miles east of Los Angeles. As we were crossing the vast, empty parking lot, Elizabeth began looking all around and she said, "I wonder where all the people are." Burton replied, "God damn it, woman, we went to all this trouble to not be seen and now you're disappointed," followed by: "I need a drink." They were going to be staying at the home belonging to Elizabeth's former husband, British movie actor Michael Wilding, while Wilding was in England.

After we arrived at the home at the end of a very long driveway, they got out of the limo and she asked me to help her look for her cat. Richard couldn't be bothered and went in the house for that drink. The things that still stand out in my mind were the unusual and beautiful color of her eyes, and her sexy voice. Unfortunately, I wasn't able to find her pussy.

Allan picking up Richard Burton and Elizabeth Taylor in 1963.

The following day was Sunday, and Kathy and I would often go for a drive after church. Kathy asked me to take her to see the estate, but I explained that the home couldn't be seen from Carolwood, the street that intersected Sunset Boulevard. The house was one lot over from the corner, which was a vacant lot with an eight-foot-high chain-link fence. Kathy then made a proposal that was gutsy even for her, because she was usually up for almost anything. She proceeded to climb over the fence and through the bushes to take a peek. She saw Elizabeth lying on a chaise lounge, while the two boys were running around the swimming pool, all of which I got on film.

Elizabeth must have been pleased with my driving, because we received a call from her male secretary, requesting me to report to his apartment in West Hollywood. He wanted to know if it was possible for me to drive him to a premiere party that weekend, with one minor hitch. He had just purchased a black London taxi in England a few months earlier and wanted to be taken to this soiree in his London cab. It appeared to be about forty years old and had a body style resembling some of our sedans produced before the war, only smaller. The really tricky part was the manual transmission and right-hand drive, which were both totally foreign to me.

Shortly after I parked in front of his apartment, he came out to greet me, wearing a formal black tux and carrying his tiny fuzzball Yorky. He and Elizabeth were very taken with this breed of dog at the time, and he wanted to drop the dog off temporarily at a lady friend's apartment. After leaving her place we headed off, and it finally dawned on me that the friend was actress Patricia Neal, who was in a number of movies in the '40s and '50s, the most memorable to me being *The Day the Earth Stood Still*. We were finally on our way to the Beverly-Wilshire Hotel where they were hosting a post-premiere party for *The Sandpiper*, a corny movie about a love triangle, starring Liz and Richard.

The security people at the entrance of the ballroom were carefully checking everyone's printed invitations. Since it didn't include their drivers, the secretary probably expected me to just sit in the limo for two or three hours. That's no fun. There had to be a way to sneak into the party, but it was going to be a real challenge. The waiters were all dressed in black suits just like me—so why not become a waiter, right? They were using a separate door from the area where the cocktails were being prepared, so that was the key to getting inside.

Once inside the ballroom, I picked up a half-filled highball glass left on a table, so it was time to act like a guest instead of a waiter. This was the perfect opportunity to become the proverbial fly on the wall. As people mingled around, many of their faces were familiar from recent movies and TV shows. What made it especially funny was when Liz's secretary approached me and said, "The drinks are pretty bad here, don't you think?" My response was "Awful." For some reason, he didn't even question that his driver was attending the party. Whooda thunk?

In the early '60s, Sophia Loren starred in a World War II movie called *Two Women*. She won an Academy Award, a Cannes Film Festival award, and a British Academy Film Award for the film. Shortly after she received these recognitions, the Movieland Wax Museum in Buena Park invited her to visit and unveil her likeness from a scene in the movie.

I picked her up at LAX with her small entourage and one man who was there to greet her. The scene from the film was heartrending and caused many viewers to tear up when they saw it. She lay on a paved highway with her young daughter in her arms after they were raped, screaming and crying as the soldiers passed by them. It seemed like a rather unconventional scene to choose for the likeness of her, but it was very moving.

She looked exceptionally beautiful that day, and her official photographer, who was sitting up front, kept leaning over the seat and taking pictures of her as we drove. Sophia immediately began complaining about an incident at a party she attended, where Frank Sinatra had made an insensitive comment to her. He suggested that instead of pursuing a movie career, she should be barefoot and pregnant at home in Italy, cooking spaghetti. She was absolutely infuriated and let everyone in the limo know how offended she was.

None of the people in this small group realized at the time that Frank had borrowed a line his character delivered in a 1959 war film called *Never So Few*. The title of the film was based on a widely reported speech that Winston Churchill made about the war, saying that never did so many people owe so much to so few. The setting in the film was war-torn Burma, with Frank Sinatra portraying an American soldier. Gina Lollobrigida played the vivacious young concubine of a much older gentleman. Frank was trying to put the make on her and told her she would stay barefoot and pregnant if she married him. This movie was playing on TV one evening, and the line rang a bell for me from chauffeuring Sophia in 1961. It only took me fifty years to discover where his remark had really come from.

This was a great drive and made even better because someone had arranged to have us escorted to the wax museum by two uniformed California Highway Patrol motorcycle officers. Talk about red carpet treatment— we never even had to stop for red lights. When we arrived back at LAX, Carlo Ponti, Sophia's husband, was waiting to return with her to Italy.

Another celebrity event in which we participated was the 1962 funeral for Ernie Kovacs,

Chauffeur Abbott in 1964.

where Frank Sinatra and Jack Lemmon were two of the pallbearers. I drove the hearse and directed the two of them and the other four pallbearers during the ceremony. At that time I didn't realize it was Frank Sinatra, but I clearly recalled one very short pallbearer with a strange profile because of his oddly shaped nose. The following month, a celebrity magazine called *Photoplay* printed a full-color cover photo of us walking to the grave. Kathy purchased the issue and asked why I hadn't told her Frank Sinatra was there.

Kim Novak also attended Ernie's funeral. She had appeared in a movie with him called *Bell, Book and Candle*, and they had apparently become good friends. The car that Ernie Kovacs was driving when he got killed was a Chevrolet Corvair, one of the first rear-engine American cars ever built. It was very controversial because many of them were wrecked when the car had gone out of control after hard braking. Shortly after his death the production of this car was discontinued, partly because of bad press and partly because of Ralph Nader's criticism of it in *Unsafe at Any Speed*.

At Ernie Kovacs' funeral, Allan leads the pallbearers, including Jack Lemmon (third from left). *Photo originally appeared in* Photoplay *magazine.*

A friend of mine, Deidi Kramer, who has listened to many of my stories, located an old copy of *Photoplay* magazine with an article about Ernie's funeral. She purchased it online and had it mailed to me directly, sight unseen and to my great surprise. It wasn't the magazine with the cover shot, but it had a spread of a different photo showing us crossing the lawn at the cemetery.

We provided the family car for the funeral of actor Robert Vaughn's mother. The services were held at Christ the King Catholic Church on Sunset Boulevard in Hollywood. Accompanying Vaughn was the most unusual entourage I'd ever encountered up until that time. There was one attractive blonde and an assortment of male groupies. The only conversation in the limo was not about the funeral or his mother, but about his blossoming career. Vaughn had a big hit with the television show *The Man From U.N.C.L.E.* and was quite good as the heavy in *Bullitt*, with Steve McQueen.

Bullitt had an outstanding car chase scene, and McQueen performed the stunt driving himself. He also did his own motorcycle riding in *The Great Escape*, except for an amazing jump that, he was told, was too dangerous for a big star like him. Ron and I were lucky to meet him at a live TV show called *Larry Finley's Strictly Informal* very early in his career. After the show we went out and saw his Jaguar, called a "D" Jag. It was built strictly as a racecar and was the prototype for the popular XKE Jaguar production car. He said the only time he ever got past second gear was at the Riverside International Raceway, because this car could easily reach sixty miles per hour in second gear alone.

The first death call we made for a well-known movie star was Peter Lorre, who died in a three-dollar-a-night fleabag hotel in Hollywood. The motion picture industry realized that many of its own ended up this way, so it founded the Motion Picture & Television Country House and Hospital in Woodland Hills. Just as the military cares for its wounded and dead, Hollywood took up the challenge for the health care of movie veterans in the twilight of their lives. We made many calls there over the years.

Another memorable service was for the funeral of David O. Selznick, the highly acclaimed movie producer-executive. His wife, actress Jennifer Jones, whom he had met while making a movie together, was the only occupant in my limo. The funeral concluded in the hallway of the mausoleum at Forest Lawn Glendale, where his casket was to be placed into the marble-covered wall. The funeral director instructed me to drive her home, but as we pulled out of the cemetery she asked me why the casket hadn't been placed in the crypt while she was there. The crypt closing is normally done after the family has left, because it is difficult for a family to watch. Nevertheless, she told me to turn around because she wanted to witness the closing personally. After returning to the garage, the crew who cleaned our cars each night found a boar-bristle hairbrush on the rear seat of the limo she was in and gave it to me. It was marked Harrods, so she probably purchased it in London. Kathy kept it as a souvenir.

On a private limo drive, my instructions were to pick up a Mr. and Mrs. Stacy in Hollywood. They immediately stood out as some of Hollywood's "beautiful people." The girl was wearing a green skin-tight dress and the man an expensive imported suit. He eventually called her Connie, which made me realize who they were. It was singer and actress Connie Stevens and her husband, James Stacy. During the ride to the airport she handed me a few letters and asked me to mail them for her. The name on the return address was Concetta Ingolia, her birth name.

Many years later, Stacy's life was changed dramatically when he and his girlfriend were riding his motorcycle down the very curvy Mulholland Drive. A drunk driver crossed the centerline and struck them almost head-on. His girlfriend was killed outright and his left arm and leg were torn off by the impact. The medical expenses wiped out his savings so some friends and his ex-wife Connie gathered for a benefit, which raised a great deal of money for him. Because Stacy was a well-known movie star, a state law was passed making any bartender serving a customer alcohol after he can no longer drive safely liable for any accident occurring from that customer's intoxication.

The biggest funeral we ever worked on after Marilyn Monroe's was a few years later, for William H. Parker, the highly respected Los Angeles police chief. Even Sam Yorty was there, the colorful mayor of "Los Ang-gah-leez," as he pronounced it. Parker's service was held at Saint Vibiana's Cathedral, beautiful but located in what had become the center of downtown's skid row.

We routinely took funeral processions on the Los Angeles freeways, and Ron became the official liaison between the CHP and the Los Angeles County Funeral Directors Association. We had to maintain a speed of at least fifty-five miles per hour on the freeway and have at least one escort for each of the twelve cars.

At Chief Parker's funeral, we took freeways to reach the San Fernando Mission Cemetery at the north end of the valley. When we pulled up onto the freeway we saw that the CHP had completely closed the northbound side, with motorcycle officers blocking every on-ramp. It was an amazing display of respect for Chief Parker, for whom the Parker Center Police Building was named, depicted on many TV programs and movies such as Jack Webb's *Dragnet*.

Over the years, the most well-attended funerals in which we were involved were those of policemen. This was especially true in cases where the officer had been killed in the line of duty. It wasn't unusual to have as many as thirty black and whites show up with the names of their city or county displayed, many of whom had arrived from hundreds of miles away. In the case of one fallen officer from Torrance, California, we were barely able to fit all the flowers into our largest truck. The church was only about eight miles from the cemetery, but this was the only time I ever had CHP motorcycle officers breaking red lights and escorting me in our flower truck all the way to the cemetery, so I would have sufficient time to set up the flowers before the funeral attendees arrived.

19

Going into Overdrive

We were eventually transporting so many remains up and down the state that I had to design a truck with an electrically operated platform. This enabled the driver to put two remains on it and raise it halfway up from the floor, which then enabled us to place two more cases underneath. As usual, my expertise in building something without consulting a knowledgeable designer wasn't the best, but it served the purpose.

The platform was steel, with four collapsed legs in the down position. Our mechanic welded a steel A-frame mount between the bucket seats, using my drawing as a guide. We purchased a cable wench that could be powered by the van's twelve-volt battery, which pulled the table halfway to the roof. This allowed the truck to carry four bodies at a time. Jack LeVan, who had worked for us in the late '50s, built the second lift van. He powered it with two small aircraft landing-gear actuators under the truck, with legs that came up through slots in the floor. Later, he informed me that my first, somewhat inefficient design was based on an engineering principle called a "dead man's lift." That was certainly appropriate.

We became aware that a man named Russ Monroe had a long-distance transportation company operating in Northern California. We made an agreement with him to work together and exchange cases in mid-state, which saved us both a great deal of additional driving. We determined halfway points along the highways. Through this system, both drivers would meet at a designated place and time, make the switch, and head back to home territory. Our arrangement lasted for over fifteen years, with each of us tabulating our ongoing charges. When we discontinued this service, the balances owed to each other came to less than $200.

Automobile leasing was pretty much in its infancy at this time, and it had some real benefits compared to purchasing vehicles outright. With leased cars it wasn't necessary to come up with a down payment, as most leasing agencies now require. We had been purchasing Dodge station wagons from a dealership called Harger-Haldeman, which had established a leasing division within the dealership, so we decided to make the switch to leasing.

We would put only about 30,000 miles a year on the ten smaller local wagons, but as much as 120,000 miles on our long-distance lift vans. One year we put an incredible 135,000 miles on a large Dodge Polara wagon. Car-leasing companies all use similar calculations to determine the number of miles you are allowed to accrue on any given vehicle over the length of the lease period. If you run over the predetermined allowable mileage, a penalty is assessed when the car is returned. Because of their high mileage and excessive wear, our vehicles were rarely turned back to the leasing company at the end of the one-year lease, so I would sell them to a wholesaler.

One of our employees took such good care of his vehicle that we assigned it to him for his exclusive use. Vern Steen had owned Steen Mortuary in North Hollywood, which we served for many years before he sold his mortuary. He said that he had retired much too young and decided to ask us for a driving job. When it was time to retire his vehicle, it was so pristine that I decided to return it to Sam Conrad, who owned the leasing company. When Sam came out to inspect Vern's big Dodge wagon, he immediately commented on its nice condition. He stuck his head in the driver's window to check the odometer and commented with surprise in his voice, "Oh, 35,000 miles!" I replied, "No, Sam, it has 135,000 miles." In those days, vehicles had only five digits on the odometer, so if a vehicle ever reached 99,999 miles, it would then zero out again. Sam still took the car back and gave us a fair price for it. I'm *sure* that the true mileage was disclosed to the next purchaser of the vehicle.

Each time we changed to a new model, it was necessary for me to remove and install the radios and the necessary hardware, and extend the rear doors. This was not my favorite time of year, because all this work took up many hours. As the cost of converting a growing number of wagons increased, it was time to come up with a less expensive approach, while still ensuring privacy inside each vehicle. After placing half-inch masking tape strips on the inside of the side and tailgate windows, I sprayed them with cans of black spray paint. When the paint dried it was simply a matter of pulling off the tape, leaving very nice stripes on the windows, much like Venetian blinds. The driver could easily see out the windows, but the public could not see inside the darkened interior. With a helper, I could complete all ten cars in just two days.

One day, a first-call driver of ours was pulled over by the police and given a citation for having painted windows. After a quick trip to Georgia Street Receiving Hospital with my camera, I showed the judge photos of Los Angeles' ambulances, which had all the windows behind the driver completely painted out. The judge dismissed the charges and admonished the officer about issuing any more invalid citations. You've got to love that.

An Abbott & Hast 1967 Dodge Coronet conversion.

20

Where Have All the Graveyards Gone?

Many people have commented to me about cemeteries over the years because they knew of my profession, saying things like "I learned how to drive a car in a cemetery" or "That's my favorite place to walk my dog." Many people jog or picnic in cemeteries because there is no traffic and exhaust fumes are absent. In fact, it seems that many people over the years have had pleasant experiences in this serene environment.

In the past fifty years, there have been more changes in funeral customs and the accompanying terminology than there were in the entire century before that. In the United States, there are two common names for burial grounds, depending on age. Older ones are called "cemeteries," while the more modern ones are referred to as "memorial parks," coined by Dr. Hubert Eaton, the visionary behind Forest Lawn Memorial Parks. Most cemeteries have an old and a newer section. The older ones have standing headstones and monuments, while the new sections have flat grave markers.

The older cemeteries also have aboveground tombs, which are capable of holding as many as six caskets. Gypsies often purchased plots in these sections because they perceived great value in their monuments. In their unique tribal culture, they still refer to their community leader as "king." For many years in Los Angeles it was the Adams clan, and the family tomb was marked "Adams—King of the Gypsies." Inglewood Park Cemetery was one of their favorite cemeteries because they had space for such tombs.

Rosedale and Evergreen Cemeteries were both over a hundred years old when we began our business, and reading names on the oldest family grave markers is like reading a who's who in early California history. One recognizable family name was Lankershim, after whom one of the main streets in North Hollywood was named. Another famous name was Hollenbeck, whose name was given to the Los Angeles Police

Department's Hollenbeck Division, a fifteen-square-mile downtown hot spot for some of the worst gang violence in Los Angeles.

In the early 1900s, Forest Lawn Glendale changed the face of cemeteries across the country. This happened because of Dr. Eaton. He imagined that rather than a forest of standing stones, called "marble orchards" in the industry, a flowing, friendly, "memorial park" setting could be created. This new concept emphasized tranquility and beauty instead of heartbreak and sorrow. Forest Lawn was started by a group of businessmen in 1906 in Tropico, just before the area was annexed by the city of Glendale. Dr. Eaton gained management control in 1917 and set out to completely change the concept of how these cemeteries were designed. The grounds were decorated with beautiful statuary, many of which were re-created from famous examples in Europe. Most cemeteries now use only flat grave markers their lawnmowers can travel over, rather than maneuvering around each monument, and this technique was copied by most cemeteries.

Forest Lawn also featured magnificent artwork and quaint chapels, some of which were modeled after famous English ones, like "Wee Kirk o' the Heather" and "Little Church of the Flowers." To add to the charm, some of the chapels' ceilings were made from materials carved hundreds of years ago. Dr. Eaton collected, shipped, and reinstalled a number of these at the Glendale facility. They also have some spectacular structures like "The Church of the Recessional," where I drove a family car for the funerals of Clark Gable and David O. Selznick. Forest Lawn Glendale boasts a very large stained glass window depicting Leonardo da Vinci's *Last Supper* in the Memorial Terrace of its Great Mausoleum, and its Hall of the Crucifixion-Resurrection features a painting of Christ's ascension. Ron and I attended Dr. Eaton's funeral in this hall. During his funeral, the hall was filled to capacity and they had even arranged for the famous Mitchell Boys Choir to sing at the service.

At one point, Forest Lawn was the center of a great controversy when they proposed to open a new cemetery in Covina Hills, an unincorporated county area just east of Los Angeles. The local residents of Covina Hills vowed that they would fight to the end to prevent the creation of a cemetery in their exclusive neighborhood. A lot of the controversy was the result of plotting by Lee McNitt of Rose Hills. Lee arranged for horseback riders to parade up and down the street before a city council hearing on the matter. The horse riders did not want any type of development on the property as they had been using it for horseback riding while it was raw land. The riders were also tasked with patrolling the grounds to obstruct any burials, because of a provision in the law that designated an area as a cemetery if it already had six interments. However, very quickly after securing zoning approval from the County of Los Angeles, Forest Lawn surreptitiously conducted enough burials to ensure its legal status as a cemetery.

Forest Lawns memorial parks are the only ones with a booth at the entrance, where an attendant will give you a printed map showing the many points of interest. This is where we would pick up the "take man" to direct us. Very often they would tell us to go to the Doheny Memorial (which is an aboveground, vault-like structure covered with an elaborate white gazebo made of wrought iron) and bear right or left. Our drivers passed this memorial hundreds of times and all knew its location. There was always a large fresh floral piece shaped like a star, made out of red and white carnations.

The name Doheny is well known to anyone interested in California history. The family's prominence grew when they funded the building of the beautiful St. Vincent's Catholic Church in Los Angeles. The surprising thing was that Forest Lawn isn't a Catholic cemetery, which would have been a requirement for Catholic burials at the time. One of their employees informed me that a priest had gone there and consecrated the plot of ground on which the memorial stands, because of the family's closeness to the Catholic Church.

Everyone remembers the Y2K scare as we approached the year 2000. Fortunately, many computer engineers predicted the problem well in advance and took measures to prevent computers everywhere from crashing. Not so in the cemetery business. When people purchased a family plot or adjoining graves, it was common to purchase only one grave marker. It usually had the family name in bold letters and two places beneath to etch the names of husbands and wives. For the first one interred, the marker would give birth dates and a death date, but also the birth date of the spouse, and then the first two digits ("19") of the spouse's future year of death. However, if the spouse passed away after 1999, those digits would be filled with epoxy and a new date of death carved. It never made sense to me to have a spouse's information inscribed on the head-stone while they were still alive, unless someone was afraid that inflation would make it more costly to complete the work in the future.

21

Another Day at the Office

When the Watts Riots broke out in 1965, none of us were too happy with our chosen profession. The riots took place in South Central Los Angeles, and we ended up having to send one of our new conversions to pick up remains near the hot zone. One of our drivers, Newlyn Brunton, came around a corner, and to his surprise, the locals had dragged some old furniture and trash into the middle of the street and set it ablaze. Rioters were running all over and started hurling objects at the car. Newlyn had people rushing him from behind, and with a raging fire blocking the street, he made a quick decision to drive the car over the curb and down the sidewalk. Needless to say, the car sustained a great deal of damage from flying debris.

At one point the riots got so far out of hand that the National Guard had to be called in. Even though our office was at least ten miles from Watts, an army jeep was parked in the center of the intersection of Figueroa Street and Washington Boulevard, with a large-caliber machine gun mounted on it. This was only fifty yards from our office, and everyone was on edge about our proximity to this roadblock. A woman tried to crash into the jeep, but a reservist unloaded his machine gun into the vehicle and the woman.

Our worst incident during the riots was when one of our drivers dropped off a body he had picked up for McGlynn's Mortuary. They were located approximately a mile from the edge of Watts, and we didn't feel good about reentering the area after what had already happened. One of our employees volunteered to do the drive and said he would be especially careful. After he dropped off the remains, he made a beeline for the office along a main business street. He even began running red lights, because along the way he could see looters breaking into stores. Then he noticed in his rearview mirror that a police car was about half a block behind him. Reasoning that he had better start observing the law, he stopped at the next red light. Four young men rushed out, opened the car door, and dragged him from the car.

One of the guys said, "Do you have anything to say before you die, white boy?" He realized that the only way he was going to survive this terrifying situation was to talk his way out of it. As fast as he could, he explained: "I'm just doing my job, which is transporting bodies. I have no axe to grind with you guys." At this point, the rioter who was holding him released his grip. Our driver dove into the car and sped off. Apparently, the police car had turned off Vermont just before the assault took place. But our fellow wasn't taking any more chances, so he didn't stop for another red light all the way back to the office.

There was a hospital in Culver City where we made numerous removals over many years. Newlyn made a call at the hospital, after which we received a serious complaint about him. Veteran movie actor Jeff Chandler had died there from a staphylococcus (staph) infection following minor surgery. The hospital was found guilty of malpractice, and the notoriety was so severe that its name was changed from Culver City Memorial Hospital to Brotman Medical Center. Newlyn was there just after the name change, and while a nurse was giving him some information, he jokingly remarked that they should have named it Jeff Chandler Memorial Hospital. After hearing that comment, the nursing supervisor called Ron and raked him over the coals.

Chandler's death caused the media to start asking some hard questions, which ultimately revealed that you are about ten times more likely to get exposed to staphylococcus germs in a hospital than you are in your own home. Americans didn't seem to learn the lessons provided by the Civil War. If a soldier was taken to a field hospital to be treated surgically, he was eight times more likely to die from infections or gangrene than he was from dying in battle.

22

Flying into the Unknown

In 1965, California passed a law allowing families to have the ashes of their loved ones scattered at sea. The new regulation required that it be done from an aircraft that was three miles out from the shore and flying at an altitude of 5,000 feet. This was the only procedure allowed for ocean scattering at that time. Seizing the opportunity to offer this service, we purchased a new red and white Piper Cherokee airplane. If we were going to buy an airplane, I wanted it to look like a World War II fighter. The Cessna was a less expensive alternative, but it looked hokey to me.

We signed a lease with Pacific Airmotive Corporation, which had a private area at Lockheed-Burbank Airport. We rented space there, where we had the plane fueled and maintained. They also provided us with an instructor and flight school training. For our first lesson, our flight instructor, Don Lorenti, told us that he had to make a pickup at LAX in their company plane. Rather than cancel our lesson, he said we would have to pay only for the instruction time and nothing extra for using the company plane. On the way there Don let me fly the plane, which was really nothing but holding the stick steady. I was shocked when he said he was going to have me land the plane at LAX. My first thought was, "Are you out of your frickin' mind?" This seemed like a daunting task on my first instructional flight.

I could feel the sweat running down my sides as we made the final approach, while Don just sat there and calmly told me what to do. He never touched his stick, but as soon as the wheels touched down, he took over and taxied quickly at this busy airport. At this time my brain was running at full tilt, wondering if my second instructional flight was going to require a carrier landing.

Don was a former fighter pilot instructor in the United States Air Force, but not even he had a clue about the Lockheed "Skunk Works" that produced the spy planes our country used to protect America and gather

Allan in front of their 1965 Piper Cherokee "Air Hearse," used for scattering ashes.

intelligence on the Soviet Union. These planes included the brainchild of Clarence "Kelly" Johnson, the SR-71 Blackbird, which still holds the world's record for the fastest plane ever built, and the U-2, which was responsible for taking pictures of the missile sites in Cuba and flyovers of Russia authorized by President Eisenhower during the Cold War.

Kathy didn't know we were taking lessons, and our dispatchers knew not to say anything. One day, she called the office and one of our hearse drivers answered the phone. Not knowing about my policy, he said he would have me call after my flying lesson was over. By the time I walked in the door that evening, she had the shotgun locked and loaded—speaking figuratively. We debated and she finally agreed to my continuing the lessons, but in the following two weeks she lost four pounds, so I quit.

Cremation was starting to become a very popular alternative, and we knew that scattering ashes at sea was going to be the wave of the future. I designed a container to hold ashes prior to disposal, with a long snout and two end caps. My prototype was made of cardboard, so I had a sheet metal shop use the pattern to construct one out of stainless steel. It looked very professional, and the extension at the bottom fit perfectly out the small opening in the plane's left window.

We hired Ray Champion as a pilot to do all our air scatterings. We knew him because his family had a casket-manufacturing business. We went through the entire procedure with Ray and couldn't think of any possible complications. On his first day, Ray picked up three members of a family and flew the plane to the proper location three miles out to sea. He picked up the container holding the cremains, removed the lower end cap, pushed the snout out the small opening, and tipped it up to let gravity and wind take over. It worked perfectly, just as I knew it would. However, as soon as the ashes reached the rear of the plane, they passed by the ventilation scoop, which brought some ash back inside the plane. The family had to brush "Uncle Charlie" off their clothing. A family member even joked that it was just like him to stick around. From that day on, Ray was paranoid about checking the air vent to make sure it was not open.

Several years later, California passed a new law that allowed scattering at sea by boat, which was a much smarter way to do it. We sold the plane and purchased a yacht that we named *Tribute*. The Piper still looked almost new, but before selling it we had the tail assembly painted because it was sandblasted from all the scatterings we had done.

23

New Beginnings

While Kathy was pregnant with our first child, we bought our first home, which was in the Hollywood Hills. One of the most interesting things about living in Nichols Canyon was its history. This newly developed area, which had been used as a Boy Scout ranch for years, soon became almost as famous as Laurel Canyon because of the many movie stars who moved into homes there. They included Morgan Fairchild, Doc Severinsen, director William Friedkin, and Jaclyn Smith and her actor husband, Dennis Cole.

On May 12, 1966, Kathy gave birth to Michael, whom we called by his Russian nickname, Mischa. I still remember my twenty-one hours in the waiting room at Daniel Freeman Memorial Hospital in Inglewood, because that's where I had my first ulcer attack. When my brother and mom showed up at the hospital, my stomach was hurting so bad I could barely sit up. A combination of worrying and no food for almost twenty-four hours had really done me in, so they talked me into going to the hospital cafeteria. John also gave me a pain pill he had left over from a recent root canal, but a painful dental procedure would have been preferable to this waiting. Kathy's stay at Daniel Freeman did have its upside. Her second-floor window had a panoramic view of Inglewood Park Cemetery, so I felt right at home.

I took a two-week vacation to be with Kathy and help out with our new baby, but we were both quite anxious with this new addition to the family. I'm not sure how most parents react to having their first child, but after running a twenty-four-hour-a-day business for years, I thought this was going to be a piece of cake. Wrong! By the end of the two weeks we couldn't believe that one little baby could cause such chaos in our lives.

After that vacation, Kathy resumed her job with the United States Air Force, and Mischa was taken to Kathy's mother daily. Vera's apartment was on my way to work, so it was convenient for me to drop him off and pick him up. Meanwhile, my mom lived on the next block from us and would babysit him when we went to a movie. One evening we returned to find that Mischa had given her a bad time. She immediately asked us what a "slonik" was, because he had tried to get her to retrieve it when he was placed in his crib. When she didn't respond, he kept repeating the word, being very careful to pronounce each syllable. He repeated "slow-neek" multiple times and looked at her as if to say, "What's the matter with you? Aren't you listening to me?" Like most young children, Mischa had a favorite toy that he slept with, which was his stuffed elephant. The Russian diminutive word for elephant is "slonik." Now, wasn't that simple?

At one point, even Kathy couldn't understand what he wanted when he kept asking for an "akameaner." She finally figured it out when he hummed the melody of the song that says, "Oh I wish I were an Oscar Mayer Wiener, that is what I'd truly like to be." Tell me that sponsors aren't getting their message through to our kids.

One unfortunate thing that marked this year for us was when our manager, Jimmy Houston, passed away. He never made first calls, but one slow day he decided to go with Newlyn Brunton on one. As they were carrying a loaded cot down a long stairway, Jimmy collapsed. By the time the ambulance arrived, he had died. There can't be too many people who have died while making a death call.

Before we moved into our Hollywood Hills home, just a few weeks after Mischa was born, we were not aware of the area's significance in California's history. Nichols Canyon runs north from just above Hollywood Boulevard to Mulholland Drive, at the crest of the mountain. Our home was near to where the road ends in a cul-de-sac called Nichols Canyon Place. At the top of a dirt trail is a landmark commemorating the burial of James Lankershim, who owned much of the ranchland that eventually became the communities of Studio City, Universal City, and North Hollywood.

In addition to memorializing Lankershim, the fifteen-foot obelisk contains two other inscriptions commemorating prominent aspects of the area's history. The first plaque reads, "Near here on the banks of the Los Angeles River was fought the Battle of Cahuenga, Feb. 22, 1845." This battle was fought between California governor Manuel Micheltorena, appointed by the Mexican government, and the previous governor, Juan Bautista Alvarado. Micheltorena was unpopular with the citizens of California, and a revolt formed to unseat him from the office of governor.

A man named Pío Pico would be the last Mexican governor of California before its independence.

The monument's other inscription states, "The Treaty of Peace between Gen. John C. Fremont and Gen. Andres Pico was signed 1½ miles north at Cahuenga on Jan. 13, 1847." After the Bear Flag Revolt in 1846, in which Fremont assisted the uprising of American settlers against the Mexican government, Fremont was appointed lieutenant colonel of the California Battalion. It was composed of his survey crew and settlers from Monterey, California. They marched south to Los Angeles and defeated Pío Pico's forces, led by his brother, Andres Pico. The Treaty of Cahuenga was not a formal treaty between nations, but an informal agreement that ended the Mexican-American War in California. It wasn't until the Treaty of Guadalupe Hidalgo in 1848 that Mexico formally ceded California to the United States.

Also of historical significance, Mulholland Drive was named after William Mulholland, who brought water hundreds of miles from Northern California by way of an aqueduct from the Owens Valley to Los Angeles. This changed Los Angeles from a desert town to a thriving community. Even though the aqueduct was an engineering masterpiece, there was great controversy, especially from the people living in Owens Valley, who attempted to sabotage the aqueduct because it drew their water away. Their resentment was captured in a popular local sign at the time: "Flush your toilet, LA needs the water." The movie *Chinatown*, starring Jack Nicholson, was loosely based on Mulholland's career.

Mulholland is also remembered for designing and constructing the San Francisquito, or Saint Francis, Dam, which came to a catastrophic ending. When the dam started to leak, he was contacted and subsequently inspected the dam. He announced that there was nothing wrong with it and proclaimed, "All gravity dams leak a little." It broke a few hours later and many lives were lost. Mulholland never recovered from the guilt he felt about the tragedy.

Old Hollywood had many of its brightest stars living on or near Mulholland, including Marlon Brando, Dan Duryea, Barry Sullivan, Charlton Heston, and Rudy Vallee, who was one of TV's earliest celebrities. Vallee lived on Macapa Drive, a cul-de-sac branching off Mulholland that he attempted to get renamed Rue de Vallee, which was French for "Street of Vallee." Some of the newer arrivals in the area included Warren Beatty and Hugh O'Brian, who had a cute sign on his property reading "HOB Hill" for his initials.

Around the corner from us lived Mama Cass Elliot, of The Mamas and the Papas, who died in 1974 of a heart attack that may have been brought on by her drug use and obesity. Ringo Starr later purchased the house. To get home from the Hollywood side of Nichols Canyon, we would always take Franklin Avenue to Outpost Road, which winds its way up the mountain to Mulholland. Just before turning on Outpost, we would always pass the hotel on Franklin Avenue where Janis Joplin died of a heroin overdose. It was always a little eerie to think of all the ghosts of Hollywood who had passed these same roads in bygone years.

Another couple living just off Mulholland was actress Joanna Pettet and her husband, actor Alex Cord. Mischa and their son Damian became friends while attending Valley View Elementary School. One day while playing at their house, Damian showed Mischa a stash of marijuana hidden under his parents' bed. I guess his mother never heard Tom Lehrer's song "Be Prepared," about the Boy Scout motto. He sings, "Be prepared, that's the Boy Scout's marching song, be prepared as through life you march along, be prepared to hold your liquor pretty well, don't write naughty words on walls if you can't spell. Keep those reefers hidden where they won't be found and be careful not to smoke them when the scoutmaster's around, for he'll insist that they be shared."

Since my mother lived so close, we would often take her to dinner with us. One evening, while dropping her off, I tapped my horn and waved good-bye to her. A neighbor two doors away was just getting out of his Cadillac. He shouted, "Who the hell do you think you're blowing your horn at?" I paused a moment and replied, "I wasn't beeping at you, Mr. Axton, it was just to say good-night to my mom, Louise. You know her, she's the mother of my brother, John, who your dog bit last month." Hoyt Axton, the singer, songwriter, and movie actor, lived just two doors up from her. His lack of response reminded me of a line from one of his hit records, "Della and the Dealer": "The dealer had a dog named Jake and a cat named Kalamazoo, who was cool and never said a mumblin' word."

Errol Flynn had a large ranch on Mulholland that was subdivided after his death. A corner of the estate was used to construct a few new homes, and Ricky Nelson built one there. When Kathy and I would take an evening walk, we could hear his sons practicing with their band called Nelson. Two blocks farther up the hill was the famous architectural Mushroom House that was prominently featured in the film *Body Double*.

When Kathy was in junior high, she had a girlfriend named Beverly Aadland. One movie star's secret that wasn't kept secret for long was that Errol Flynn would pick up Beverly after school, when she was only about 14. Beverly's mother knew about their "relationship" but did nothing to stop it. Many years later, Beverly appeared at a San Fernando Valley nightclub. Undoubtedly, many people just came to see her because of the scandal. Her name was well known to the public after their affair and after Flynn's autobiography, *My Wicked, Wicked Ways*, appeared.

After Beverly's performance, we went backstage and knocked on her dressing room door. When Beverly asked, "Who is it?" Kathy just said, "We'd like to talk to you," and before Beverly even opened the door she shouted, "Kathy, is that you?" We had a memorable visit. I asked her how she recognized Kathy's voice. She said it was a combination of not only her voice, but also her accent. In our thirty years of marriage a few people would ask about her accent, but it was never discernible to me.

By 1968 we had outgrown our old Auto Club facility and decided to rent the recently vacated two-story office building next door and connect the two together as one facility. I rented a jackhammer and demolished a two-foot wall between the two parking lots, which were two feet different in elevation. After my demolition work was complete, the next piece of equipment needed was a steamroller and a cubic yard of hot blacktop that was delivered on-site. This was one project that wasn't going to get done in a suit. It was summer and already hot by lunchtime. I stripped to the waist and was well into running the compactor back and forth, when our female dispatcher walked by and made a nice comment about my physique.

Our building addition was next to a Ford dealership, and we had a circular driveway in front where Ron and I parked. The parts department entrance was about twenty feet from our driveway. About once a week, we would try to leave and some car would be blocking our exit. I got so tired of having to go in and complain that I purchased a can of red paint for the curb. While painting the curb between the entrance and exit of the circular driveway, a man walking down the street paused for a moment, shook his head, and said, "Only LA would have a guy in a suit painting the curbs." I didn't bother explaining.

24

The Sky's the Limit

We were sometimes asked by suppliers to help develop technologies because of our growing experience in every aspect of the funeral industry. For years we had been assisting mortuaries transporting caskets by railroad. The caskets were placed in large redwood boxes for their protection, and these "shipping boxes," as they were known, were delivered to one of two train terminals in Los Angeles. Often the casket and shipping box would weigh as much as 400 pounds, which wasn't a problem for the rail lines, and the weight didn't change the rate. At the time it was common for a family to have their parents or other relatives shipped back east for burial. Most first- or second-generation Americans had roots in an eastern state, and many had purchased cemetery property and family plots. Now that we were in the jet age, these families wanted their loved ones transported by air since it could be done in a relatively short time.

An American Airlines executive named Harry Bate called and asked for a meeting with us. He explained that he was working on a project to get a larger share of the burgeoning funeral transportation by jet market. Harry had even set up what he called the "Jim Wilson desk." There was no Jim Wilson, but the mortuaries felt more comfortable when they called to arrange an air shipment because the phone was always answered, "Jim Wilson."

By this time, caskets were being transported by many airlines with the use of a padded canvas zippered bag from a company called Continental Mortuary Air Service, which had facilities at many airports. CMAS operated facilities much as one-way truck rental services do. We had been delivering caskets to their facility at LAX for a few years when Harry informed us about a major problem with this service. All caskets were weighed before being loaded into the jetliner, and this was calculated in the cost of transportation. CMAS bags solved the requisite problem of lightweight containers, but didn't address the more important problem of protection because the caskets were often damaged upon arrival.

Harry was on the cutting edge of developing new technologies in shipping cargo by air. At our first meeting, he said he had done research with local funeral home owners and our name kept coming up. He concluded that we were the "go-to guys," as he put it. He asked us to research and develop a lightweight, sturdy container that would protect the caskets from arriving at their destination with damage. No one knew at what point the caskets were being damaged or who was responsible, because the damage wasn't discovered until the container was opened at its final destination. He knew that whoever solved this problem would get the most business, and competition between the airlines was fierce. Many families would fly on the same aircraft to accompany the remains, so there were additional incentives to make this work.

The three criteria that we had to deal with were protection, weight, and dimensions, the latter being the most critical because all major carriers depended on what were called "feeder airlines." It wasn't a problem to ship a casket to Chicago or New York on the large aircraft, but the small airlines did the puddle-jumping from major airports to small towns. American Airlines had to know these feeder airlines had large enough cargo doors to accept a casket in a container, or they couldn't book it. Sometimes the caskets were almost as big as the loading door, so the protective container had to be as small as possible and still offer a certain level of protection. The weight was also an important factor, because the combined passenger and cargo weights were used to determine if it was safe to fly. A miscalculation could result in an aircraft being unable to lift off as it reached the end of the runway. We needed to think outside the box—or, was it inside the box?

After experimenting with a few prototypes, we finally came up with a workable design. It began with a plywood bottom and a solid wooden lower edge to protect the bottom of the casket from forklift blades. Next was the cardboard inner liner ring that protected the sides of the casket. The lid was also cardboard and resembled a large corsage box top, with hand holes in the wooden tray for easy carrying. Once a casket was placed in the tray, and the inner liner and top placed over it, the whole unit was made very compact by connecting the preinstalled straps and pulling them as tight as possible. The cardboard lid's lower edge was slightly smaller than the tray, and tightening the straps pulled the lid down inside the lower sides of the tray itself. This made the whole container only about one inch larger than the casket it contained. We called it the Casket Airtray and tried to patent it, but we were told this wasn't possible since it was only a container. We were advised that the next best thing would be to trademark the name. We promptly did this, but it did not protect our invention. Within a short time it was being copied all across the country, and all they had to do was change the name.

We nearly hit the big time when the United States government started purchasing airtrays from us and shipping them to Vietnam. The opening order was for 200 and the government had its own specifications, including a plastic curtain coating to protect the casket from rainy weather there. However, it wasn't long before a general came into Graves Registration, the branch of the military in charge of embalming and identification, and saw our units being used. He got very upset and said he didn't want any of his soldiers being sent back to the states in a "cardboard box." I assumed he was aware that as soon as the airtray arrived in Dover, Delaware, the remains would be transferred to a very nice metal casket, and this was just an inexpensive way to transport fallen soldiers back to the United States. In spite of this lucrative contract's loss, I understood his motivation and respected his decision.

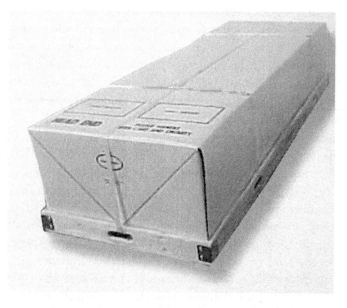

Allan and Ron invented the Casket Airtray in 1968.

During this same time period it was becoming obvious that the funeral industry was going through a major metamorphosis. Not only were new laws raising the overhead of the funeral business, but people's perception of the value of traditional funerals was also transitioning downward. A new law was enacted mandating that all employees working for a mortuary must be paid for each hour that they were restricted to the premises. The reason that many mortuaries are called "funeral homes" is that for many generations, business owners or an employee would sleep there and answer phones throughout the night. It didn't even matter if their sleep hadn't been interrupted all night—the law required the firm to pay the employee overtime for every hour after their normal workday ended.

In a bold move, one mortuary broke with the tradition of twenty-four-hour availability and hired an answering service, which seemed almost scandalous to many in the industry. On its face it must have sounded very impersonal to a family not to be able to speak to someone who owned or worked for the mortuary, particularly if it led to the automated response systems with which we are now plagued.

Imagine this scenario. Your doctor tells you that you have an inoperable cancer. You don't know how much time you have left, so you decide to make your own funeral arrangements to save your family the burden at a very emotional time. You get out the Yellow Pages and decide what firm you'd like to use. A cheerful recording announces that you have reached your friendly neighborhood funeral home. It informs you that you have some options. "Please press one if you want to arrange a funeral for a family member or a loved one. Press two if you are doing this for yourself. If you want to make a pre-need funeral arrangement, using the keypad on your telephone, enter the letters 'FUN.' Now press one for burial, two for cremation, or three if you desire entombment in a crypt. If you wish to charge this to your credit card, please enter the number. Now enter your expiration date." By this time you are thinking, "Damn, the doctor didn't tell me exactly when I was going to expire," so you think the hell with it and hang up in sheer frustration.

25

Handling the Big One

The next momentous occurrence was the outbreak of the Hong Kong influenza epidemic of 1968. Since Southern California was densely populated, this pandemic spread quickly. In the late '60s we were making more removals from homes than institutions. House calls required two men instead of the usual one, and when the outbreak hit, we became inundated with these calls. Under ordinary circumstances, we were expected to have our men on the road in seven to eight minutes after receiving such a call. However, at the height of the frenzy, our dispatchers were quoting as much as an hour to respond to house calls, which always took precedence over institutional calls.

At any given time for over two months, removal orders were stacked up on the dispatch counter eight pages deep, waiting for the next available crew. This was the only time we literally went to DEFCON 2. Many of our staff didn't return to the office during their entire shift but were given instructions over their radios. It's my sincere belief that the news media downplayed the severity of this outbreak because they didn't want to incite panic. In truth, the Hong Kong flu epidemic was a worldwide pandemic, although not categorized as such at the time. Thankfully, the World Health Organization (WHO) and other agencies have since become aware of the necessity of warning the public to wear face masks and take other precautions, as in the case of the 2003 severe acute respiratory syndrome (SARS) epidemic.

Many of our drivers were up for thirty-six hours straight. They would drive until they couldn't stay awake any longer, then switch with a second man, sleep in the passenger's seat, and be awakened upon arrival at the next residence. Once the body was in the car, the passenger was out like a light again. All of our cars were equipped with two cots, and some of us actually crawled up on the empty cot next to a body for some much-needed sleep. One time our driver was pulled over for doing ninety while

I was asleep on a cot. The police officer told him that anyone traveling at that speed could be arrested on the spot, but after the driver explained the dire circumstances to the officer, he just issued a citation for going eighty.

Not only were we going crazy picking up bodies, but we were also trying to back up every mortuary in town with funeral cars, and this became a dispatcher's nightmare. We would start laying out the schedules for the next day's drives about 4 P.M. and finish after midnight. It was a very difficult job, so only Ron, our manager, Pat Lind, and I could complete the task. We would schedule a single hearse driver to as many as four services per day as opposed to the usual two. We would go home, sleep for five or six hours, and start again the next morning.

We never routinely farmed out any first calls, but as the death toll grew, we realized that we were going to need the cooperation of every mortuary in a four-county area to help us with hearses and limos. Imagine us calling mortuaries at midnight asking if they could cover a service for us the next day and never having anyone ever getting upset for these middle-of-the-night calls. We asked for assistance from mortuaries in Ventura, Oxnard, San Diego, and Santa Barbara, some of which were 100 or more miles away.

During this six-week siege, things got so intense that we pressed every mortuary in Southern California into service. We sent competitors to help each other, colored cars, old cars, young drivers—and no one ever complained. They willingly ignored the usual rules, knowing the only way we were going to survive this pandemic was through cooperation. The death rate in densely populated areas like LA had gone up to at least six to eight times the normal rate.

An ordinary day's work for us during the holiday season would be a combination of sixty drives. During the influenza outbreak, on the day before Christmas and the day after New Year's, we covered over 220 services with the cooperation of each of our many friends in the business. Most people are unaware that the death rate increases every year around the holidays. There are several reasons for this phenomenon—illness increases because of inclement weather, the suicide rate rises, and fatal accidents occur more often during rain and snow conditions. It has even been confirmed statistically that ill family members are often able to hold out until reaching a significant holiday, and afterward quite literally give up the ghost.

On one extremely busy day, it was necessary for me to schedule myself to drive on four services. A delay on your first service could have consequences throughout the day. My first service was a High Mass and ran about one hour. At Resurrection Cemetery in South San Gabriel there was no take-man waiting at the gate—the first time that this had ever happened to me. About fifteen cars were in the procession behind me and, fortunately, the motorcycle escorts had stopped all the traffic. This gave me a chance to run into the cemetery office in a panic, where I insisted that the girl show me where the grave was on a large cemetery map.

We finally pulled up to the grave, but a glance at my watch told me that my next service was about to begin at a mortuary ten miles away. Tradition dictates that the coach driver leads the pallbearers to the grave and gives them more instructions after placing the casket on the lowering device. Opening the hearse doors up and hustling some of the pallbearers into position, I gave them the usual instructions, but the second they picked up the casket, the hearse doors were closed and I was gone with the wind.

Fortunately, this part of town was not densely populated, so the only real danger would have been someone pulling onto the highway as I drove eighty miles per hour most of the way, with one foot on the brake. When I arrived at Carter-Cram Mortuary in nearby Monterey Park, people were coming out the side door of the chapel, so that told me that the service was over. I ran in to locate the owner, Art Cram, to let him know I had arrived. Instead, his wife, Ruth, came running in from where the hearse was parked and yelled, "Your hearse is on fire!" I ran back outside with her and saw billows of white smoke coming from the rear wheels. I assured her that the car wasn't on fire, but that I had merely fried the rear brakes.

After my fourth service it was back to the garage, where our mechanic was working. He immediately commented on the smell of overheated brakes. He pulled a rear wheel off and showed me the drum. He told me that in all his years working as a mechanic he had never seen the brake drum turn blue, as this one had from such high temperature. He then proceeded to give me a concerned look as if to say, "Are you out of your mind?" Well, I might have been out of my mind, but I wasn't crazy. Besides, just like this hectic day, we somehow managed to just make it through this entire calamity.

26

Dealing with the Unexpected

As we continued to expand, we employed twenty-five people and had many new mortuaries seeking our assistance. Hardly a week went by that I didn't get a call at home by a night dispatcher, informing me that a car had been involved in an accident or broken down, or that someone hadn't reported for the night shift.

Late one night our dispatcher called, telling me that Bobby Kennedy had just been shot. The coroner's office wanted to know if we were prepared to have two men ready to leave immediately in the event he died. We had been making calls for the coroner's office for about eight years by then, and it seemed rather strange for them to be putting us on alert about a call that might not come. As it turned out, Bobby survived just long enough for someone on his staff to recommend the Armstrong Family Mortuary. They made the removal and between them and the coroner's office, his body was prepared for shipment back east.

We had been assisting our friends at Armstrong Family through three generations of the family. After this momentous event, they had little signs made for the windows in their hearse that read, "On June 8, 1968, the body of Robert F. Kennedy was transported to the Los Angeles Airport in this vehicle." This hearse was traded to me about ten years later, as part of a transaction with them for a newer model. I later rented it to a studio making a movie called *Wired*, about the life and death of John Belushi. Sadly, no one seemed to want it for its historical value. I eventually sold it to an Iranian man who couldn't have cared less about its past.

One of my most memorable limo drives was to pick up singer-songwriter Carly Simon, along with a female friend, from her swanky home in Brentwood. I drove them to the Shrine Auditorium, where she was going to be a presenter at the Grammy Awards that night.

About halfway there, Carly opened her purse and retrieved two joints, which they lit up and began smoking. I'm no prude, but I thought that this was pretty inconsiderate. My only choice was to raise the divider window or risk getting stoned myself. With the window up it was no longer possible to hear their conversation, which had been quite interesting. Carly was telling her companion that she and her boyfriend had quarreled over a song she had written. Apparently, he resented it, but she told him that the song was not about him. It must have been a one-in-a-million chance to actually hear her talking about this subject.

During his senior year at Dorsey High School, Ron had gotten to know Mike Love of the Beach Boys. Mike would occasionally visit our office and started using our limo service. He was a product of the hippie generation who believed he could enhance his self-awareness by following gurus like the Hindu Maharishi Mahesh Yogi. Mike did come off as being extremely calm and mellow the few times he visited us. On a number of occasions, our drivers would drop him off at Ron's house after a night of partying so he could sleep off whatever was influencing him. This continued until we received a call from the group's manager, instructing us to stop taking orders from Mike because the manager was going to discontinue authorizing limo service payments for him.

For years we had a verbal contract with the manager of Diana Ross and the Supremes, whom we furnished limo service to when they were performing locally or arriving in Los Angeles from out-of-state concerts. They had signed a deal to perform at a casino in Lake Tahoe's South Shore. He wanted to know if we could transport all their band equipment to a hotel, and some of Diana's personal items to the private home at which she would be staying. We had a walk-in van that we used on large flower deliveries that could easily do the job, so we accepted the order.

Steve Nimz was a relatively new driver of ours in his teens, and he volunteered to make the trip. Steve was told to report to the band equipment company in Los Angeles to pick up instruments that afternoon. After that stop, he continued on to the residence of Diana Ross to pick up her luggage and other personal items. She greeted Steve in a nightgown, smoking a cigarette, with no makeup on and cussing like a drunken sailor.

Steve drove all night, and around 6 A.M. he was almost to the town of Truckee when he heard a loud bang, and the truck wouldn't go any further. After an inspection, it was determined that the rear axle had broken. There was a U-Haul truck rental facility nearby, and he was able to transfer all the contents from our van to the rental truck, but that delayed him. He didn't arrive in Lake Tahoe until noon the following day.

Steve's trip back to the rental company took him through the Donner Pass, named for the Donner Party that became stranded in the winter of 1846 on their trek west to California. It was bad enough that Steve's rental truck had no air conditioning to combat the summer heat, but to make matters worse, he hadn't slept for about thirty hours. As fate would have it, he fell asleep at the wheel and crashed into three parked cars, damaging them badly. The truck was still drivable, but Steve was required to stay in Truckee to wait for the California Highway Patrol to make their report. At least Steve didn't have to resort to cannibalism to survive, as the Donner Party had.

27

Onward and Upward

On January 21, 1969, Kathy had our second son, Greg, and the delivery was much more peaceful for her. It was enjoyable witnessing how the kids learned to speak and hearing the cute creations they came up with. When Greg could recite the whole alphabet, he couldn't pronounce the letter *r*, which would come out as "cow." Even when you would coach him by clearly enunciating the sound "arr," he would follow slowly and repeat the sound correctly, but when he went back through the entire alphabet, it was back to "cow." Meanwhile, Mischa could not pronounce the Russian version of Greg's name, Greisha, so he called him Geeta instead, and that became his permanent nickname.

Either my mom or Kathy's would babysit, but it was a lot more convenient for us to take them to Ron's house because he lived only about five minutes away, near Lake Hollywood. The first time we asked Ron to babysit for us, I think he was a little nervous, but eventually he sat for both of the kids, mostly when Kathy and I would go to a movie. Since Greg was almost three years younger, he gave Ron a bit more of a challenge. One night Ron had been trying to entertain him but wasn't having much

Kathy and Allan with their sons, Greg (left) and Michael, in 1974.

luck. He had given him a large serving spoon to play with. That didn't turn out to be a good idea, because Greg whacked Ron on the head with it, catching him just above his eye. The following evening, Ron spoke at a large function sponsored by the Los Angeles County Funeral Directors Association. His whole eye had turned a deep purple. He explained to the audience how he got the shiner, so Kathy and I got a recap in front of the whole crowd.

The single biggest leap forward in our business also took place about this time when our next-door neighbors, the Frank Taylor Ford dealership, started pressuring us to move out of our location so they could expand into it. In compensation for leaving, Ron asked them for $30,000 to take over the remaining seven years of our twenty-year lease. They thought his request was unreasonable, but this was on Figueroa Street in downtown Los Angeles, with dealers that represented almost every major car manufacturer. In the thirteen years we had been at this location rents in the area had skyrocketed, while we had been getting only small increases in our rent each year. Therefore, if we relinquished our lease to them, they would save a tremendous amount over the remaining years. The lease we had signed in the '60s did not prevent us from transferring the lease to a second party. After conceding this point, they agreed and we began our fourth search for a new base of operations.

It wasn't long before we started inquiring about a glorious old abandoned funeral home. It was one of the most beautiful mortuary buildings in California, colonial in style, with two stories and large white columns across the front. We knew it would cost a great deal of money and take a lot of work to get it into usable condition, because it had been sitting unused for a very long time. The building dated back to the '30s and in its heyday was the home of the Edwards Brothers Colonial Mortuary. The chapel seated about 100 people and every Sunday the mortuary hosted a religious radio broadcast from there, which included religious music performed by the well-known Edwards Brothers Singers.

As times changed, the mortuary's business started to wane. Typically, the three most important events to be celebrated in the first half of the twentieth century were weddings, births, and deaths. In those days, funeral arrangements had a very simple fee structure. A family would purchase a casket and that price included almost everything provided by the funeral home, including the hearse, limo, casket, embalming, makeup, hairdressing, visitation, and flower delivery to the cemetery, whose internment costs were separate from the funeral home.

During the mid-'60s, the significance of funerals lessened and the industry fell under tremendous scrutiny after Jessica Mitford's book, *The American Way of Death*, appeared. The book heavily criticized the funeral industry and evidently struck a chord with the American people. Even before the book was published, the trend began to shift toward lower-cost services. When President Dwight D. Eisenhower died in 1961, he was placed in an inexpensive casket. The news media took notice of this in the many articles appearing across the country. Many families even asked mortuaries if they had an "Eisenhower" casket they could purchase for their loved one. After all, if it was good enough for him, it had to be acceptable for them as well.

A large San Diego firm called Goodbody Mortuary had purchased the Edwards Brothers business after the owners had passed on. They had contracted with a married couple to run the business. We had been providing Edwards Brothers with equipment and staff for years, and we realized that they were having financial difficulties when it became harder to collect what they owed us each month. Everything in the mortuary was leased, right down to the drapes and carpets.

One day there was a big buzz in the industry because the couple had apparently absconded with $80,000 from the pre-need funds—prepaid funeral arrangements held in trust accounts at a bank. They were both in their sixties and must have decided it was time to retire in sunny Mexico. As a result, the State Board of Funeral Directors and Embalmers (as it was then called) had an investigation and pulled their license to practice as Edwards Brothers. The San Diego office realized that the main draw of the mortuary had been its name recognition and that even under a new name, the mortuary would still have to furnish free funerals to all the swindled families, so they just shut it down.

Goodbody Mortuary didn't know what to do with the property, so it sat empty for years. Homeless people started living in the building and drug addicts were also taking refuge inside, so the police department wanted the building torn down. We contacted the San Diego firm to see if the property might be for sale, and they were delighted. Owing to its deplorable condition we were able to purchase it for just over $100,000, although it would take many months and thousands of dollars to refurbish it.

Since the property had been abandoned for so long, the weeds had grown tall and most of the windows had been broken. Someone even broke into the building after it had been locked up, dismantled the entire marble fireplace, and carted it off. An extremely large casket display room took up about one-third of the second floor. Since we had no use for it, we had a hallway constructed down its center with four small rooms built on each side. That gave us dormitory rooms for our students and night help.

This building, which we called "The Mansion," became our livery service base of operations for many years. It had more than twice the square footage of our previous location, but the garage had space for ten cars only, and we had thirty, so we still needed a garage for our other twenty cars.

We purchased a large garage not far from our office, which was ideal for us because it could accommodate about twenty-five cars and a mechanic's facility. We acquired a great deal of equipment that made us totally self-sufficient in handling all of our repairs. We also added a body and paint shop, which allowed me to further expand our activities. With our own body shop, we could refurbish funeral cars for mortuaries that could not afford to buy new ones. It also made it possible for me to purchase older hearses to fix up and export to other countries. After the word got out, we received much more of this type of business, most often from callers overseas, including Guam, American Samoa, and the Philippines.

EDWARDS BROTHERS COLONIAL MORTUARY — 1000 VENICE BOULEVARD — LOS ANGELES

In 1973, Allan and Ron purchased the Edwards Brothers Colonial Mortuary, featured on this postcard in its heyday.

28

Embarrassing Moments

People in the funeral profession have to be particularly mindful of the emotional state of families when they are bereaved. An incident that may be insignificant under different circumstances may become a serious issue at a time when emotions run high and tolerance low. Inevitably, things go wrong and mistakes are made in this business, just as in any other.

A family-owned mortuary that we assisted for years gave us an order for a hearse. One of their employees told me that the firm had purchased some caskets that might have been freight damaged or have other defects. Inexpensive caskets have six small metal handles and are referred to as cloth-covered caskets, or just "cloths." They are made from inexpensive wood, which is why you never see the wood itself, only the fabric covering it. The more expensive hardwood or polished woods have one long handle on each side, which may be wood or metal. The casket for the service this day appeared to be expensive because the handles were made of extruded metal, which is very sturdy—but the decorative end caps were pot metal, about two inches in diameter.

At the cemetery, I instructed the pallbearers to carry the casket down a fairly steep hill. By the time we reached the lowering device, I saw that the fancy knobs at each end of the handles had broken off. The pallbearers didn't seem to know what to do with them, so one man placed the broken knob on the "casket piece," which is what the floral arrangement on top of the casket is called, and the other three men did the same. Fortunately, the other family members seemed unaware that this had happened.

Another embarrassing event occurred on a military service at Fort Rosecrans National Cemetery in San Diego. We had just leased six new Dodge station wagons and had not yet received the license plates. Almost all car dealers deliver a car to you with a temporary license plate insert showing the name of the dealership or the manufacturer, as a way to get some free advertising. A male family member came up to me just as the pallbearers were about to step up to the rear of the conversion. He was visibly angry and told me that he was extremely upset over the license plate insert. Having never really paid any attention to it, I was caught totally off-guard. That year, Chrysler Corporation's national slogan was "Something wonderful is happening." I tore the license inserts off the car and apologized profusely.

At the conclusion of a veteran's funeral, the final procedure is presenting the folded American flag to a member of the family and telling them, "On behalf of the president of the United States and a grateful nation, we are presenting you with this flag." The person chosen to receive it is usually the closest relative. On one occasion there were two daughters, resulting in a very emotional fight between them as to who would get the flag.

When film director John Farrow died, I drove the family car for his big celebrity funeral. I picked up his actress wife, Maureen O'Sullivan, and daughter Mia Farrow, who was still in her teens. She hadn't started making films yet, so I had no idea who she was. It had rained most of the morning when we arrived at a church in Beverly Hills. When the Mass ended, the family was instructed to return to the limo for the trip to Holy Cross Cemetery. However, a friend of the family decided that since it had been raining and the grass was wet, the children first had to be taken a few blocks away to a store to buy galoshes. Meanwhile, everyone who had attended the funeral waited for us to return before they started forming the procession.

Another incident of *funeralis interruptus* also occurred at Holy Cross Cemetery. The priest had given the usual committal service, but when he finished everyone remained at the graveside, apparently waiting for something. I finally asked the funeral director what was going on. He informed me that actor Peter Fonda was supposed to give the eulogy. Peter finally showed up twenty minutes later, and the graveside service continued.

Forest Lawn owned the most famous mortuary and cemetery combinations in the country, located in Glendale and the Hollywood Hills. They also owned Mount Sinai Mortuary & Cemetery, in the same area, which did nothing but Jewish funerals, and the staff there was well trained in those traditions.

We had been furnishing Mount Sinai with family cars and first calls for years. The mortuary chapel was just outside the entrance of the cemetery, and I will never forget the day that every funeral director dreads. There was a special portico to park the family limo just outside the chapel door, where people would walk to their cars and form a procession to drive into the cemetery grounds. Everything seemed normal that day, as the people filed out and walked past me without saying a word. Then the side door was closed to give the immediate family a few minutes of privacy. A minute later I heard a woman screaming, "That's not my Hoiman!"

It was apparent that they had placed the wrong body in the chapel. This was confirmed a minute later, when the side door flew open and the director, sweating profusely, came outside. He asked everyone to get out of their cars and come back into the chapel. They had two male cases that were in the same gray octagon casket, and they placed the wrong one in the chapel. After some hastily spoken prayers, people started filing out again, and they were all talking a mile a minute. You would think someone would have noticed it was the wrong body as they filed past the casket, but if the widow hadn't recognized him, they might have buried the wrong person.

Another factor that could seriously hamper a funeral service was the traffic accidents that inevitably took place, because processions didn't stop for red lights. The motorcycle escorts didn't always stay in the intersection but would often race ahead to break the next stoplight.

At one funeral that concluded with a graveside service at the Veterans Administration cemetery in Westwood, I drove a limo behind one of our own hearses. It was a miracle we didn't have a disastrous chain-reaction pileup that day. We were traveling along in the second lane from the fastest on the San Diego Freeway, which comes to a peak at the Mulholland Bridge. Just before we reached the hump, a small Porsche blew past us in the fast lane.

Moments later we passed over the peak, enabling us to see down the freeway, and it wasn't pretty. The traffic ahead of us was at a dead stop so the Porsche driver slammed on his brakes, spun around 180 degrees and came to rest directly in the lane of the hearse ahead of me. White smoke was coming off the hearse's rear tires as the driver, Wayne Beckner, locked up the brakes and started to skid. There was only a split second to check if I could switch into the fast lane and prevent the limo full of family members from crashing into the back of the hearse. Just as I swerved over, there was a thundering crash as the hearse slammed into the Porsche. I heard the young girl in the back seat of the limo yell out, "Hail Mary full of grace the Lord is with thee, blessed art thou amongst women and blessed is the fruit of thy womb, Jesus." If it hadn't been so frightening and I'd heard these incantations bursting out under some less severe circumstances, it might have actually been funny. When I later recalled the incident with my son Greg, he remarked hilariously, "Your karma ran over her dogma!"

The whole freeway came to a screeching halt. I piled out of my limo to see if Wayne was okay. The front end of the hearse was caved in, and huge billows of steam were pouring out of it. I let the people in the procession know we would have to pull over to the side of the freeway and noticed that about twelve cars behind us a tow truck was sitting in the backed-up traffic. I ran and asked him if he could tow the damaged hearse to the VA cemetery at the bottom of the hill. Wayne, who was not injured, got into my limo and proceeded to take the rest of the procession to the cemetery. We hooked up the hearse to the tow truck in about ten minutes, and the driver was willing to take me as well. When we arrived at the cemetery with the smashed vehicle, Wayne had all the cars lined up and parked in front of the cemetery office.

As luck would have it, there was a hearse exiting the cemetery driven by an old friend from Utter-McKinley. I told him what had happened and that I needed to borrow his hearse. Wayne and I transferred the casket into his hearse and we drove it to the grave. The tow truck driver agreed to take the mangled hearse back to our body shop. Back at the office, Wayne said he hadn't had this much excitement since he had retired from the Los Angeles Police Department's vice squad.

On other occasions, accidents occurred at cemeteries with surprising results. A director who worked for one of the Jewish mortuaries had just concluded a service at Hillside Cemetery. Milton Glatt was Groman Mortuary's most senior employee and one of the nicest, friendliest individuals imaginable. The cemetery was fairly new and had storm drains just like the ones on city streets. One day Milton stepped from a curb and slid down into one of the drains, which had no grate covering it. They finally pulled him out and sent him to the hospital. Steel grates were installed the following week.

In sharp contrast to Milton was another of Groman's directors whom all of our drivers hated to work with, Leon Gerber. Not only was he very demanding, he never had a kind word for anyone. We provided the cars for Jack Benny's service and by that time had assisted Groman's for over fifteen years. Leon called on the phone the day before the service and told our dispatcher, "If you guys f*** up on the Benny service tomorrow, you can kiss your ass good-bye."

All cemeteries provide 2" x 12" wooden planks, placed parallel to the length of the grave, so the pallbearers can walk on either side of the lowering device. After a grave is opened, the soil on either side of the grave is inherently unstable. On a few occasions, when one of the pallbearers stepped a little off the plank as they were placing the casket on the lowering device, that side of the grave would cave in. On rare occasions, even a pallbearer would slip into the grave up to his hips. Kind of gives new meaning to expression *grave* danger.

When the patriarch of the Utter-McKinley Mortuaries chain died, we were called upon to furnish the equipment. The first thing they asked was "How much weight can your hearses accommodate?" We told them we had some coaches with airlift shocks that could be inflated to carry about 900 pounds. Maytor McKinley was placed in a silver deposit casket that had been flown in from Texas. All metal caskets with which we were familiar were made from sheets of copper, bronze, or steel. However, Maytor's casket was cast in much the same manner as statuary. When you *cast* something, it ends up being much thicker than sheet metal. His casket weighed in at about 850 pounds, and it took ten pallbearers to carry it instead of the usual six. I drove a limo, but it was not the primary family car. They used Maytor's own Rolls-Royce, which I followed to Inglewood Park Cemetery. Ron drove the hearse that day and was instructed to pull up to the family plot. The casket was to be placed into one of two above-ground concrete vaults beneath an ornate wrought-iron gazebo. One had Maytor's name on it and the other had that of his wife, Varri.

One of the cemetery workers was helping with the alignment of the casket into the vault. When it seemed correctly positioned, the pallbearers started lowering it. Unfortunately, the workman had gripped the bottom of the casket just as this was being done and the heavy casket chopped off one of his fingers. Ron loaded him into the hearse quickly and took him to nearby Daniel Freeman Hospital. At the hospital, they asked if Ron could retrieve the finger, so he made a mad dash back to the cemetery On his hasty return trip to the hospital, he ran into a woman's car. He explained his mission to her as fast as possible, which shook her up so much that she didn't even ask him for insurance information.

Afterward, the Rolls and my limo were driven to another part of the cemetery to wait until everyone left, before returning to the grave. At Maytor's request, they opened the trunk of the Rolls and got out some silver chalices to toast him with champagne.

29

Life Gets "Tegious"

Maintaining a large fleet of cars took a great deal of ancillary support, including mechanics and a cleaning crew. From the time we had purchased our large garage, most of my days were spent there—overseeing the fleet, keeping records, going on movie drives, and converting station wagons. Ron was at his desk every day, staying in touch with our clients, brainstorming on opportunities, and conducting all manner of PR activities. He was the businessman extraordinaire. Every day around noon he would call me at the garage to say that he was on his way to pick me up for lunch, which was often the only time we would see each other. We would typically discuss business then. It seemed the only way we were going to stay in the game was to be more competitive than anyone else.

For me, automotive costs were something that had to be watched at every turn, so my mission was to be tighter than the bark on a tree. My childhood was spent watching my family struggle through the war years. This no-frills lifestyle hardened my resolve to not spend money on anything that I could do myself. My credo was: If it's broke, fix it. If you don't know how, keep at it until you do.

Our garage was equipped with fifty-five-gallon drums of oil and transmission fluid. A truck would deliver motor oil in bulk every few months. Large quantities of waste oil eventually made it necessary to create a place to store it. The garage had a mechanic's pit that was never used, so I capped it with a 4' x 8' half-inch steel plate, poured concrete over it, and added a center hole, creating a reservoir that could hold over 1,000 gallons of used oil. Every six months a vacuum truck would come and pump it out to be recycled. We would get compensated with a bag of absorbent material, called dry sweep, to mop up spilled oil. Today, that much waste oil would fetch a pretty penny.

During our first eight years, taking cars to the tire shop took up much of my time. An inventory one year revealed that we had purchased 365 tires that year, which meant we were wearing them out at a rate of one per day. Just standing around getting them installed was wasting time, so I purchased a machine for mounting and balancing and started doing it myself. Purchasing twenty to thirty tires at a time brought the price down substantially as well. Some of the mortuaries also started asking me if they could purchase their hearse tires from us, because they had difficulty finding the odd-ball size whitewall tires.

There came a point at which we were consuming so much fuel that I contacted Atlantic Richfield Company (ARCO) about buying gasoline wholesale. They had a program where they would install a tank with a pump, and the fuel would cost three cents a gallon above wholesale. The tank held 6,500 gallons, which lasted only ninety days.

The 1973 oil crisis severely affected the price and availability of gasoline, which took a particular toll on our business because it was so transportation oriented. The crisis arose when the Arab members of the Organization of Petroleum Exporting Countries (OPEC) began an oil embargo in response to the United States assisting Israel during the Yom Kippur War.

We could not take a chance on one of our vehicles being unable to refill at a station that had run out of fuel, so I had extra gas tanks installed in ten of our wagons. Our drivers would go along until the engine started to sputter, and then they could reach down on the floor to flip a lever that would change tanks. We also acquired thirty-gallon fuel cells made of a heavy rubberized canvas that were being used in the racing industry. These were placed in any car or out-of-town vans that didn't have a second tank permanently installed in them.

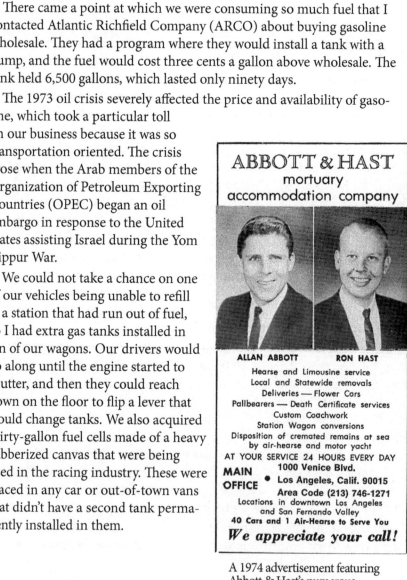

ABBOTT & HAST
mortuary
accommodation company

ALLAN ABBOTT   RON HAST

Hearse and Limousine service
Local and Statewide removals
Deliveries — Flower Cars
Pallbearers — Death Certificate services
Custom Coachwork
Station Wagon conversions
Disposition of cremated remains at sea
by air-hearse and motor yacht
AT YOUR SERVICE 24 HOURS EVERY DAY

MAIN   1000 Venice Blvd.
OFFICE   ● Los Angeles, Calif. 90015
               Area Code (213) 746-1271
Locations in downtown Los Angeles
and San Fernando Valley
40 Cars and 1 Air-Hearse to Serve You

We appreciate your call!

A 1974 advertisement featuring Abbott & Hast's numerous mortuary accommodation services.

The lifeblood of our company was a continuing supply of fuel. For months during the gas crisis, most of my time was spent on the phone trying to locate fuel. I managed to talk a few gas station owners into letting me purchase their entire inventory, enabling them to close for a few days and reduce their cost of operation.

I put the word out to everyone we knew to keep an eye out for fuel we could buy from unconventional sources. One of my contacts alerted me to a gas station that had unearthed three partly filled old metal tanks, intending to replace them with plastic tanks that would not rust. Vacuum truck companies in Los Angeles were moving gas twenty-four hours a day during the shortage, and the driver they sent on our behalf arrived at the location about three in the morning. He dumped a little over 1,000 gallons into our tank and, as he finished, informed our dispatcher that another truck had arrived to pump some gas. He told the just-arrived driver where he was taking it. The next day, two Los Angeles police detectives came to our office and questioned me about a report of grand theft.

Shortly thereafter, the owner of the station contacted me and demanded we return the gasoline, which I refused to do. I offered him more than the going rate, which he turned down. He finally called me, after all my efforts to settle this matter in an amicable way, and surprised me by saying it wasn't necessary for us to pay him as his insurance company had already compensated him. It would have been very interesting to know how many gallons of stolen gas the station owner reported.

The closest we ever came to running out was when a customer from the Philippines purchased a hearse through the use of a financial instrument called a letter of credit. As soon as the hearse was loaded on the ship and it had set sail, they would give me signed copies of the bills of lading. I could then apply for funds from the bank listed on the letter of credit. On this occasion the ship was loaded and ready to go, but the Maritime Union called a strike that lasted for weeks. As long as the ship was sitting idle in the harbor, we couldn't obtain the funds. To make matters worse, ARCO had put me on COD status because of a late payment caused by this strike. It was pretty frustrating having a $6,000 check sit on my desk that couldn't be cashed and ARCO refusing to bring us any more gas. I was sweating bullets until the strike ended and the check was issued.

Gas was in such short supply that cemeteries couldn't get enough to keep their lawn mowers running. And we thought that we had problems! People often complain about the high price of gas prices, but they have no idea how bad it is when you can't get it at any price.

30

More Disasters Than an Irwin Allen Production

In the early '70s there was a large earthquake in Los Angeles, the epicenter of which was in the San Fernando Valley, at Sylmar. The most severely damaged structure there was the large complex of buildings called the Olive View Sanitarium and Hospital. It was three stories tall and all the floors had pancaked. It was still dark, and everyone in Los Angeles awoke from the horrendous noise produced by the severe shaking that seemed to go on forever. It was obvious to me that we were going to get very busy.

Even before the sun came up, the coroner's office was getting calls from all over Los Angeles County. They were dispatching deputies, who began picking up bodies as dawn broke. The calls they got were for people who had already died, but it was going to take a long time to get rescue crews to perform the body recoveries from this multistory building. They assigned us as their official representatives to report to Olive View with our men and cars. Because of the complexity of the job, I requested a signed document from them naming us as their official representative while we remained there. I called it our "Writ of Hideous Corpses." Our vans and wagons were there around the clock for three days as the building's layers were uncovered. As each body was recovered, we transported it to the downtown morgue.

One of the tragedies that resulted from this horrific event involved some friends who routinely carpooled to work each morning. The earthquake struck as they passed under a freeway bridge, which collapsed and crushed them in a pickup truck. When our men arrived at that scene they knew it was going to be difficult, because the whole truck was crushed to less than three feet of twisted metal. They told me that the only way they could tell body parts from truck parts was to squeeze whatever they saw—if it was hard, it was part of the truck, and if it was squishy, it was probably part of a body.

The startling part of the story came when we found out that these friends always traveled with a third worker, whose wife informed them that he wasn't feeling well that morning and wouldn't be going with them. His friends didn't have the same luck. Had the victims left one minute sooner or later, they probably wouldn't have died that day. It makes you wonder: If you were given the opportunity to know the date of your death, would you want to know? Pondering questions like these about mortality can be mind-numbing—a condition that for us was an occupational hazard.

Fortunately, a positive result of the Sylmar quake was the wakeup call that Los Angeles got about all of its unreinforced masonry buildings. The most common ones were large warehouse and factory buildings. This marked the beginning of reinforcement and removal of parapets, a short section of wall that extends higher than the roof of a building. These modifications probably prevented a great deal of death from the Northridge earthquake decades later.

Another disaster we worked on was a plane crash in Pago Pago, American Samoa, which is part of the island archipelago of Polynesia. As commercial aircraft grew larger and transported greater numbers of passengers, the death tolls from crashes were beginning to increase as well. Even if the airline wasn't at fault, it was customary for them to purchase a casket and transport the remains, or what was left of the deceased, back to their families wherever they lived.

When the decision of which mortuary to use for this air disaster came up, one of the executives chose the Douglass Mortuary in El Segundo, across the street from the south runway at LAX. Owner Sam Douglass's wife, Jackie, had worked for the airline and knew many of their executives. Sam and Jackie were asked if they would be willing to fly to Dover, Delaware, and oversee all of the identification, embalming, casketing, and funerals for the victims. With our ongoing assistance, it was handled very efficiently and the airline was quite satisfied. From that time on Douglass Mortuary became the official airplane disaster mortuary in the nation, while we served as their support team.

The deadliest airline disaster in history occurred in 1977 on the island of Tenerife in the Canary Islands, probably best known for the French sailors who sighted a giant squid there in the seventeenth century. Many aircraft were being diverted from the island of Gran Canaria because of a bomb threat. Tenerife had a smaller airport called Los Rodeos. These two islands were in proximity to each other, so Los Rodeos received most of the diverted planes. It had no working ground radar and only one short runway and a taxiway. Planes were stacking up, and only incoming aircraft were allowed to use this runway. By the time everything got sorted out it had become foggy, but they decided to let some of the diverted planes take off.

A KLM Royal Dutch Airlines senior pilot had landed in Tenerife and was approaching his limit of flight time, so he was eager to get airborne after the long delay. The pilot was "pushing up"—the airline jargon for advancing the aircraft into a position for takeoff. The KLM aircraft was a Boeing 747, which was the largest aircraft built at that time. At the other end of the runway was a Pan Am 747 that had just landed. The Pan Am pilot had been instructed to turn off the runway at the third exit, which he missed because of fog. The pilot transmitted to the tower that they were still on the runway, but the message was interrupted.

In the meantime, the tower had instructed the KLM pilot to remain holding, but the pilot believed they had given him permission to take off. The copilot disagreed and told him that they had not received such instructions, but the pilot overruled him and commenced with his takeoff. When the KLM jet started to become airborne, they saw the Pan Am airplane still taxiing on the runway, so the pilot pulled up as steep as he could with full throttle. He nearly cleared the other aircraft, but the landing gear struck the top of the other aircraft, causing them both to crash and burn up. Some passengers were killed instantly by the collision, while many others died in the conflagration that ensued. All told, 583 people perished.

The National Transportation Safety Board (NTSB) investigated the disaster for months and concluded it was caused by pilot error and a communications problem. When two people key their microphones simultaneously it causes a heterodyne, or combination of two frequencies. The NTSB found this had happened when they recovered the black box, which is actually a fluorescent orange color.

This transmission phenomenon was something with which we were very familiar. All our first-call cars were equipped with two-way radios, so the dispatchers at our office were in constant contact with our drivers. Because there were not enough frequencies available for commercial use, we shared ours with a firm called Western Trucking Company. Many times when our drivers were trying to communicate, they would get "stepped on" by a heterodyne.

Just like the Pago Pago disaster, the remains from both aircraft on Tenerife were once again sent to the Dover Air Force Base, where the Douglasses had to report and begin their labor-intensive process. Sam and Jackie were working sixteen-hour days, and they asked us to help with the arrangements on our end in Los Angeles. All casketing and identifications, whenever possible, were being done at Dover. Many of the remains were not whole, so it was decided that they would be buried in one mass grave.

Their small staff needed our assistance because so much of this procedure involved transportation to and from LAX. Many of the victims were from California, so Ron contacted Westminster Memorial Park in Orange County. It agreed to furnish one large grave space at no charge. He also arranged for a priest, a minister, and a rabbi to conduct the graveside service.

At Douglass Mortuary you could stand on their front porch and observe the activities at LAX. Carroll Shelby had his test track parallel to the runway on a private portion of the airport and I saw them test his latest creation, the Shelby Ford Cobra. Sometimes their driver would see a jet was taking off and he would accelerate down the test track, leaving the jet plane in the dust.

The last plane crash that we worked on occurred in the skies over Cerritos, California. An Aeroméxico airliner had collided with a small private plane. Douglass Mortuary once again called on us to coordinate every aspect of the disaster. The airline supplied all the caskets, which in some cases contained as little as one limb. We furnished the cars for the funeral, and I drove a limo to pick up six Aeroméxico pilots who had flown in for the service. The emotion these fellow pilots felt was palpable.

31

Someone's Gotta Do It

The first of many United States national cemeteries was the Soldiers' National Cemetery in Gettysburg, Pennsylvania. It was dedicated in 1863 by Abraham Lincoln in his Gettysburg Address, four and a half months after the battle there that changed the tide of the Civil War. The Veterans Administration, which was established in 1930, assumed responsibility for the National Cemetery System from the Department of the Army in 1973.

Because we had become so well known in the funeral industry, the VA cemetery in Westwood often contacted us for assistance. We had already furnished most of the funeral homes in Los Angeles with cars for burials at this sole VA cemetery in Los Angeles County. When the wife of a veteran would die, even twenty or more years after her husband, the family would contact the VA to inquire if she could be interred in the same grave. Double-interment burials became popular in the late '60s, but when these graves were originally dug, they were not excavated to the required depth of ten feet to accommodate the second burial.

In cases like these, it was necessary to open the original grave and lift the casket out in one piece. Then it was just a matter of removing the rest of the grave liner and digging another four feet of earth out with a backhoe. When this was accomplished, a new liner was installed, the original casket was replaced, and some of the extra dirt was used to cover the top, leaving the required six feet of space available for the second casket. The one thing that hadn't been considered was what to do if the original casket had deteriorated and could not be removed in one piece. The cemetery's first few attempts had gone fairly smoothly, but eventually it turned into a real crapshoot when some of the caskets began to crumble, and the cemetery workers refused to climb down and finish the job.

That's where we came in—again. Our crew of four would get to work after the cemetery workers finished with the backhoe. Call me a latent archaeologist, because this job never seemed boring to me. I was always fascinated by the idea of digging up prehistoric bones. In this case, they just weren't that old.

We went on to complete many more of these procedures over the following years. That resulted in our disinterring the famous mountain man John "Liver-Eating" Johnston, portrayed by Robert Redford in the film *Jeremiah Johnson*. By the time we were hired by a historical society for this job in 1974, Johnston had been buried about eighty years. All we were able to recover were small pieces of the fibula and tibia, the lower leg bones. Although there wasn't much left of him, the historical society was delighted to take what we had recovered back to Cody, Wyoming. The bone fragments were placed beneath a monument in his memory, and Robert Redford served as the pallbearer. History has recorded that Johnson had cannibalized as many as 200 Crow Indians. I wonder if that was the origin of the expression "eating crow"? Naah.

The government was paying a paltry $245 benefit to families of veterans to cover burial costs, which was used to pay for a casket and transportation. Whenever possible, we would try to schedule two services on the same day. There was no charge for the plot or the color guard, which consisted of six uniformed soldiers acting as casket bearers and a bugler.

Another seven soldiers firing three times consecutively performed the twenty-one-gun salute. The origin of this ritual dates back over 200 years and has experienced some modifications or additions. During the time when the great world powers were fighting major sea battles, each side knew the names of their enemy's ships and how many cannons each ship possessed. Upon approaching a foreign port they would fire their cannons into the open sea, as a gesture of good faith. The opposition knew that reloading was slow, putting them in range of their own cannons.

The tradition that later arose began as a naval salute alone, but it evolved into the demonstration of honor that it is today. After the salute has been completed, the color guard tri-folds the flag and the bugler plays. Friends and family seem to be able to hold it together until the haunting sound of "Taps" begins. That always evokes an outpouring of emotion.

The Westwood VA cemetery was filled by 1976. We continued our services for the $245 allowance, but now we were transporting bodies to the next-nearest VA facility, Fort Rosecrans National Cemetery in San Diego. Eventually, Fort Rosecrans was also nearing capacity. Then, the next-nearest VA cemetery was in the Willamette Valley, near Eugene, Oregon, almost 1,000 miles from Los Angeles. It greatly upset the veterans organizations as no California mortuary would consider making such a trip for the $245 fee that the government allowed. The politicians finally got the message and started to plan a new VA cemetery in California, but it was expected to take about three years.

We felt this was unacceptable for our veterans, so we decided that the only way to correct this injustice was to come up with an interim solution. We purchased a large truck and equipped it with a heavy-duty hydraulic lift at the rear. I designed and ordered six three-tiered racks with large rubber wheels and had them custom built to our specifications by our friends at Ferno. This would enable us to transport up to eighteen caskets. We then informed all the mortuaries of our new service.

It would take two days to get to the Willamette Valley, followed by one full day at the cemetery and two days to return. We made the same trip each week and in three years put 120,000 miles on the truck. Finally, the new national cemetery was ready to open in Riverside, California, so we sold our truck and began taking four at a time to Riverside in a lift van.

When the VA realized that we had been providing veterans services for years, they called us directly about the possibility of having a program for indigent veterans. We informed them that we were willing to furnish a casket and transport the deceased seventy miles to Riverside for the amount allowed by the government, which had been adjusted from the paltry $245 to a whopping $255. Nevertheless, we always felt privileged to serve our country's veterans and their families.

Abbott & Hast's Ford truck, used for transporting veterans to VA cemeteries.

32

Expanding Our Business

We rented hearses every year for Halloween parties, birthdays, and weddings. Our most unusual hearse rental was to a group of guys who wanted our driver to take them to a hospital to pick up their friend as a joke. He had jumped off the roof of his friend's house trying to land in the swimming pool but was about two feet short. The man didn't quite appreciate the humorous side of the gesture, especially when our driver took a detour through a cemetery, as requested.

In the '70s, the California Department of Transportation created a dedicated carpool lane on the Santa Monica Freeway. Intended to promote ride sharing, this "diamond lane" was only for vehicles carrying multiple passengers. Many people viewed it as discriminatory, so they formed a group of volunteers to drive in the diamond lane with only one occupant per car, in violation of the law. They hired me to drive a hearse leading the procession, with my stipulation that one of their volunteers ride in the hearse with me. The rest of them received citations, and they didn't achieve their objective of changing the law.

That same year, a funeral director went to court to explain that he had been given an erroneous ticket for using the diamond lane. He pointed out that there was nothing in the law that said his passenger had to be alive, so he was found not guilty. His argument worked, but it didn't work so well for several pregnant women who claimed they had passengers as well.

While movie rentals were a nice supplement, the core of our business was still accommodations. A mortuary has a variety of ways to advertise its business, but a funeral car livery service doesn't. We were well known in our local industry, but we needed to get more statewide exposure. A trade journal published in LA called *Mortuary Management* had subscribers all over the United States, especially on the West Coast. Many industry suppliers, like casket manufacturers, funeral car builders, and embalming fluid chemical companies, ran half- or full-page ads in this magazine.

We weren't sure how effective a half-page display ad would be, and we couldn't afford one anyway, so Ron got the publisher, William Berg, to let us run a series of business-card-size ads. This provided us with great exposure because every third or fourth page had our small ad on it, featuring headshots of Ron and me with the captions: "Call Abbott & Hast for hearse service," "Call Abbott & Hast for limousine service," and so on. This was at a time when magazines set up their pages with a cut-and-paste format, so it worked out well for their art director, since many page layouts contained gaps that could be filled with a repetition of our many small ads.

Each year at the state conventions we attended, funeral directors would approach us asking if we owned the magazine because of our numerous ads. In spite of our assurance that we didn't, it was assumed by many that we did. Then, in 1975, we got a call from Mr. Berg, who was retiring and thought we might want to purchase the publication. We acquired the company and changed the name from Berg Publications to Abbott & Hast Publications. Ironically, our acquisition just confirmed some people's belief that we had owned it all along.

With a nationwide industry trade journal added to our business, we had become a sort of clearinghouse for anything that was going on in the funeral industry, and were often consulted on issues involving the funeral trade. Companies would also consult with us when a new technology was developed, including the first cryonics (frozen body preservation) firms in the mid-'70s. One company had developed a prototype and delivered a huge cylinder to our facility to be put on display. They held meetings and invited businesspeople to come and see the unit in an effort to attract investors. By the late '70s, one of the companies, Cryonics Society of California, ran out of funds. Their machines were turned off, resulting in thawing and decomposing bodies.

As our business continued to expand, we wanted to design a new business card that people would keep and not just throw away. We went to our printer and asked him to print an imitation $50 bill, with a drawing of our new building in place of the United States Capitol building that is on the back of the real $50 note. The other side had numerous lines where people could write down their most often-called phone numbers. The business card was a big hit with everyone—except the U.S. Treasury. Two government agents came to our mortuary and confiscated every bill we had. They even fined our printer. We still liked the idea, so we had new ones printed with an image of our building on just half the bill. When folded in half twice, it looked like a real $50.

When Mischa was asked as a youth if he would ever be interested in working for our mortuary, his answer was an unequivocal no. He reminded me of one occasion when we were both going upstairs on the freight elevator. A decomposed body on a cot was being taken up to the prep room. A sheet covered the body, so the only thing showing was the man's feet, which reminded him of the Incredible Hulk, with his bilious green color. He said that being close to that body convinced him to never consider working in the business. However, during their high school years, Mischa and Greg were both interested in working for our magazine, which was next door to the mortuary.

The "News Briefs" section of *Mortuary Management*, which Greg began editing when he was 16, always reported on issues concerned with lawsuits, criminal investigations, or anything else of interest in the funeral industry. Over the last thirty-five years, we have published enough bizarre and fascinating stories to fill an entire book. For instance, we reported on the amazing fact that some books at the nation's most prestigious libraries are bound in human skin, including a collection at Harvard University's library. Because human skin was cheap, durable, and waterproof, doctors were asked to retrieve it from amputations or unclaimed bodies.

We also ran some articles about body farms, the most famous of which is the University of Tennessee Forensic Anthropology Facility. More than 1,000 people have willed their remains to these farms in the last ten years, and a large number of crimes have been solved as a result of thorough examination and documentation of insect life cycles and other natural indicators on the collected corpses. A proposal from a Texas university to start a similar body farm was turned down because of the phenomenon known as "NIMBY," or "Not In My Back Yard." It would have been especially disturbing to people who lived downwind.

The covers of *Mortuary Management* have always been well known for featuring scenic photographs. We always provided a description of where the photo was taken and tried to have the covers reflect the seasons, like flowers in spring and snow scenes in winter. Over the years, Greg and I furnished the majority of the photographs, but we also acquired photos that we would have been unlikely to take ourselves, including underwater scenes, volcanoes, lightning, and fireworks.

One photo that Greg acquired from another source was the best example of its subject that we had ever seen. It was an upward-facing shot of the top half of the Statue of Liberty, which clearly showed the beautiful green patina that copper turns to as it weathers. Cover photos were always chosen far in advance of publication, so it was poignant when readers called in after 9/11 to say they were moved to see that photo appear on our September 2001 issue.

Our magazine covers became so popular that some readers requested prints suitable for framing, a service we were happy to accommodate. One such reader, Guy Thompson of Thompson's Harveson & Cole in Fort Worth, Texas, ordered six framed prints of religious structures that had appeared on various covers. He put them on display at his funeral home. To complete this collection, he included a watercolor of a restored cathedral in Baltimore, Maryland, and then graciously sent us a photo of his church gallery wall.

Funeral director Guy Thompson's gallery wall, displaying several *Mortuary Management* cover photos.

33

Rental Carmageddon

I've always been fascinated by movie productions. Even as kids, when my brother and I wanted to do something exciting, we would ride our bikes to the back lots of some of the movie studios in the area and climb over the fence. We would also go to the movies almost every Saturday. In many films they would show a late-model 1940s cars speeding down a highway, but as it was about to get in a wreck or go over a cliff, it would become a tall, square 1930 model, because of budget restrictions. I couldn't have imagined at the time that I would eventually be providing Hollywood with funeral cars for demolition in crashes and other disasters.

We provided two matching hearses for a production that was being filmed at a mortuary in downtown LA that we had served for many years on their larger funerals, including those of Mario Lanza and Jimmy Durante. The mortuary was almost unrecognizable because the set decorators had already covered the outside of the building with a trellis and climbing vines.

The reason the studio needed two vehicles, or "doubles," was that they wanted to have a clean one as the "picture car" and a high-mileage cheap one as the "crash car" they could damage, which saves the studio from wrecking an expensive car. They had already picked up the two hearses, which looked identical. My concern was that you couldn't tell them apart, and there was a chance the studio might use the wrong one for the crash. One hearse was in our current rental fleet and the other one was a rust bucket from the East Coast that I had cleaned up and painted. After I explained my concern, the transportation captain used a grease pencil to write in the upper left corner of the windshield of the good hearse "picture car" and on the other, "crash car."

The heroine in the story, played by Nanette Fabray, was going to run from the mortuary into their garage, jump into the hearse, and crash through the door as she made her getaway. They had replaced the original garage door with one that would easily break apart. Since filming is frequently shot out of sequence, the director decided to first shoot the scene showing the hearse *after* it was supposed to have crashed through the garage door. He instructed the female stunt driver to make a hard turn from the side street, where the garage faced onto Washington Boulevard, a main thoroughfare. For some unknown reason, he instructed her to drive the hearse that had been marked as the picture car.

The traffic had been stopped and replaced by cars with stunt drivers. As she came barreling around the corner, the hearse got away from her and she struck two of the stunt cars. Obviously, she had never driven anything like this hearse, which weighed in at over 6,000 pounds. Once the picture car got damaged, the director used it to crash through the garage door as well. All of their trouble could have been avoided if they had just given me a wig and put me at the wheel, because I was used to driving a hearse like a maniac.

Another production, called *The Outside Man*, with Angie Dickinson and French actor Jean-Louis Trintignant, featured several limousines and a hearse for a funeral scene. It was being filmed in the town of Calabasas at a Catholic retreat that was to double as a cemetery. I arrived at 6 A.M. with nary a soul from the studio present. There were rolling hills covered in grass and a Spanish-style structure well back from the entrance, but it didn't look much like a cemetery. Soon the prop trucks arrived, fully stocked with flat grave markers and flowers in vases. They dyed the grass greener and set out the props. In an hour, it looked exactly like a real cemetery.

In addition to our vehicles, they rented a Mercedes stretch limo from another vendor to serve as the main family car. I had also arranged for a friend of mine, John Brady, who was a real funeral escort, to arrive in full uniform on his motorcycle for a procession scene. His equipment included a two-way radio and handset for the hearse driver. The director, who was French and spoke almost no English, really liked the radio because he could communicate with the escort directly. *Bad idea!*

After a couple of shots of the procession entering the cemetery, he kept insisting that the vehicles get closer together and increase their speed. I walked over to the assistant director and stated my concern about this risky request, but he told me the director was insistent on doing everything his way. Then, as if on cue, an employee of the retreat got in her car and started driving away, apparently unaware that she was about to cross directly in front of the procession. The director suddenly spotted her and yelled, "Stop!" into the radio. He knew that word! John slammed on his brakes and threw up a hand signal for the other drivers. Everyone tried to stop, but it happened too fast. Bam, bam, bam! Two limos and the Mercedes got creamed.

The transportation captain came over to me and asked if we could come up with two more identical limos for the next day. My immediate concern was about our two limos that were already smashed. He told me to turn a claim into my insurance company, to which my reply was "No pay, no cars tomorrow." He reconsidered the matter and agreed to cover the damages. That was the last time we ever released a vehicle or prop to any studio without requiring that they obtain an insurance policy that covered all rentals up to $1 million.

In the film, Jean-Louis played a hit man brought over from France to handle a killing for the Mob. Just after a shootout at the cemetery, the police came roaring in. They screeched to a halt as Jean-Louis jumped into the hearse and drove across the cemetery grass for his getaway. On this day, I brought Kathy and the boys, who were about 6 and 4, to watch the film being shot. As we sat observing this scene unfold, Mischa got up and brought back a big cup of lemonade from the craft table. When the police began firing their shotguns at the fleeing hearse, the shots were so loud that he threw the whole cup up in the air and drenched himself in lemonade.

Studios typically wanted the newest cars for their shots. Since Cadillac would sometimes go many years without a major body change, it was possible for me to match our limousines to the newest models by installing updated components. These parts were typically the grille and rear bumper, which housed the taillights. The retail price of a Cadillac rear bumper and grille was about $1,500, but a growing number of wrecking yards would allow customers to remove parts themselves. I would frequent these yards, taking along a large piece of cardboard for lying on my back. Other mechanics would walk by wearing their grubbies and look bewildered by the sight of me lying on this cardboard in suit pants, white shirt, and tie. I could obtain a complete Cadillac rear bumper and grille for only $150 after removing it myself.

The studios always thought they were getting limos that were newer than they actually were because they couldn't tell the difference. They wouldn't have cared anyway because the public's perception of what they were seeing was the only thing that really mattered.

In 1977, Cadillac and all the other auto manufacturers were required to downsize their cars because gasoline consumption had become a significant issue. As a result, the 1977 Cadillac limo was smaller than the 1976 Cadillac Sedan DeVille. Funeral directors were totally dissatisfied with the new smaller version, which held only five passengers instead of the previous seven.

This downsizing triggered the birth of the stretch limo. A company called Lehmann-Peterson had been producing stretch limos for many years, but they were special-order presidential and executive bulletproof cars. Now that the standard Cadillac limos had been reduced to little more than a sedan, the industry kicked into gear to produce what the car manufacturers could no longer make. Companies called cut-and-stretch builders started popping up across the country. They began by cutting a Sedan DeVille in half and adding thirty-six inches in the center. Next, they added an additional forty-eight inches, or sixty inches, and so on to the limos, which were known as super-stretches. From this point on, no government restriction would limit the size of a limo. Providing identical cars had been simple until the advent of the stretch. After that, the same year, make, and model didn't match because the amount of stretch varied with each builder.

Studios usually preferred to order stretch limos once they become prevalent. We got an order to furnish two identical limos to serve as picture car and crash car, but they hadn't specified that they wanted stretch limos. After locating a high-mileage standard limo, it was painted black to match one of the factory limos in our fleet. Two days after the studio picked them up, the limos were returned because the director wanted a more impressive-looking stretch. I was pretty committed to having this work out after purchasing the second car. We had a high-mileage Lincoln stretch limo, but no identical second car. I told the transportation captain that I had purchased this second standard one for them and spent money to make it match our good limo, so he finally agreed to swap the two cars for our Lincoln stretch to be used for both shots.

For many small communities across the country, mortuaries offered both funeral and ambulance service. For small-town funeral homes that couldn't afford a separate hearse and ambulance, the manufacturers produced a limousine-style hearse with windows all around, referred to as a "combination." It was painted black but wired to accommodate a portable red light on the roof, held in place by a magnet.

Cadillac hearses lasted for many years because of their limited mileage, but ambulances rolled out twenty-four hours a day, making it necessary to replace them more frequently. As a result, a company called Stoner Manufacturing in Santa Fe Springs set the pace for major changes in ambulance production. This was the dawning of the modular ambulance, which was a truck cab and chassis to which they added a large box, or "module," filled with all the necessary equipment. The cab, engine, and chassis had to be upgraded every so often to meet the standards of the municipalities, but the modular part could still do the job for many years by installing it on a new front end.

We had four limos in a film called *Scavenger Hunt* that had many well-known actors but did not do well at the box office. I had worked with the transportation captain before, and he was delighted when all the cars were ready for pickup. They all ended up being destroyed during filming.

In 1981, United Artists made a film called *True Confessions*, starring Robert De Niro and Robert Duvall. It was a period film about a murder in Los Angeles that was committed in the 1940s. They rented our vintage hearse and filmed it arriving at Union Station to deliver a casket for a rail shipment. The casket wasn't in a shipping box as it would have been, but it was nice watching the scene play out. Ron's 1949 Pontiac hearse pulled into the LA train station and passed in front of the camera, with our Abbott & Hast Mortuary nameplates showing clearly in the hearse window. When the manager of Bob's Tire Town saw the movie, he recognized our nameplate and asked me if we had been in business in the 1940s. Come on, I'm not *that* old.

The studio that produced the popular series *Dynasty* was trying to locate a Lincoln stretch that they could blow up. On my trips to different studios it was helpful to always keep my eyes peeled for anything that might be acquired for future use. I knew of an abandoned stretch being stored by a studio. I acquired the limo, but it was not in running condition, so I suggested towing it to where they were filming the show. In the episode, the lead character, Blake Carrington, is being pressured by the Mob to sell his interest in a football franchise. When he refuses, they give him a dire warning. Since the limo did not run, they just filmed the actors walking away from it after they had arrived at their destination. To demonstrate that they were deadly serious, a mobster drives by and throws a bomb into his limo, knocking everyone down and blinding Blake Carrington.

All the cemetery shots on *Dallas* that featured our vehicles were filmed at Valhalla Cemetery in Burbank, just one block away from the end of the runway at Lockheed-Burbank Airport. Every time an airplane took off they would have to stop filming because of the noise. On one occasion Larry Hagman said to the cameraman, "Next time a plane takes off, catch it on camera and I can probably get free airline tickets for the rest of my life." His joke was a reference to product placement, a multimillion-dollar business in which the studios are paid to show a specific brand on camera.

The various studios kept such a hectic pace of trying to shoot new episodes each week that having multiple cars allowed them to film in different locations at the same time. For one episode of the popular TV series *Knight Rider*, they rented four identical limos.

One hearse we furnished for the popular Lee Majors TV series *The Fall Guy* was going to be used to make a jump. This show always opened with a clip of his four-wheel-drive truck doing a jump, but hearses don't jump well. It came back from the studio on a flat-bed truck, looking quite "V" shaped and well beyond repair.

Universal called one day, asking for something that we would not normally have provided. They were trying to locate two ten-year-old Cadillac Coupe DeVilles to use as double cars for a new detective series called *Crazy Like a Fox* starring Jack Warden. My friend Doug Scott was a licensed car dealer as well as a funeral car salesman. I asked him to bid on a couple of Caddies at a big dealer's auction, and he was the high bidder on two sedans.

The only problem was that the cars weren't the same color, so I took the dark brown car to Thompson Lacquer and asked them to mix up a gallon of paint to be used on the light brown one. George, our painter, picked up the paint later that day and began prepping the beige one the same day, because the studio was in a big hurry to get them. After he finished painting the car he called me at the office to say it was ready, but to my total disbelief it was the wrong color.

The paint store representative had just used the color code from the tag on the driver's door of the dark brown car to save time matching the color, but he had no idea that a previous owner had changed the original factory color. The next day, George painted the car again, and this time it was correct. In the pilot episode, Warden is involved in a high-speed chase and loses control of the car, rolling it over and destroying it, along with its two new paint jobs.

150

It is surprising how seemingly intelligent dictators—I mean directors—make some really dumb decisions because they get so used to having their way. In an episode of *Mickey Spillane's Mike Hammer*, starring Stacy Keach, the studio said they needed a 1970 hearse, which was going to be stolen from a graveside service. The script called for a scene where Hammer shoots at the criminal, who is trying to flee from the cemetery in the hearse. They were going to attach a device to the inside of the car that would blow three holes in the windshield to simulate the hearse being hit by his bullets. They agreed to put their own glass in the car, do the shot, and then replace the original glass. Since my hearses were newer models, it was necessary for me to get an older car from another mortuary, but I assured the owner that it wouldn't get damaged.

I was emphatic with the transportation captain that they not damage the car. He told me not to worry. Oh, sure. As they proceeded with the shot, Mike Hammer starts shooting at the hearse. The director decided that if the driver had gotten shot, the hearse would go out of control and hit something. He directed the stunt driver to slam the hearse into a massive oak tree. The transportation captain protested but was overruled by the director, which was always the case. If you run a normal car into a large tree, you expect to get a certain bang for your buck, but with a 6,200-pound hearse there is just a dull thud. The studio must have bemoaned that bill, because after we replaced most of the front end and repainted the whole car, the repairs cost about fifteen times the daily rental rate.

When a studio needed a vehicle that they knew would be damaged, they wanted to simply purchase it. Instead, I devised a system in which they could purchase the rights to the car. It didn't matter how badly they damaged it, because they could return it in any condition and pay no more. Apparently, no one in the industry had proposed this idea before. It was often necessary to explain that they were buying the rights to do anything they wanted to the vehicle before they returned it. Every so often a car would come back with only a few hundred dollars' worth of damage, so it could get repaired fairly cheaply and be ready for the next destructive production.

When we were asked to supply a limo for one of the Charles Bronson *Death Wish* sequels, they invited me to come to the VA Hospital grounds in Westwood at midnight. In the story, Bronson had been sent a limo and driver to take him to a meeting with a crime boss at a remote location. As soon as the driver stopped and exited the limo, Bronson realized it was a trap because the rear door handles had been removed so that he couldn't escape. He shot out the rear window and fled just before the car exploded. The studio worked on the limo for hours, doing all their safety tricks so a flying hood or trunk wouldn't injure someone.

In another sequel to *Death Wish*, they drove one of our limos off a pier and into the ocean. When the car was returned, the engine and drivetrain had been removed. The engine compartment and trunk were completely filled with Styrofoam so the limo would sink more slowly for the shot. I was curious how they had gotten it to drive off the pier without an engine. Paying close attention to the completed film, I caught a glimpse of a cable that flew by at the bottom of the limo as it became airborne.

The studio filming *Scarecrow and Mrs. King* called and wanted a hearse to blow up in Griffith Park, where the park's famous observatory telescope resides. The plot had some Russian spies transporting an explosive device in a hearse that was to be detonated in an American cemetery. To achieve the most spectacular explosion, they would often have a crew member break all of the windows out beforehand so the flames would travel farther.

The special-effects man went from one window to the next, using a spring-loaded center punch. What he didn't know was that one of the windows had been replaced with Plexiglas after the regular one was broken on a rental. When he got around to a Plexiglas window, it wouldn't break. After several unsuccessful attempts he picked up a lug wrench and started whacking it to no avail. When it finally broke he looked over at me as if to say, "What the hell is going on here?" I shrugged and said, "Who knows? I'm just the driver."

The detonation device was attached to a wire about 100 yards long being dragged behind the hearse as it came down the roadway. It was connected to something called a naphtha bomb, which blew up at the instant the car crashed in a ditch. When they returned this hearse, we had the tow truck driver drop it in the farthest stall possible. The exterior damage didn't look that bad. The problem was that naphtha is a petroleum extract with a terribly strong chemical smell. For the next two months our parking lot reeked of mothballs, which are made from the same chemical. A man eventually purchased it to build it into a tow vehicle for towing competitions. I'm sure everyone could smell him coming.

Paramount Pictures wanted to find a custom limo for a production called *The Zamunda Project*, starring Eddie Murphy. They were attempting to duplicate some scenes that had been filmed earlier in New York with a rare Mercedes stretch limo. We didn't have such a car, but since all they needed were some interior shots it seemed possible to match it if they brought me some photos for comparison.

I removed the center seat from one of our stretch limos to make space to accommodate a cameraman and his equipment. The New York Mercedes had a much smaller rear window with an opaque white curtain covering it, whereas ours had a very large one, so I made a template to hide the large window and cut the proper size opening in it. Once they covered it with an identical curtain, it was a close match. They returned our limo on New Year's Eve, and it was scheduled to be used New Year's Day for the celebrated Rose Parade. That evening, in pouring rain, I reconnected the seat from under the limo on my back in my drenched driveway.

About a year later, we went to see an Eddie Murphy movie called *Coming to America*, in which a prince comes to the United States from his country of Zamunda, which sounded familiar to me. Then I realized that *The Zamunda Project* had been the working title for *Coming to America*.

A studio that had given us numerous orders purchased the rights to a limo for a series called *Hardball*. They said that a motorcycle was going to hit it head on. When the car came back it had a metal ramp bolted to the front bumper, which they didn't even bother removing. The windshield itself wasn't damaged, but it appeared to have gotten shattered. They had created the illusion by shooting a capsule filled with clear petroleum jelly at the windshield. After they removed the metal ramp and cleaned off the jelly, the car was ready for the next show.

34

Not Your Typical Used-Car Salesman

I never set out to become a used-hearse salesman, but that's what happened. To many people, used-car salesmen rate somewhere just slightly above politicians and attorneys, but at least in my case it wasn't necessary to tell the hearse buyer how great he would look behind the wheel. All of my sales were strictly word of mouth or referrals from other funeral directors.

Sales had picked up dramatically after 1971 because of a film called *Harold and Maude*, in which the main character drove around in a 1959 Cadillac hearse. The '59 Cadillac was probably the most outrageous example of large fins and bullet taillights. After the film's release, it seemed like every kid in town wanted one, which tripled the price of that model.

By the mid-'70s, people were contacting me from places like American Samoa, Guam, Australia, Sri Lanka, and especially the Philippines, where my name was being passed around from one mortuary to another. The purchase price of a hearse was used to calculate the amount of import duty that the Philippine government levied on the purchaser. Unfortunately, the mortuary owners had to pay 100 percent of the cost of the hearse by way of this tax, which doubled the total price.

Being sympathetic to my customers' needs, it occurred to me to reduce the price of the hearses and make up the difference by charging more freight, which wasn't taxed. That worked for a while, but eventually the government began to suspect something. Almost all of the hearses arriving in Manila had come from me, with a noticeable drop in their value. The Philippine government then set up an office in Long Beach, where all of my shipments departed.

From that point, each car had to be inspected before shipment. The first time I followed this new procedure, the inspector asked me why this hearse was being sold so cheaply. I explained that the car was a rust bucket from an eastern state where they used salt to reduce ice and snow, causing the undercarriage and some parts of the body to rust away. It had also come from a large city, where it had been owned by a funeral car livery service like ours and therefore had an inordinate amount of miles on it. He didn't dispute it further.

Another way to help my loyal customers was to suggest that the space between the wheel wells and the back of the front seat could be used to bring in extra mortuary hardware without having to pay any customs duty. The most unusual item I ever hid in the hearse for a customer was an entire collection of *Playboy* magazines. Not exactly the mortuary equipment I was thinking of.

In 1982, a lady called saying she understood that we sold limos to movie studios. She went on to explain that she needed a limo with no roof, no bumper, no fenders, and no hood. My only question was her budget. She asked if she had been clear about what she wanted. After I told her that she had been very precise, she said, "That's funny, because the five people I talked to before you didn't seem to get what I wanted."

After locating a good candidate, she was quoted the price and seemed delighted. I purchased the limo and prepared it for the shot. It was necessary to rent an industrial-grade chop saw and cut away. The grinder was extremely powerful and threw out a stream of sparks at least fifteen feet. Of course, the sparks just had to land on a couple of shop towels in the corner that immediately broke out in a small fire because I had used them to wipe up some spilled gas. Just another exciting day at the office!

The limo was going to be used to promote the fourth Cheech and Chong movie, *Things Are Tough All Over*. It was about two dope-smoking hippies traveling across the country, selling parts of their Cadillac to have enough money to continue their trip. A flatbed truck delivered the stripped-down limo to a studio in Hollywood while I followed to make sure everything went well.

They opened a large garage door from a rear alley at the photo studio, and we pushed the limo inside a large, flat white, three-sided room. There were no ninety-degree corners in the entire room because all of the corners were curved for a seamless backdrop. If you walked far enough into the room, you lost your peripheral vision and all points of reference. It was very disorienting.

I told the photographer about my uneasiness, and he related a story to me about a telephone repairman sent over to check his phone lines. He had inadvertently walked from the front office into this area while looking down at his clipboard. When he finally looked up, he fell to the floor and started screaming. As soon as he looked away, he got his bearings back and realized he wasn't losing his mind.

The very successful Hard Rock Cafe chain wanted me to help them locate a 1959 Cadillac hearse as the centerpiece for their forthcoming location in Honolulu, Hawaii. Their Los Angeles location featured a 1959 Cadillac Coupe DeVille sticking halfway out of the roof, as if it had come off an elevated road and crashed there. For Hawaii, they wanted a limousine-style hearse, which has windows in the rear instead of metal panels.

I explained that this would be a very difficult car to find and if I located one, my finder's fee would be $200. My friend Paul Nix was able to locate exactly what they wanted. They were in a great hurry to get it shipped to Hawaii because they had already started construction on the café. They could not put the roof on until the hearse arrived because it was to be lowered inside by crane. In the end, Hard Rock stiffed me on my commission because they said they thought that my fee was included in the purchase price.

The 1959 Cadillac hearse featured in Hard Rock Cafe's Honolulu location.

When our family went to Hawaii several years later we had lunch there, and it was amazing to see what a stunning job they had done on it. They had covered the exterior of the car with simulated wood paneling, much like the old Woodie station wagons of the '50s. It was suspended above the central bar in all its glory, with two surfboards sticking out of the rear window.

Every hearse purchased and shipped overseas went in its own forty-foot container. The freight alone was about $2,000. Hearses are about twenty-three feet long, so only one could be placed in the standard container. It occurred to me that it might be possible to construct a special wooden ramp as a solution to the single-car problem. The first hearse could be driven into the container backward until it touched the rear wall, followed by the wooden ramp, and then the second hearse could have its front end hang up over the front end of the first car. The cost of freight stayed the same whether there were one or two cars. From that point on they were sold in pairs because a mortuary in their country could then defray much of its outlay by selling the second hearse to another firm in the Philippines. The government eventually considered these mortuaries to be used-hearse dealers, so they were allowed to bring only two cars into the country per year.

About half of all my sales were to people who did business with me repeatedly over the years. One of these repeat customers was June Amarao, who also shipped forty-foot containers full of car parts to the Philippines and suffered a great loss when one such container on the dock fell into the sea during the 1995 Kobe earthquake in Japan.

Bernie Ileto was another repeat customer. He was the son of a family that owned several mortuaries in the Philippines. The bills of lading for these shipments always showed the destination as "Metro Manila," but on one occasion I asked Bernie where these two hearses would end up. When he said "Cabanatuan," a shiver went down my spine. The Bataan Death March in World War II began there and continued for sixty miles in extremely hot weather without food or water. Most of the victims were already suffering with malnutrition and war-related diseases. An estimated 10,000 American and Philippine prisoners of war died on that forced march.

Another Filipino dealer named Ray was in the process of buying his fifth hearse from me, but said it could not be shipped right away because of the two-cars-per-year rule. He picked out a fairly late model from my inventory but asked me to hold the car for about four months. Three months later, Ray called me and asked if it was possible to get a refund because the farm that his family owned was buried under fifteen feet of volcanic ash from the Mount Pinatubo eruption and he was going to have to help them recover financially. The same eruption caused the closure of Clark Air Base, which was about nine miles away and had been used by the United States for decades. The commanding officer of the base was slow to react during the volcano's early warning signs, so the government's geologist told him that he better have plenty of jam in his pockets because he was going to be toast. He got the message.

Our neighbors in the Hollywood Hills didn't seem to get upset seeing funeral cars in our driveway, although seeing me unloading bags of groceries from the back of a hearse would occasionally raise some eyebrows. Kathy was fairly tolerant of my shenanigans as long as she could distance herself from them. One night, I drove a used station wagon home that was being converted for a mortuary. The only visible modification so far was the installation of the full vinyl top. The landau bars hadn't been installed; it had no curtains and no sandblasted palm leafs on the tailgate window yet.

Kathy said she wanted to go out to dinner that night, so I suggested that we use the wagon because my car had been left at work. I told her that no one would ever pay attention to it. Kathy finally agreed, but she let me know that she did not like driving around in a funeral car as we did when we were dating.

At the restaurant, the host seated us in a booth that faced the street where the wagon was parked. A short time later, two old ladies were seated in the booth next to us. One of them spotted the car and said, "Look, someone parked a hearse in front of the restaurant. That's disgusting!" I thought Kathy was going to throw her fettuccine at me.

I always drove old station wagons so that I could haul broken cots home for repairs. After my fourth one, Kathy said that I would reincarnate as a *drundulet*, which is Russian for jalopy.

35

Digging in the Dirt

In early 1978, there was a continuous three-week rain in Los Angeles. Our office received a call at five in the morning from the owner of the Verdugo Hills Cemetery in Tujunga. This cemetery belonged to a man who also owned the Los Angeles Mortuary. He said that there had been a massive mudslide at the cemetery and that caskets and bodies were scattered everywhere. As usual, the night dispatcher called me for instructions. I called several of our crew members and requested they meet me at the cemetery with shovels, knee boots, and raincoats.

The night before, someone a mile down from the cemetery had called the police department and reported finding a body in the gutter as he walked his dog. The coroner picked up the body, and it was taken downtown. The embalmer washed the mud off the body and prepared to make an incision, but to his great surprise there was a sutured incision on the body, telling him that this corpse had already been embalmed.

In the pale light that precedes the morning sun, residents in the area started calling the police department as body parts were being discovered in the streets and yards of homes downhill from the cemetery. Doug Scott and I arrived at the same time just before the sun was coming up. Through the mist it was barely possible to see much more than the gentle rolling hills coming into view. As we drove closer the silhouette of many half-buried caskets became eerily visible, like the set of some gruesome horror movie.

Dr. Thomas Noguchi showed up at 9 A.M. and immediately started making the obligatory introductions to the many representatives who had arrived from various city and county departments. He included me because I was representing the cemetery owner. Filmed and recorded by all the news media, Dr. Noguchi stated that he would be taking over this operation and that all remains were going to be transported downtown for identification.

After the news conference concluded, I took him aside and brought to his attention that he really didn't have any jurisdiction in this matter. These people had been legally buried under permits issued by the Los Angeles County Health Department. I reminded him that a coroner could only perform an exhumation with a court order signed by a judge. Since this was definitely not his purview and that of his staff, he deferred to my assessment. He even seemed to be somewhat relieved that this burden had been removed from his office, which was understaffed and under-funded, and sent me a thank you letter for assuming responsibility of the job.

One of his deputies informed me that there was a body in a residential area a mile down the hill. They had placed a sheet over it and told us its exact location. We drove down to where the body was and found the neighborhood kids all sitting astride their bikes waiting to get a cheap thrill. The kids weren't about to leave and miss all the fun, but I told my assistant to watch them scatter when we exposed the corpse. They were in a semicircle about six feet away when I pulled the sheet off. The body of an elderly man was nude, quite dehydrated, and white as a sheet. His eyes were sunken in and his mouth was open. A movie special-effects department could not have created a more grotesque sight. To my amazement, the kids just sat there and didn't even blink. I guess the younger generations have been exposed to so much TV and movie gore that they're jaded.

The Verdugo Hills Cemetery mudslide had its roots in an engineering miscalculation. When a grave is opened, more dirt is set aside than will go back in when the grave is closed. Over the years, all this extra dirt was dumped in one corner of the cemetery that had a steep incline, and they didn't use a compactor to properly compress the side of this hill. When the cemetery was nearing its capacity, the owner made a fateful decision to start doing burials in this hillside. This set the stage for the inevitable, after a few weeks of steady rain.

Because a large portion of the hillside was still unstable, LA County officials realized they would have to step in and remove all the remaining bodies. Another slide would surely happen if nothing were done to prevent it. We were already quite involved, so they asked us to put in a bid to do the job. We proposed to disinter and reinter all the bodies, place them in disaster pouches, and bury them in a special, mass burial grave located in a stable part of the cemetery. We proposed a cost of $250 per body, which included everything, and they gave us the contract.

We knew that these were not going to be simple disinterments, since many of the caskets had been in the ground for years and few would be in concrete vaults. The county assigned a supervisor to oversee the task and make sure they got a correct tally. We rented a forty-foot office trailer, had it delivered on-site, and began the arduous task of uncovering an entire corner of the cemetery.

It took approximately four months to complete the project, and Ron practically lived in the trailer the entire time. By midsummer, the ground had hardened considerably because of the claylike consistency of the earth. An area of 400 square feet was opened on a flat part of the cemetery to inter the more than 200 bodies. In recognition of this considerable undertaking, Ron received a framed certificate of achievement from a grateful LA County.

One evening, Kathy and I settled in to watch *Quincy, M.E.*, starring Jack Klugman. All of a sudden, the same scene that was so vivid in my memory came to life. As dawn broke, a hillside slowly emerged into view shrouded in the early morning mist, with numerous caskets protruding from the ground. A chill ran through me. The thing that surprised me the most was seeing something exactly as it appeared on that foggy morning. It never occurred to me that that scene would someday be re-created in such a realistic and graphic manner. They had captured the very essence of what we had seen at dawn, when we first arrived at the cemetery. The set decorator did an outstanding job creating a realistic scene, although the plot of the episode deviated from the actual event.

36

Open to the Public

Sometimes events in life cause abrupt and major turnarounds. These changes often come as a shock and are perceived as misfortune, but as they say, when one door closes, another opens.

One morning while working at the garage, our manager, Steve McAninch, called to notify me that there was a fire at the mansion. It was balls to the wall around every street corner. I had with me a small hand-held fire extinguisher from the garage to put out what was probably no more than a wastebasket fire. The scene that struck me as I rounded the final corner was a sky filled with smoke and flames billowing out of the building's second floor.

Three employees were standing on the parking lot and, thankfully, our other drivers were all out on services. Steve didn't even know if anyone was still inside because students would sometimes sleep in their dorm rooms after their night shifts were over. I ran into the building and upstairs to the dormitory rooms. Everything was dark because the fire had already cut the power. The hallway to the dorm rooms was engulfed in flames, and there were no responses to my calls. After I inhaled a lot of smoke, dizziness set in, along with the realization that this could end up being my own funeral pyre. I had to crouch down low to get enough air to get back downstairs.

Steve suspected that one of our student employees caused the fire after having been wakened to make a first call. He had apparently lit a cigarette while preparing himself but neglected to put it out when leaving his room. The fire must have been burning for at least fifteen minutes while the dispatchers downstairs were totally unaware.

Fortunately, another student was asleep upstairs who had worked the night shift and was no longer on call. He kept hearing some crackling noises, which he thought was just the sound of rain, since it had rained the night before. The sound got louder, so he looked up from his bed and noticed an orange glow coming from under his door. When he got out of bed and opened his door, he saw that the whole left side of the hallway was on fire. He grabbed his raincoat and ran through the flames, down the stairs, and into the dispatch office.

The fire investigators said that based on the time the original driver left and the onset of the fire, the cigarette had burned down until it fell from the ashtray. After a half hour of smoldering on the floor, the fire ignited. All the destruction occurred in only half of the upstairs, but smoke and water had damaged the entire building. It cost our insurance company $130,000 to completely redo everything, inside and out.

The biggest change came when we found out that we could not rebuild the separate dormitory rooms because of fire regulations, so that area was returned to its original state as one large room. As a result of no longer having a dorm, we discontinued doing first calls and body transportation. It was obvious we needed to replace the income we were going to lose.

The funereal procedures we had been performing for over twenty years were analogous to those performed by a mortuary, and that made us feel completely qualified to operate our own stand-alone business. The problem was that we would be going into competition with our own customers. We contacted all the mortuaries that we served and invited them to a meeting at our newly refurbished building. Representatives of most of the firms showed up. We gave them our word that we would never let any of their patrons know that we had our own mortuary if they continued to support our funeral livery service.

About sixty people attended the meeting. After listening to our proposal, one mortuary owner spoke up and asked the inevitable

The Abbott & Hast colonial mansion in 1978.

question: "Why should we continue using you under these circumstances?" Before we could answer, Phil Bagues stood up to comment on our behalf. He was the nephew of Manuel Bagues, who owned a very successful mortuary in East Los Angeles that we had been serving for years. Phil said, "I'm sure a lot of you are upset about this decision, but when push comes to shove and equipment becomes much more expensive, you're not going to be the ones who are going to have to incur those costs, so just deal with it."

About a third of our customers didn't even own their own funeral cars, and the ones who did often had more than one service at the same time, in which case we filled in. Of all our customers, only three firms stopped using us, and even they were all back in less than a year.

After the renovation, we ordered a sign that read "Abbott and Hast— Funeral Directors." We had never had a sign before because we were never open to the public, but now we needed to identify ourselves as a mortuary. The day the sign was being installed, Ron and I were standing on the corner of the property watching with great pride as a crane picked up the sign and placed it into the hole that was dug for it.

We had such good relations with many of the owners of family mortuaries that every year, at Christmas time, Ron would throw a party at his house. He would always try to have some new twist to make it more interesting. One year, he rented a commercial video recorder and taped everyone without his or her knowledge. This was before that kind of equipment was available to the public, and video recorders were very expensive. Ron didn't play the tape until the end of the party, which was after he had served his guests drinks all evening. Although there was a slight degree of embarrassment for some, most seemed to enjoy the good-natured spirit of it. Another year, he had a drawing, the door prize being "two round-trip tickets to Paris." When the winner was announced, the couple were given an envelope, which contained Greyhound Bus tickets to the dusty desert town of Perris, California.

Without a doubt, the best prank he ever played was to purchase a live chicken from a poultry market. Ron wrapped it up, and because it was in the dark, the chicken never made a sound. The lady who won that year's drawing opened the box and out came the white chicken, clucking and flapping. For some reason, the lady who won it decided not to take it. Ron promised it to his longtime housekeeper/cook Louisa. When my kids found out that Louisa was planning on cooking it, they asked if we could take it home, so we ended up with a new member of the family. Ron had to go and buy another one for Louisa.

The chicken, which came to be known as Lulubell, had a surprisingly good nature and the kids loved her. She resided in a cage on our patio but caught a cold one particularly chilly winter's night. I gave her medicine from an eyedropper for a few days and she was able to recover. From that time on, the cage sat in the corner of our kitchen, where it was always toasty warm. Loodle, as the kids called her, stayed in her cage at night, but we put her on top of the cage during the day. When we went out for dinner and she heard me open the front door upon our return, she would always greet us from the kitchen with a loud squawk.

ONE THOUSAND VENICE / LOS ANGELES   (213) 746-1271

Abbott & Hast postcard, similar to the one made by the business before theirs.

37

Natalie Wood

One weekend in 1981 we were driving back home from a trip to Santa Barbara and the news on the radio reported that Natalie Wood's body had just been recovered from the waters off Catalina Island. Kathy immediately began sobbing uncontrollably. Not only had she and Natalie grown up in the same church, but Natalie's birth name was Natalia Nikolaevna Zakharenko, very similar to Kathy's maiden name Katerina Pavlana Zarenko, so she probably felt some degree of kinship. Needless to say, it was a big shock for her.

Natalie's superstitious mother, Maria Gurdin, grew up in Harbin, China, where a Gypsy fortune-teller prophesized before her daughter's birth that she would be famous around the world, but that she would die in "dark water," a warning that Maria often used to frighten Natalie with. Understandably, water became Natalie's greatest fear, and she echoed this in a 1980 television interview, saying, "I've always been terrified of water, dark water, sea water...." This happened just one year before she drowned off Catalina.

When Natalie married British movie actor Richard Gregson, the ceremony was held at the same Russian Orthodox church we attended, Holy Virgin Mary Church in Silver Lake. Father Dimitri Gazetti, the same priest who had married Kathy and me, performed their marriage, so naturally we attended. Only two well-known actors were at the service, Robert Redford and David Niven, and we got some good photos of everyone present.

After Natalie's death, Westwood Village gave us the order, so I drove the family car and picked up Natalie's mother and her sister, Lana Wood. The security provisions at her service were the highest of any funeral we had ever witnessed and were overseen by Gavin de Becker, who had provided security for President Reagan's inauguration. Each security man had a microphone up his sleeve to communicate with other security men in the

Robert Redford stands next to Richard Gregson and Natalie Wood at their wedding in 1969.

cemetery. With their gray suits and cropped hair, these guys all looked like FBI agents.

When Robert Wagner and his family arrived in their own car for the graveside service, everyone ignored Natalie's mother and sister. Even James and Clarence Pierce weren't attentive to them, which upset me. So I went back to my limo, where the funeral director would have normally greeted them, and personally escorted them to their graveside chairs.

After giving the pallbearers some instructions, we carried the casket from the hearse and placed it on the lowering device. Then they lined up at the foot of the grave while I stepped to the head of the casket to assist the priest. Moments before the service began, a man wearing a plaid sports jacket came over and stood next to me. At the time, I didn't know who he was or why he had chosen to stand next to me instead of joining the rest of the people behind the chairs.

The science fiction movie that Natalie had been working on when she died, *Brainstorm*, was nearly complete, but the dilemma was to edit the story and finish it without her. Kathy and I went to see it, and when her love interest came on the scene, I realized he was the one standing next to me at her funeral. It was Christopher Walken.

There has been a tremendous amount of speculation from the media because on the evening she died, Natalie and Robert hosted Christopher at Catalina Island aboard their yacht, *Splendour*. The controversy was about an argument that allegedly took place at a restaurant that evening and the drinking that was done as well. That may have accounted for his decision not to stand with the others.

Natalie's body had gotten battered on the rocks. The coroner's pathologists had surgically removed some bruised tissue that was examined very closely. Bill Pierce, the son of one of the mortuary's owners, was a licensed embalmer who dressed her and did the cosmetology. He spoke with me later about some of the details. He said that the bruised areas were not visible while the casket was open because she was dressed in a full-length fur coat. Next to Marilyn Monroe's funeral, Natalie Wood's service was the most memorable and every bit as sad for me.

Many years later, a movie aired on TV with a beautiful girl who looked to be in her early twenties. When the credits came up I wanted to see who this attractive actress was. Her name was Natasha Gregson Wagner, and I suddenly realized this was Natalie's daughter by Richard Gregson. I imagine that Robert Wagner adopted Natasha when Natalie remarried him some years later. It seemed like so few years since we had attended her wedding to Richard, but considering Natasha's age, it really made me think about how quickly time passes.

38

Curious Happenings

Bizarre events occurred periodically in our business, but one seemed as though it was choreographed by some tortured soul. A young man contacted me about the possibility of purchasing an inexpensive old hearse. I had one worth about $1,200 that was available, so he came in to see it. He explained that he had only $700 available in cash and asked if he could make two payments. I agreed but said that he wouldn't get the title until the bill was totally paid. In a few months, a money order arrived with the balance, so I mailed him the pink slip.

About eight months later, I gathered up some old files and threw them out. Three days later, a call came in from a Northern California police investigator, asking if we had sold a hearse to a young man by the name of Sanders. When I confirmed that fact, he asked if I knew the man's address. After I explained that the envelope had been discarded a few days earlier, it occurred to me that the trash might not have been picked up yet. The detective held the line while I reluctantly went dumpster diving, and he was extremely pleased when the information he needed was provided.

Some months later, a detective pulled into our garage to thank me for my assistance in the case. He said that because of my information they were able to arrest a real sicko. Sanders used the hearse to discreetly enter the Pacific Crest Cemetery in nearby Redondo Beach, dig up the casket containing the body of his male lover, place the casket in the hearse, and drive it to a location in Northern California.

Later, he bragged to some patrons in a gay bar about what he had done. One of them went to the police. The person didn't know where Sanders lived but did recall him saying that he had purchased the hearse in LA. The police had spoken to some funeral homes in our area, and two or three had mentioned my name. Armed with the information I provided, the police got a search warrant and went to the address. They found a hidden compartment in a wall that contained the casket and body he had snatched.

The detective showed me a plaque presented to him, acknowledging his skill as an investigator, with a small casket handle mounted on it. As usual, the local newspapers had a field day with the story, but they couldn't explain everything. Sanders must have dug up the grave a few days after the burial, but it seems strange that he could have pulled the casket out of the ground without some help. It also seemed impossible that workers at the cemetery hadn't noticed that the grave had been tampered with. If I hadn't experienced this kind of bizarre story firsthand, it would be difficult for me to believe that such a strange thing could even take place.

One evening I observed something that looked out of place, based solely on my years in the funeral business. Kathy's parents lived in Hollywood, where we had gone for the evening to have dinner together. Moments after we left, something caught my eye. I noticed a man standing on the corner holding a large calculator, and for some reason he was wearing pallbearer's gloves. They were very familiar to me because we had been issuing them for years. My curiosity was aroused, so I called the Hollywood division of the LAPD. Within a few minutes, two undercover police officers arrived in an unmarked car. After I explained my suspicion and gave them his description, they spotted him half a block down the street, where they arrested him. They were able to determine that he had broken into the Carver Escrow Company and stolen their calculator.

There were no other witnesses, so they had only my testimony at his trial. The public defender tried to discredit my story because the police never recovered the gloves. He told the jury that anyone could have been wearing gloves, so seeing them was of no consequence and certainly no basis for probable cause. I explained that it wasn't cold that night and that these gloves are thin and disposable, intended for a single use at funerals. He was subsequently found guilty.

Another interesting situation occurred when one of our staff made a first call in the middle of the night. Early the next morning, the family called and said they had changed their minds and wanted to have the body returned, so naturally we assumed another mortuary would be making the pickup. Relatives of the deceased arrived at our mortuary in a small Honda. When we inquired who would be contacting us to transport the body, to our utter disbelief they responded, "We're going to put him in the trunk of our car."

There had been no preparation of the body since the family hadn't made their wishes known, so what we didn't realize was that the deceased's legs had been amputated as a result of poor circulation brought on by severe diabetes. The couple couldn't understand our confusion because they didn't know that we were not in possession of all the facts. With no legs, he fit nicely in the trunk.

Another funeral director showed up from out of town in a beautiful motor home, pulling a small trailer, and requested that a body we were holding be placed in the trailer. Ron inquired and was told that the director and his wife had decided to make this trip in conjunction with a pickup they had to make in the LA area. His wife agreed to this arrangement only if the body was not carried in the motor home.

There was also one occasion when a family went into a mortuary client of ours to make funeral arrangements. The counselor asked where the death had occurred so he could dispatch someone to remove the deceased and bring the body to the mortuary. They said it wouldn't be necessary to pick him up because they had him sitting in the backseat of the car. The director walked out to the car and there he was, still wearing his hat.

One of our client mortuaries was in a part of Los Angeles known as Hyde Park. After many years the owner retired and sold the business to a gentleman we had known for years, Bob Bonefoy. He and his wife were in their fifties and lived in an apartment above the funeral home. Hyde Park had seen a big increase in crime. One night, the couple heard noises coming from downstairs, so Bob went down to investigate. His wife heard a gunshot and went down to see what had happened. She found him on the floor of the embalming room, and he whispered to her, "They finally got me." Strangely, Bob had told his wife that sooner or later they were going to be the victims of the criminal element that had inundated the neighborhood. His gunshot wound turned out to be fatal. The LAPD conducted an extensive investigation, but they were not able to determine who had committed the crime.

A few years went by and the case had gone cold. Acting on a tip, the narcotics division of the police department discovered a drug dealer's lab close to the mortuary. Along with many drug-producing materials were boxes of embalming fluid that had the name of Bob's mortuary printed on the cartons. Apparently, drug dealers had discovered that marijuana dipped in formaldehyde made the drug much more potent. The drug dealer must have been using too much of his own products because he didn't discard the empty boxes but simply used them to store some of his equipment. He was subsequently convicted of burglary and murder.

I'm sure that many people assumed that Ron and I were wealthy because of all the business we conducted. Someone at a local gym overheard two men in the next row of lockers discussing a home invasion they were planning. The eavesdropper clearly heard them discussing the fact that one of the owners of Abbott & Hast had a safe in his house that probably contained a great deal of money. The man contacted the LAPD and informed them about what he had overheard.

A detective called our home that evening and informed me that they were conducting an investigation of this apparent plot. He asked if our home was in the Hollywood Hills and if we had a safe in the house, both of which were correct. He gave me his name and instructed me to lock all the doors and windows and turn on all our outside lights.

The kids were very frightened, so I had Kathy take them into our den and close the door. To confirm everything, I made a quick call to the police, who told me that one of their detectives was in the field investigating just such a case. They verified his name. I placed a chair in the center of the living room and sat there with my shotgun.

Almost an hour went by before they called back and told me they had determined that Ron was the target. When three detectives arrived at Ron's house, they filled him in on what was afoot and said they were going to hide in his bedroom until the perpetrators arrived. Sure enough, two young men showed up and said they were friends of someone Ron knew. He served them drinks and waited to see what would develop. That evening, some other friends showed up shortly after the would-be home invaders. Two hours later, the detectives got tired of waiting so they came out of the bedroom and confronted the two individuals, who denied everything. The detectives told them that if anything happened, they would be the first to be arrested.

39

The Devil's in the Details

In most states, to become a licensed embalmer you must attend an accredited college of mortuary science and serve an apprenticeship under the direction of a licensed embalmer. After becoming licensed, the embalmer is required to sign the death certificates. There is quite an art to preparing a body, so the classes cover not only arterial embalming, but also facial reconstruction, cosmetology, and hair preparation.

Before the embalming process is started, it is necessary to "set the features," which is accomplished through a number of procedures. A product developed in the late '40s was used to glue the lips together after the jaw is pinned and wired closed. That glue was sold under the brand name Lip Lock, well before that expression took on a whole different meaning. Now, it is amusing (at least to those in the funeral business) to hear someone use that phrase in describing a prolonged kiss.

After the lips are glued, a type of mild stain is applied, which in the trade is called "orange juice." When the body is drained of blood, the deceased becomes very pale, so the stain compensates for the lack of natural color. Next, cotton is packed into the nasal passages and pink eye caps are inserted, which look like half ping-pong balls with barbs on them. The reason the eye caps are pink is to provide color to the closed eyelids. These are secured over the eyeballs and the lids are pulled down so that the undersides of the eyelids are held in place by these barbed caps.

A deceased man is clean-shaven during preparation, since the myth persisted for decades that the beard can continue to grow for a short time after death. The subject was addressed factually on *CSI*. Beards don't grow after death, but when the skin on the face starts to dehydrate it causes shrinkage and exposes the whiskers.

Nearly everyone has heard the term rigor mortis, which is used to describe the rigidity that occurs in the body after death. Many crime scene investigators use this rigidity to help determine how long a person has been deceased, but in about eight hours it goes away. This flaccidity, or softening of the muscles, can also be used to determine when the death occurred.

CSI is one of my favorite TV shows. No big surprise there. I'm sure they spend a great deal of money on special effects, and they constantly use terms and jargon that we have been hearing for over forty years. The shows are usually very accurate, except when the investigator declares that the death occurred twelve hours earlier, as determined by the liver temperature. This is technically known as algor mortis. In order to perform this test, clothing must be removed to access the abdomen, but the bodies on the show are usually fully dressed when this procedure is conducted.

The body loses two degrees of temperature the first hour and one degree per hour after death, but this is not always constant, due to extremes in ambient temperature. To determine "liver temp," they take a long, thin, pointed metal rod with a temperature gauge on the opposite end, much like one you would use to check if your holiday turkey was thoroughly cooked. The liver is the body's largest internal organ, so it is the best choice to use in determining approximate time of death. The first time I went on a coroner's call and arrived before the deputy coroner had performed this test, I had no choice but to stand there and observe the procedure.

The embalming colleges hold detailed classes on these subjects, as well as facial restoration for victims of traumatic incidents. This is needed when the family requests a viewing, and the hope is to have the deceased look the way the family remembers him or her. Restoration is accomplished through a procedure that involves the application of wax to fill in wounds, which are then covered by cosmetics.

Before an artery and vein are raised, the embalming machine is filled with several gallons of water and formaldehyde. The larger the body, the more fluid it takes, at approximately one gallon for each forty pounds of body weight. The embalming machine is a simple pump that has a pressure of only eight to ten pounds. Some people think that embalming is a fairly recent technique, but it began back in 1867, when August Wilhelm von Hofmann used pressure embalming during the Civil War to preserve soldiers' bodies for transport back home.

Neither Ron nor I ever became embalmers, but we always had one or more on staff after we opened our own funeral home. Not all mortuaries have an embalmer on staff, so they call an independent trade embalmer, who works for many firms. We, too, used a trade embalmer for after-hours procedures.

An embalmer can sometimes be put at risk when he is not notified that the deceased died of a communicable disease, the most common of these being active tuberculosis, which can be highly contagious. Tests for TB even forty-eight hours after embalming showed the pathogen that causes the disease still present. In the '80s, the most common risk to embalmers was exposure to AIDS. Hospitals were supposed to put red toe-tags on such cases, but it wasn't always done.

For the first few years of the disease, embalmers had been unknow-ingly preparing these cases while no one knew the underlying cause of death. Doctors were signing DCs on AIDS cases with the COD as Kaposi's sarcoma, malignant tumors that grow in different parts of the anatomy's connective tissue, but most notably appear as facial lesions. For this reason the industry standardized universal preventive measures that obligated embalmers to wear additional protective gear.

Doctors in the United States and France simultaneously discovered the virus that causes AIDS. Almost immediately, some mortuaries started charging extra fees for these cases or refused to handle them, but we continued serving these families. We even started getting referrals from a hospice in LA for the medical care of its AIDS victims.

The Los Angeles County Coroner's Office was an interesting place to visit because of the fascinating stories told by the deputies during my frequent stops there. The business office consisted of many individual desks, where the deputies sat and took telephone notifications of deaths that were called in each day by police officers, as well as funeral directors when a DC signing took a wrong turn or was disallowed by the county health department.

The original coroner's offices were on the ground floor of the Los Angeles County Hall of Records, while the embalming room was on another floor. The coroner's office was rapidly outgrowing the entire facility, so a decision was made to build a much larger facility right next to the USC County General Hospital. The new business office entrance was on North Mission Road, but in order to access the area where the prep room and refrigerators were, you had to pull into the driveway on Marengo Street. As soon as you backed into the removal area at the rear of the building and exited your vehicle, you would notice that the air was heavy with a terrible smell. There was an industrial-grade bug zapper at this rear entrance, which continually emitted buzzing noises as it killed the flying insects.

This entrance took you into a room that was the heart of most of the activity and where all the paperwork was processed. At the rear of the room was a door that led to a hallway. Refrigerated body storage areas were on the left side and a larger room was on the right side, where there were multiple embalming tables and lab facilities. I'm sure that this large new facility was badly needed, but the original coroner's office was quite pleasant compared to this one with all the rank odors flowing into the room where DCs were obtained. This office alone has handled as many as 20,000 cases per year and inspired the TV series *North Mission Road*.

Not everyone could tolerate the situations often encountered in this profession. Many people over the years told me that they knew at a fairly young age that the funeral business interested them. Vocational tests were given to all seniors in our high school, but if they had me rank a list of potential career choices that included funeral director it would probably have come in near the end of my list. The upside of the profession is being able to assist people in situations that would be imponderable for them without someone's experienced assistance.

40

Strange Traditions

Los Angeles is well known for its ethnic diversity, and the nature of our business enabled us to have unique relationships with a wide variety of clients. Few businesses provide exposure to as many people of different faiths and traditions as we encountered. Serving so many different people enabled us to see varied aspects of their cultures, particularly the interesting ways they care for their dead.

Russians were among the many cultures in LA. The most unusual Russians were called Molokan, the old believers, whose name was derived from *moloko*, the Russian word for milk. The Molokan religion dates back several hundred years when its people were being persecuted for many reasons, including the drinking of milk during Russian Orthodox fasting periods. Furthermore, many of their gatherings had been originally held in caves along the shore of a river that appeared to be white because of its high mineral content.

Dave Malloy was the only funeral director who conducted their funerals because he knew exactly how to accommodate them. They always purchased the same white octagon casket that he would order from a casket company that knew how to custom-fabricate them. These caskets allowed Dave to completely remove the entire one-piece lid. The funerals were conducted in large meeting halls with nothing to indicate their function. Nothing in the room resembled a place of worship, only wooden benches. The casket was placed in the center of the room, with the lid set to the side. A deceased male was always dressed in all-white clothing and shoes.

There were two Asian funeral homes in LA, but Gutierrez & Weber, a Hispanic mortuary, did a great many Chinese services because of their location, which was directly across the street from Chinatown. Fukui Mortuary exclusively served the Japanese community, but the Mission Nisei Mortuary, with its Chinese manager, served both cultures. All of our evening services were either Japanese funerals or Catholic rosaries. The Japanese always had their graveside services the following morning, which were very traditional rituals, exactly like the ones conducted in their homeland, with incense burning, gong ringing, and exotic chanting.

The Chinese would often hire a marching band to congregate in Chinatown. The band would play while everyone marched through the main street as a black convertible carried a 3' x 5' photo of the deceased through downtown. This car drove in front of the hearse, followed by two or three limos. Ron would purchase a black Cadillac convertible every year as his personal vehicle for these services.

At many Chinese services, a limousine was designated for the ancestors and carried no passengers, while another one transported the paid professional mourners. Our drivers didn't like to drive the mourner's limo because the women, all dressed in black, would wail all the way from Chinatown to the cemetery. At the conclusion of the service, everyone was given a small white envelope containing a piece of candy and a nickel, unless the deceased was 80 or older, in which case the envelopes were red and contained the candy and a dime.

Ernie Quan was the manager of a mortuary doing many of these Chinese services, and over the years we became good friends. While Kathy and I were dancing at our wedding reception, Ernie came up to us and handed me a red envelope containing a $100 bill and a piece of candy. It was a very nice gesture, but I wasn't sure if he was trying to send me some sort of subtle message about marriage.

Fukui Mortuary conducted many funerals and our drivers, who were not Japanese, got the same respect as anyone else conducting the service. As each family walked up the steps of the temple, they would bow at the waist and we would reciprocate the gesture. The Fukui family had been held in an internment camp during World War II. After all they endured, they still managed to open a mortuary in downtown LA.

When we started serving the Fukuis, the parents had their son, Soichi, manage the business. His mother still lived in the upstairs apartment and would answer the phones at night. She would call us in the middle of the night and give me an order to make a removal. She spoke broken English, and on one occasion she told me that the deceased was at the Paco Ima Hospital. Confused, I wrote the name as it sounded and realized that it was the Pacoima Hospital. Another time she called and said the case was at the Tanu Prima Hospital. The name didn't sound familiar to me at all, so after repeating the name two or three times she hung up in frustration. The phone rang about two minutes later and Soichi Fukui asked me, "Don't you know where Daniel Freeman Hospital is?" I apologized and told him we would make the call immediately.

Later, Soichi's son, Jerry, became the manager, making him the third generation we had served. One day, Jerry called about an upcoming funeral for a man who had possibly committed suicide. In our conversation, he mentioned how rare suicide was among the Japanese community. We were good friends so I jokingly told him that I always thought that the Japanese had practically invented ritual suicide, or seppuku, as their culture calls it.

One of our biggest supporters over the years was Groman Mortuary, which did the greatest number of Orthodox Jewish funerals. They owned one hearse and no limousines, so we picked up all their families for every funeral. When Groman's completed a death call, sometimes their staff became aware that the deceased was not Jewish. The remains were immediately taken down the street and left in their parking garage until the family could contact a Gentile funeral home.

Orthodox funerals are very different from Reform Jewish services. In Orthodox services, the blood is saved in jars and buried with the deceased. Often, this all had to be accomplished before the sun set, depending on the time of day that the person had died.

Most rabbis performed traditional services, which concluded with everyone reciting a funeral prayer, or Kaddish, with the rabbi. The rabbi would then approach one or more members of the family and cut the man's lapel or the woman's blouse with a small pocketknife. During a few Orthodox services, the families were apparently unaware of this custom and were visibly upset when it happened. Eventually, they began using black Kriah ribbons that were pinned on family members and cut, instead of damaging someone's clothing.

At one Orthodox service, many attendees were surprised when the rabbi lifted the artificial grass covering the mound of dirt and used a shovel to break the metal handles from the wooden casket. Orthodox caskets are not supposed to have any metal used in the manufacturing process, so they're assembled with glue and dowels, much like fine furniture.

Whenever our drivers would return a family to their home we would give them a Shiva candle in a glass container. They explained to the family that it was to be lit and would burn for seven days and nights. We trained our drivers to explain the significance of the candle, because some of the families were not aware of its purpose.

The person who almost single-handedly changed the way Jewish funerals were conducted in LA was an unconventional rabbi named Edgar Magnin. He was at the helm of the well-known Wilshire Temple, where many famous entertainers and Hollywood's elite attended funerals. He was also the only rabbi who had a limousine drive him to every cemetery chapel service. Rabbi Magnin was part of the I. Magnin department store family and was extremely colorful. He referred to his particular style of funerals as "reformed teachings." I drove him many times as the sole occupant of the limo, and he always sat in the front seat. He had some really great stories to tell and it was always a pleasure driving him.

One day a director from Groman Mortuary arrived at Home of Peace Jewish Cemetery and stopped momentarily to turn in the burial permit at the office just inside the front gate. He left the engine running and when he came out the hearse was gone, casket and all! We got an emergency call from them asking if we had a gray cloth-covered octagon casket in our display room, which we did. They requested that we put it into a hearse and get it to the cemetery ASAP. They informed the family about the problem, but they decided to go on with the ceremony using our empty casket.

Three hours later, Groman called again and asked if we had a car and two drivers who could leave immediately for Indio, California, near Palm Springs. The man who had stolen the hearse stopped there for gas and then drove off without paying for it. The gas station attendant called the CHP, who spotted the hearse and gave chase. Hearses don't exactly blend in, so he was caught about twenty miles down the road. They arrested an illegal alien trying to get back to Mexico. The lesson here is that if you're going to steal a vehicle, make sure it's not a big black hearse.

During our years of delivering flowers, we worked on a number of Gypsy funerals. The Gypsies were, without a doubt, the most unusual people whom we ever encountered. They are very loyal if you give them good service, and we had gotten fairly accustomed to their many peculiarities. Holman & Sons mortuary, which performed many Gypsy funerals, would sometimes buy freight-damaged caskets very cheaply and have them repaired. At the conclusion of one of their services, we were gathering up the flowers as the pallbearers carried the casket from the chapel to the hearse. Without any warning, the bottom of the casket gave way and the body fell to the ground. As a result, the Gypsies stopped using that mortuary, which set the groundwork for us to become the new official Gypsy mortuary.

The original casket display room that we had turned into dorm rooms before the fire once again became one very large room that the Gypsies loved to use for their wakes. It was like a large living room with easy chairs, couches, and Ron's baby grand piano.

Many of the observations we had made over the years in the industry helped us avoid making the same mistakes when we opened our own mortuary. When we did our first Gypsy funeral, we knew it would be necessary to explain that certain rules had to be followed or we would not serve them. It was important to be very firm with the Gypsies because, left unchecked, almost anything could happen at one of their gatherings. They would bring kegs of beer, set up barbecue grills on our parking lot, and often rent a large tent under which the chairs were placed.

Gypsies are nomadic people from the Indian subcontinent who established themselves primarily in Eastern Europe. The word "Gypsy" has a negative connotation and has taken on another definition, describing someone who has no home or wanders endlessly. In the many conversations we had with them over the years, it was obvious that they have pride in their culture, although they had some rather strange practices. We paid an employee $100 to stay with them for the entirety of the wake, which would last all night. Their belief was that you should become so exhausted by the experience that when it was over, you could go home, collapse in bed, and forget your sorrow.

Gypsies believe in a variation of resurrection, so they want the deceased to have all the necessities for the next life, known by anthropologists as "grave goods." They would often buy a brand-new Stetson hat that was placed on the chest of their male loved one, and during the wake everyone would place items of importance in the casket. There was no limit to what was given the deceased—cash, boots, candles, incense, and bottled liquor. Women received even better treatment than men because the casket would end up full of jewelry, perfume, cosmetics, money and even an ivory-handled brush and mirror set once. I was really flabbergasted when a family member put a hot turkey sandwich in the casket just before we left for the cemetery. I suppose an unscrupulous funeral director could have collected all the cash in the casket and replaced it with a check made out to the deceased. I *know* what you're thinking—and no, we never did that.

An advance group of friends or family would always come in before the visitation to make sure that everything was in good order. One evening, two young men arrived and were escorted to our large display room by Bob Halverson, to make sure the deceased looked exactly right before the rest of the family arrived. Bob heard them talking and knew from past experience that they would often request something extra, so he waited a few moments. One young man was asking the other one if he had the gold cigarette lighter they were going to place in the deceased's pocket. The other man produced a lighter, but then his friend asked, "Where did you get this lighter?" When his friend hesitated he exclaimed, "You stole this lighter, didn't you? You know we can't use a stolen lighter, so you have to go buy one."

Gypsies are not so much religious as they are superstitious. One time, a Gypsy man had his leg amputated as a result of diabetes. His son brought the leg into the mortuary and asked us to embalm it. He said his father wasn't expected to live very long and requested we store the embalmed leg in our body refrigerator. After a year of seeing the father in his wheel-chair at a number of subsequent funerals, the son agreed that we could cremate the leg. When the father finally died, the son insisted that we get a replacement leg for him. Ron went downtown to a company and purchased a damaged manikin. I sawed the leg off and we duct-taped it to the man's leg stump before dressing him. At the funeral, we asked the son why it was so important to attach this artificial leg, and he said that when his dad got to heaven he didn't want God to think he was a cripple.

A Gypsy client came to me one afternoon and insisted something be done about his deceased brother in our care. The deceased had committed suicide with a gunshot just below the hairline. Our embalmer, Jerry Hendrix, had done a pretty good job waxing the wound and covering it with makeup, but it was still slightly visible. The brother said he didn't care whom we had to call or how much it would cost but the problem absolutely had to be remedied.

I'm not trained in cosmetology, but I had an idea. Mischa was operating *Mortuary Management* from the building next door to the mortuary, and his girlfriend assisted him there, so I requested that she come upstairs to the prep room. She had long black hair, and I asked her if it would be possible for me to cut off a piece. She leaned over and exposed the nape of her neck so some could be cut off where it wouldn't show. It was affixed to his scalp with a little wax, combed over the wound, and held in place with hair spray. When the brother was shown the result that afternoon, he was delighted and tucked a $100 bill into my suit coat pocket. I told him that this was not necessary, but he insisted.

Most Gypsies are not affiliated with any particular church, so we approached the priest at Saint Sophia Cathedral, where Kathy and I were married, about referring our Gypsy clientele to him. He agreed to conduct their services for $150 but made it very clear that he would not tolerate disrespectful behavior. Many times it was necessary to admonish the attendees to stop talking in church. They would comply, but it wasn't that they were concerned about being asked to leave; it was that their disrespectful behavior during the ceremony might jeopardize the deceased's chances of being received in heaven.

41

A Good Laugh in a Somber Profession

People's emotions about death can cause unusual reactions on certain occasions. Once, on my way back from Las Vegas, I was in one of our special black lift vans. The only thing that identified this as a funeral car was the pair of fourteen-inch chrome wreaths on either side. This was back when a gas attendant would actually come out and fill your tank. When he came to my window, I told him to fill it up. While I was stretching my legs after hours of driving, the attendant began with some small talk until he noticed one of the wreaths on the van. That was when he finally made the connection between a black van with chrome wreaths and a funeral car.

He looked at me strangely and asked if the van was some kind of a mortuary car, which I confirmed. Next, he asked if it was used to carry dead people, and I told him that was true as well. Then came the $64,000 question: Is there a dead person inside the truck now? Once again the answer was affirmative. He let go of the gas nozzle as if it had just given him a huge electrical shock and ran into the garage. After topping off the tank myself, I figured he was not coming out to collect the money, so I walked into the garage, where he asked me to place the money on the workbench. With a terrified expression on his face, he looked as though he had just had an encounter with the Grim Reaper.

Some of the funniest reactions to my hearse came from the girls handing me lunch at a drive-up window, but the most hilarious one came from a man running a recycling operation. When he saw me exit the hearse and open the back door, he didn't even wait to see what I was getting out. I heard him say, "You've got to be kidding me!" I wonder what he thought I had for him. He had probably seen the movie *Soylent Green* too many times.

On another occasion I was waiting for my hearse to complete its cycle at our local car wash, where the workers were used to my coming in.

While I sat and read a newspaper, two employees were drying the hearse. One of them whistled and waved a towel to let me know the car was ready, except he pointed at something in the open back door of the hearse that apparently needed my attention. I walked over, and for a fleeting moment, the unthinkable seemed to have happened. There was a fully clothed man on the floor with his arms crossed over his chest. It was just his buddy lying there, but for a split second my brain registered that someone at the mortuary had left a body in the car. This time, the laugh was on me.

In an environment where loss and grief walk hand in hand, a little light-heartedness is always helpful to keep your sanity. One family had an unusual epitaph placed on a family member's headstone that read, "He was a waiter and the good Lord finally caught his eye." One of my favorites simply says, "I told you I was sick." However, the all-time classic epitaph comes from a grave-yard in England: "Remember, as you walk by, as you are now, so once was I. As I am now, so shall you be. Remember this and follow me." Sure enough, someone replied to the message, by scribbling on the tombstone, "To follow you, I'll not consent, until I know which way you went."

An infusion of gallows humor into my talks with the people whom we did business with always lightened up our conversations. My trips to Thomas Cadillac and auto supply shops always got everyone laughing when they would ask me, "How's business?" My answer was always "Dead." The other comment that garnered the greatest laughter was telling someone, "We'll be the last ones to let you down."

One day a man called and asked if we would be interested in purchasing two cases of embalming fluid. Naturally, I wanted to determine how he had come into possession of them. He said he had been the highest bidder at an auction. One of the largest companies producing embalming fluid was the Champion Company, and when he saw this name in bold red letters on the cases, he thought it said Champagne. When the auctioneer stated that these cartons contained bottles of embalming fluid, he thought that it was just a humorous way of describing the alcohol. This guy needed to consider going back to school.

Inglewood Cemetery Mortuary offered to provide professional pall-bearers as an option to their clients, as opposed to having family members fill this role, so three or four times each month they requested pallbearer service from us. Once, after placing a casket on the lowering device, we lined up in our usual position in a straight line at the foot of the casket, as we had hundreds of times on previous graveside services. As we stood there in total silence, Al Hartman observed an extremely large cockroach walking directly in front of him. As it walked by, he raised the front of his nearest shoe to let it pass under and then raised his other shoe so it could continue on its way. This did not go unnoticed by the other pallbearers and me. Sometimes, in the most serious of circumstances, the harder you try not to crack up, the worse it gets. One of our men tried very hard not to react but wasn't able to stifle a quiet laugh, which caused the rest of us to start busting up as well.

Because we purchased three or four new hearses each year, we got to know all the salesmen who represented the four major hearse manufacturers: Superior, Miller-Meteor, Eureka, and S&S. These factories each had salesmen in every state, and we had gotten to know all of them quite well at the conventions. One of our favorites was a character named Ken Frink. Ken was not your ordinary salesman. He was slightly irreverent, joked all the time, and always had funny stories to tell. After we had known him for many years, he told us that he had been diagnosed with an inoperable cancer. He also mentioned that he had just made his own funeral arrangements with White's Funeral Home.

Ken liked and respected the mortuary owner, an elderly gentleman everyone called "Shorty" White. On the day that we attended Ken's funeral, Shorty told us that Ken had sold them the hearse that was to be used that day for his funeral. Ironically, when the service ended and they prepared to form a procession, the hearse wouldn't start. A quick call was made to the funeral home's friendly competitor, and within ten minutes a replacement hearse arrived, allowing us to leave for the cemetery. We found out later that when they called to have the hearse towed to the dealership, the tow truck driver got into the hearse to see if he could determine the problem. As soon as he turned the key, the engine fired up immediately and the problem never occurred again. Who knows? Maybe it was just the spirit of Ken, joking around as usual.

A funeral director we knew was making an arrangement for a woman who requested something that wasn't all that unusual in and of itself, considering the number of people who have left their entire estate to their pet. In this case, she wanted to have her pet dog euthanized and placed in the casket with her. He then had to ask her what her instructions would be if the dog died first.

A studio brought some rental caskets back after filming a movie and no one thought to look inside them. Months later, we got another rental order for caskets, so it was necessary to check that they each had a pillow inside. When an employee opened one of the caskets, he jumped back at the sight of an authentic-looking mummified body. It had obviously been left in there from the previous rental.

The rubber dummy was badly in need of repair. Both hands were missing and it had other areas of damage. I spent three weeks working on it in the evenings. When it was finished, I took it to show everyone at work. Our employee Alfred Estrada suggested we pull a prank on our manager, Jerry. We put it in the walk-in refrigerator on a dressing table and then Alfred buzzed Jerry on the intercom, "You better come down right away and look at the deplorable condition of this public administrator's case." We actually had a PA case in-house at the time, or it wouldn't have worked.

Usually on these cases no one attends the funeral, but we would go through the formalities anyway, which included a service in our chapel. Jerry came downstairs and entered the refrigerator. When he saw the dummy on the dressing table, thinking it was a real corpse, he yelled out loud, "Give me a f***ing break!" and ran over to the phone to complain to the coroner's office. From behind the stairwell we couldn't hold back any longer and busted out laughing, so Jerry realized what was afoot. With his years of experience, it was surprising that he had fallen for the prank.

Later that same day, a friend of ours arrived to officiate at the service for the real PA case. Bob Richards was a Lutheran minister whom everyone called Zeke. He always performed these ceremonies for us with only Ron, an employee, or me sitting in the chapel. After the service I asked him for a special favor. He followed me into the prep room where I had placed a crucifix on top of another casket. He was then asked to bless it and place it inside the casket. He dutifully said a prayer and made the sign of the cross over it while holding it in his other hand. When I opened the lid and he saw the dummy, he just stood there for a few moments with a shocked look until I told him it was a prank. Thankfully, forgiveness is his stock-in-trade.

In the late '50s, the LA rock station KRLA had a contest where listeners would get a chance to guess how many times their call letters were stenciled on an old hearse, and whoever got closest to the correct number won the hearse. The contest begged the question of who would want an old hearse anyway, aside from the people who used them to smuggle illegal booze during Prohibition.

Actually, very few people seem to appreciate the tremendous versatility of a hearse. Not only are they extremely spacious for hauling large items, but they can sometimes be a person's home. After country singer David Allan Coe was released from a state penitentiary, he moved to Nashville and lived in a hearse until he began his recording career. And after all, we began our careers after purchasing a hearse for reasons that had nothing to do with its intended purpose.

Our mechanic for twenty-six years was Mike Lampros, who was so well trained that we never had to farm work out for our fleet. Mike could completely rebuild any engine or transmission in-house, and I even purchased an alignment rack so he could also do front-end alignments. His work on hearses must have rubbed off because he eventually bought one as his personal vehicle. He had me order him a set of hearse name-plates for the windows that simply read, "THE END."

A man who found out I sold hearses came into the garage one day to see what was available in my inventory. When I asked him why he wanted a hearse, he said that a station wagon wasn't large enough to hold a flag he had commissioned that measured 47' x 82' and weighed about 800 pounds. After he agreed to purchase a twenty-year-old hearse, he asked if my paint shop could paint it red, white, and blue, and install a stainless-steel roof rack.

His name was Thomas Demski, but everyone just called him "Ski." When the hearse was ready, I personally delivered it to his home near Long Beach and was surprised to see a 132-foot-tall flagpole with the gigantic American flag proudly flying, which his friends had dubbed the "Ski Pole." One of his neighbors took him to court because he said that on windy days the flag would make flapping noises, but the judge ruled in Demski's favor.

Ski told me that the flag he bought the hearse to transport was a minia-ture compared to a new one that was in the process of being produced. Called "Super Flag," this one would be 225' by 505' and weigh 6,000 pounds. Super Flag has since been unfurled in front of the Washington Monument, Hoover Dam, and a Super Bowl game.

As unconventional as Ski was, when he died at age 72, a viewing took place in the garage of his home inside a glass casket. His shirt was removed to display flags tattooed on his chest and on his back, visible from a rectangular mirror below the casket. At his request, his body was cremated and his ashes placed in the eagle atop his giant flagpole.

42

Cremation and Consolidation

The first U.S. citizen intentionally cremated was Colonel Henry Laurens, who presided over the Continental Congress of 1777–1778 and was also a member of George Washington's military staff. He was cremated at his own request upon his death in 1792 and his ashes were placed in the family plot. It was not until 1873 that the United States first held meetings to formally discuss cremation. It didn't take long until Americans were requesting how their bodies would be disposed of in their wills. Interestingly, fourteen former American presidents have been cremated, putting them well ahead of the curve compared to the national average.

In England and early America, cremation was not a popular option and carried a fairly negative connotation. The impetus against cremation in many cases was based on the belief that it was a barbaric act practiced in many third-world countries. But by the '80s, it had become apparent that cremation was taking hold and that future profitability in the funeral business was not looking very bright. Societies had popped up everywhere offering low-cost cremations. The first one in California was Telophase in San Diego. Once they had gotten their foot firmly in the door, it wasn't long before the Neptune Society began opening branches in almost every part of California. Their name was derived from the fact that they also offered ocean scattering where their namesake, the mythical god of the sea, resides.

These businesses were exclusively cremation service providers, but they were not crematories. Any funeral home can offer cremation, but almost all of them have to outsource the work to a crematory. Originally, cremation societies were cheaper than full-service mortuaries because they were nonprofit organizations formed to negotiate for the lowest prices. Some cremation businesses took to calling themselves "societies" so that potential customers would think they were one of the nonprofit services, but the state Board of Funeral Directors and Embalmers banned all new businesses from using the word.

Mortuaries did their best to resist the type of service known as "direct cremation," with no casket, no visitations, and no burial. Many of the firms we served referred to these potential customers as "shoppers," who would call on the phone inquiring about the price of different services. The reluctance of the mortuaries to offer low-cost direct cremation only encouraged the expansion of the cremation societies. By the mid-'80s, the cremation rate exploded in most large cities, while rural areas and religious communities maintained traditional funeral practices.

In the early '80s, a young man named Tim Waters contacted me because he wanted to buy a conversion. He had recently graduated from high school and told me that during his senior year he had been driving a hearse to high school. Just before purchasing the conversion, he had acquired a cremation service in Burbank called the Alpha Society. By purchasing an existing company, Tim was able to keep the "society" designation. Alpha had been doing only about thirty cremations per year and the owners had full-time jobs, so they used an answering service for their calls.

Tim started calling me at home, and we would sometimes talk for several hours. He said that he had been hearing about us for more than a year, and he had many questions about the funeral industry. Ron and I started off in this business ourselves in our late teens, and it would have been very helpful if we had been able to get answers from someone with experience in this field, instead of learning everything by trial and error as we did. Tim was very aggressive when it came to business, and within a few years he was doing about 300 cremations per year. Soon, he opened a second location in Ventura County, which was doing another 100 cases by 1984.

Cremation grew in popularity, not only because the service was less expensive, but because follow-up options, such as remains transportation, were more economical as well. Often, people on the West Coast who wanted to return their family members to eastern states would have them cremated first and ship the ashes. Obviously, this was much cheaper than shipping the remains, but it had its own problems. You can't look at cremated remains and recognize them as your relative, so you have to accept them on faith. It had become common for funeral directors to send us ashes through the U.S. Postal Service. More than once, we received a box of ashes that had been broken while going through the mail. These ashes were from mortuaries in landlocked states that had seen our scattering service advertised in *Mortuary Management.*

One thing about cremation is that it's final. If there's a mistake, that's a bell you can't unring. One of our client mortuaries once sent a body to Rosedale Cemetery and Crematory but soon realized that they had sent the wrong one. A preponderance of the crematories in Los Angeles County are located within cemeteries. Rosedale was contacted in a big panic and told to shut down the retort. By the time we got there, they had already removed the body from the furnace because the casket was nothing but charcoal. As strange as it sounds, the body was in relatively good condition, even though the furnace burns at 1,800 degrees. We estimated her weight at about eighty pounds, since all of the fat had rendered out of her body. She looked much like a Native American, because her skin was deep red and her face looked like tanned leather.

A number of lawsuits in the industry arose from misplaced or switched ashes. Sometimes families were given their loved one's ashes, only to have someone else call a while later, asking when they would be picking the ashes up. Some of these errors were caused by paperwork snafus, in conjunction with the inability to identify ashes when there was a mix-up.

Before the advent of DNA analysis, forensic odontologists identified the dead by comparing their dental records, but teeth are destroyed during cremation, so that identification process did not help in this situation. Gold teeth did not aid the identification process either, because they were usually removed from the ashes before being returned to the family. It was a well-known fact that many crematory employees sifted through cremated remains and removed the gold. The only crematory we served that consistently did not follow this practice was Forest Lawn, because we would often see gold in cremains that families would bring to our boat for scattering at sea.

To avoid any legal liabilities, most crematoriums would post a sign on their walls that read something like "All metallic objects are removed from cremated remains before packaging." I believe that any inquiries as to the meaning of this signage could be explained away by merely suggesting that it pertained only to things like screws, latches, and hinges.

One of our employees, Jack Farina, went to work for the Pierce Brothers crematorium called Chapel of the Pines, adjacent to Rosedale Cemetery. Sometimes after a service there, it was nice to stop and visit with Jack, who was now in charge of running the crematory. There was a closet in the workroom, and he showed me many shelves stacked with boxes of cremains. Some were from recent cremations in the '80s, but many dated back to the '60s. He told me that some families did not pick the cremains up after being notified that they were ready. In fact, about 5 percent of all ashes in the U.S. are never claimed. Even though we offered to scatter them at sea at no charge, Pierce Brothers didn't want to do any unauthorized disposals, so they just stored them.

During one of my visits with Jack at the crematory, I saw some strange metal objects of varied length sitting on his workbench. They looked like railroad spikes with a mushroom head. Jack told me they were artificial hip replacements that didn't melt during cremation. It seemed strange that he hadn't just disposed of them, but he said that one day he dropped one and it made a very pleasant ring, almost like a tuning fork. They all had a different pitch depending on their length, and he offered to save me a few. I told Kathy about them and jokingly explained that they could be made into a nice wind chime for our patio. She said, "Sure, you can hang them there if you want to, but that's where you'll be sleeping."

After a cremation is completed, there are always some bones still partially intact. Some crematories have an apparatus to crush them, but smaller operations crush them manually on a steel plate, using a large hammer. This is called "processing," so cremains will fit in a box once they are reduced to a fine gravel consistency. They are then strained through a wire mesh and metal objects are removed.

It was not uncommon for deceased women to have their diamond wedding ring on during a visitation. The mortuary would typically be instructed to remove it and other jewelry before proceeding to the crematory. An employee of one of the firms we served said that he had forgotten to perform this task. When the family called and asked when they could come to pick up the diamond ring, the mortuary discovered that it hadn't been removed. In a panic, they were able to locate the jewels among the ashes. Although the settings had melted, the diamonds were in perfect condition.

Our mortuary's cremation rate eventually arose to about 70 percent of our services. We had to conduct about five cremations to achieve the same amount of profit generated by a full-service funeral. We were maintaining a glorious building in the heart of downtown where it cost about $300 a month just to run the air conditioner. Over the years it had become quite apparent that radical changes in people's perception of the value of funerals were occurring.

Cremation services also conflicted with funeral homes' historical pricing structure, which was product oriented toward the casket, with the various funeral services provided as accompaniments to that purchase. The final "nail in the coffin" for the traditional funeral industry's casket-based pricing structure occurred in 1984, when the Federal Trade Commission (FTC) instituted the Funeral Rule. It required that a general price list be provided to consumers before making their arrangements, which explained the cost of individual goods and services offered by the mortuary. It was tantamount to handing the family a menu that they could selectively choose from.

Mortuaries were also required to get written permission from a family to embalm a body, which was problematic because embalming is not just for the appearance of the body, but also an important factor in keeping the remains preserved. The new law resulted in every mortuary having to install a refrigerator for the remains until the family came in and signed the necessary form.

The upheaval in the funeral industry didn't end there. This was a time when the ownership of mortuaries was evolving rapidly. There were a few publicly traded corporations that started buying up all the family-owned mortuaries in high-volume areas all over the United States. In almost every case these corporations, referred to in the industry as "consolidators," would not change the name of the firm they had purchased. In many instances, they would also keep the former owners on the payroll as managers.

Their advantage was that by operating several funeral providers in one community, they could utilize economies of scale, such as having only one embalming facility for three locations. Ron had even written an editorial in *Mortuary Management* about a man in Texas who had a chain of mortuaries with very small facilities and low prices. The article was entitled "Is There a McDonalds in the Funeral Industry?" Apparently, he didn't like the reference and filed a lawsuit against us. In all the years we had published *Mortuary Management*, this was the first time we were sued for libel. Our insurance company made an out-of-court settlement with him.

As a result of funeral price consciousness in the public and the Funeral Rule, casket retailers began popping up all over California and all they did was sell caskets, not services. We served our share of families that provided their own casket, including some that they had built, painted, and decorated themselves. We always used what was provided because a mortuary is legally required to use any casket provided by a family, even if they bought it from a competitor.

Being forced to use a casket purchased elsewhere is inherently unfair, in my humble opinion. Imagine what would happen if you took a raw steak into your local restaurant and asked the chef to cook it for you, but the restaurant charged you only for the side dishes. For that matter, what does happen if you take your favorite wine to a restaurant to accompany the meal? Wine is a major source of markup for restaurants, so many restaurants charge a corkage fee equivalent to their cheapest bottle, to recoup at least some of the potential lost revenue. However, a funeral home is prohibited from charging a handling fee, even though caskets are sometimes delivered inside a great deal of packaging that staff members have to remove and discard.

Funeral directors would call Ron to ask him if he had any thoughts about this financial threat to our industry, and he was always very candid in his response. His most frequent response was that funeral directors should price their products and services individually and competitively, rather than basing charges on the casket price, as had traditionally been done.

At one point, a funeral director went to one of these casket stores to see who was manufacturing them. He identified the caskets as being distributed by the Inland Casket Company. We had been purchasing many of our caskets from Inland, so when Ron was asked what he thought about the situation, he simply said that we would probably not be buying from them any more. As a result, we got sued for restraint of trade. We paid up because this was what the government considered a violation of antitrust laws. What a load of crap, when you can't even state your opinion about something.

43

New Ventures

One day, my friend Tim Waters called me with a business proposition. He knew a couple in North Hollywood who owned a picture car rental company called Hollywood Picture Vehicles. Among their cars were five ambulances, two detective cars, six Checker cabs, and a hearse I had sold them. They wanted to sell the business, so Tim approached me about joining with him to buy it. They agreed to take half the asking price of $20,000 as a down payment and the balance in monthly installments.

Kathy saw this as an opportunity to get involved in this business herself. She was very active and liked to exercise at least three days a week. It seemed to me that going back to work would have cramped her lifestyle, but she jumped at the chance to become the office manager for us. After we consummated the deal she started answering the phones and checking cars in and out.

Several months into the business, we received a letter from the California Secretary of State's office stating that the previous owners had used the business as collateral for a loan on which they had defaulted. We consulted an attorney and were informed that under the terms of such a lien, we would have to pay it off to keep the business. We tried to cancel the deal, but the sellers had already spent the down payment money.

The attorney said our only other option would be to break up the business. Neither one of us could use the name of the company, keep the phone number, or retain more than 49 percent of the vehicles. We finally agreed that Tim would take the ambulances and a number of other vehicles, I would take the Checker cabs, and we would sell five of the vehicles. After that, we operated independently. Kathy was out of a job, but she never mentioned working again. The cabs became part of our rental fleet, and I eventually bought four more because they were a popular rental item.

Checker Motors Corporation stopped producing Checker cabs in the early '80s and they had been slowly disappearing by attrition. They had been produced for about thirty years in Kalamazoo, Michigan, and during that entire time there were only minimal changes. The only noticeable change came after the government forced all car manufacturers to beef up their bumpers.

Checkers were really an ingenious innovation because cab companies need cars that are roomy inside, last a long time, are cheap to repair, and don't cost too much. They ran very basic, small-block Chevrolet engines. The exterior underwent some minor changes from time to time but mostly remained the same over many years. Amazingly, a number of Checkers have been documented to have a million miles on them.

It often became necessary to match existing film shots made on the East Coast with current ones taken in downtown Los Angeles, hence backgrounds were filled with lots of Checkers, looking like New York or Chicago. The TV show *Mickey Spillane's Mike Hammer*, starring Stacy Keach, was shot mostly if not entirely in LA, even though it was supposed

One of Hollywood Picture Vehicles' Checker Cab rental cars in 1984.

to take place in New York. Besides being rented for films, Checker cabs were popular in TV commercials and photo shoots. One of my Checkers was even used on the cover of a Dolly Parton album.

Tim and I continued to run our respective businesses and in time we even became what can only be described as friendly competitors. He was renting a large blue '76 limo to the studio filming weekly episodes of *Remington Steele*, starring Pierce Brosnan. At the end of the second year the studio tried to purchase the limo because the show had been doing well, so Tim said he would sell it the following year if they would continue renting it for one additional season.

The studio contacted me and said they wanted me to possibly find a match for Tim's car. A business associate of mine named Jack Rodman had an identical gray '76, so I offered to buy his limo and train him in funeral work, which would keep him very busy. Painting the limo to match Tim's dark blue limo was easy, but dying the interior proved to be more difficult. As usual, the studio wanted the car yesterday, so my painter had to do a real rush job. Instead of spraying dye on the seats and headliner as he was instructed, he used blue paint instead. The seats hardened like cardboard, but it was a perfect match! Despite Tim's losing this lucrative rental, we remained good friends and I followed the progress of his business.

The limo he had was of no use to him after he lost the rental so he sold it to me, which I ended up using once, in a very unusual way. Mischa was attending North Hollywood High School when some of the kids decided to pull a prank on a female student. She had a little stuffed pig that she carried with her at all times. As a joke, a student stole it and was showing it to his buddies, including Mischa, who brought it home and took a Polaroid picture of it bound up with twine. The student was in a panic to get it back, so she was given a ransom note instructing her to come up with $50,000 in Monopoly money for its return.

By this time word had gotten around, and much of the school was becoming aware of the scheduled hostage payoff. We put our heads together and planned to make the pickup at a specific time and place. On the day of the exchange, Mischa drove the limo with me in the backseat. I was in a black suit and a snap-brim hat, which made me look like a Mafioso. As we drove up to make the drop-off, many students gathered on the school's front lawn just after lunch break to see what was going to happen. A student approached the limo with the Monopoly money, and we turned over the pig. These silly but imaginative antics were reminiscent of the Hollywood productions with which we were involved.

In the mid-'80s, a couple of LA County funeral home owners decided to sell their businesses and retire. One was in Monterey Park and belonged to Art and Ruth Cram. After months on the market as an operating mortuary, they hadn't gotten any offers, so they sold the property by itself while agreeing to sell us the name Carter-Cram for a percentage of the revenue they had generated annually. Another funeral director, Amos DuBois in San Gabriel, was also planning to retire and was aware of our plans to take over the Monterey Park mortuary, which was only about five miles away.

Since Carter-Cram and DuBois were close to each other, it seemed reasonable that if we purchased the two well-known names, we could combine them into one facility. A property was available just around the corner from the famous San Gabriel Mission, belonging to a casket company that decided to close the facility. After the purchase we did extensive remodeling and introduced a number of arches into the building to reflect the flavor of the nearby mission. We combined the two names together to form DuBois, Carter-Cram and hired a manager, because neither one of us wanted to commute there each day.

As it turned out, we never took into consideration the fact that both of these mortuaries had been on their town's main streets, while our new mortuary was not. When the locals would drive down the main streets of the two towns, the old landmarks were not there anymore, so many people just figured that they had gone out of business. The new facility never performed very well, so after a couple of years we made the decision to sell it. The same day escrow closed, the Whittier Narrows earthquake occurred and the building sustained a great deal of damage. Maybe it was some kind of divine intervention since we had no earthquake insurance, or maybe it was just a case of the new property owner getting screwed by the fickle finger of fate.

44

Lambs to the Slaughter

Tim Waters had complained to me on a few occasions about a young man named David Sconce, who operated a cremation business in conjunction with the Lamb Funeral Home, which his parents owned. All funeral homes do a certain number of cremations, which they farm out to cemeteries with retorts. We had been sending ours out for years to Evergreen Cemetery, one of the oldest in Los Angeles.

The city had closed many crematories because of the poor local air quality. Early technology in filtering smoke from retorts was quite rudimentary. Newer models had high-efficiency scrubbers to clean the exhaust. When the Air Quality Management District (AQMD) shut down the crematory at Westwood Village Cemetery, we became concerned that Evergreen's crematory might also be shut down.

Nobody was able to determine how David Sconce could undercut the fees charged by other crematories, especially considering the convenience he offered. Normally, a mortuary had to deliver a case to a crematory and later pick up the ashes, but David would make the pickup and return the ashes, all for an extremely low fee. It was a long time before we found out about his dirty secrets—and what shockers they were. He would ultimately be charged with the worst criminal activity ever seen in the funeral industry, but for the time being things continued as usual.

David had been making the rounds to all the mortuaries attempting to solicit their business, including that of Tim Waters. In spite of his young age, Tim wasn't the type of person to get talked into anything that he was opposed to. Tim had been using the Grand View Cemetery in Glendale and he respected the people at this family-owned facility, so he wasn't about to switch and start using David's service.

Tim's manager, Don, called me one day and said that Tim had been brutally beaten at his office by two very buff guys, and he was in Kaiser Permanente Hospital in the valley. I visited him there, and he was hardly recognizable because his face was badly swollen and his nose was broken. He said he had no idea who might have done this to him or why. In just over a month, Don called again to inform me that Tim was back in the hospital, but this time he was very concerned that Tim might not make it.

He had gone to his parents' home in Camarillo, where he had become violently ill and had to be rushed to the hospital by ambulance. The hospital was about sixty miles north of LA, and when I arrived there the receptionist at the nurse's station said that she couldn't give me any information because it was hospital policy to discuss a patient's status only with family members. Having been in the funeral business for years, I knew that this could mean only one thing.

After I returned to Los Angeles, Tim's mother called, gave me the bad news, and said she wanted me to take care of his funeral. It was to be held at Saint Charles Catholic Church in North Hollywood, which everyone called "Bob Hope's Church" because he lived less than a mile away from it and had donated a great deal of money for its construction. Two days after Tim's death, I drove to the Ventura County Coroner's Office to bring Tim back to LA. Over the years transporting cases had become routine, but this time it was very strange to look in the rearview mirror and see a cot carrying somebody I knew so well, wondering how this could be at his young age of 24.

Tim had been grossly overweight, but would never discuss that with anyone. This might have contributed to or caused his death, but there was also that horrible beating that he had gotten just weeks before. The pathologist who did the autopsy told me that Tim had an enlarged heart and liver due to his obesity. All coroner's cases are immediately weighed so they would have that information on record, but my inquiry didn't shed any light on that issue. The doctor said their scale went up to only 350 pounds, and the needle was resting on the peg at that mark. The pathologist seemed to be somewhat uncertain about a distinct cause of death, even though it was attributed to heart failure. Little did we know at the time that it may have been something much more disturbing.

At his family's request, we put Tim in an African mahogany casket, the lid of which we could barely close because he was so large. He was interred in a lawn crypt at Grand View Cemetery. After the cryptside service, his father came over to me and we talked for a few minutes. Surprisingly, he told me that Tim had commented to him that the only person he couldn't out-finagle in a business deal was Allan.

Following Tim's death, the word got out that the crematory facility that David Sconce had been operating in the town of Altadena, just north of Pasadena, had recently had a big fire. David denied it and said it was only a small flare-up.

One of the hot-button industry issues at the time was a ruling from the State Board of Funeral Directors and Embalmers that no crematory could cremate more than one person at a time, and that under no circumstances could there be any commingling of ashes. Ron decided to send a letter to the Lambs about this matter and enclosed a form for them to sign and return.

David showed up at our office and demanded an explanation for the letter. Ron explained that we were merely carrying out our responsibility to the families we were serving and protecting ourselves at the same time. David claimed that Ron's letter had brought his grandmother to tears. We never did receive the form back from him, but in spite of David's resentful reaction, it would turn out that Ron was admonishing him to never do precisely what he was in fact doing.

One evening at home, Ron heard a knock on his front door. When he answered it, he found two men standing there who identified themselves as undercover LA Police Department detectives. They told him that they were investigating allegations that his car had been involved in a hit-and-run accident. Ron took them into his garage to prove that his car had no damage, but once inside the garage they beat him severely and even splashed bleach from his pool supplies all over his face. As soon as they fled, he called me.

Our homes were both in the Hollywood Hills and it took me only three minutes to get there. Upon my arrival, I saw Ron was standing in the driveway, holding a blood-soaked towel to his face. When the police arrived they asked a lot of questions about the possible motive, but for the life of us, we could not think of anyone who would have a reason to carry out such a horrible attack.

Shortly thereafter, the news broke that David had been arrested for operating an illegal retort. The allegation involved the use of a former pottery kiln in Hesperia, California. Many of the residents had complained to the authorities about a foul smell in the air that had continued for months. An AQMD officer had gone there to investigate and found the facility behind a locked chainlink fence. He buzzed the intercom and announced that he was there to do an inspection but was informed by an employee that he didn't have the authority to let anyone in. The inspector told him that if he didn't open the gate immediately he would have a sheriff's deputy there in ten minutes with a pair of bolt cutters and arrest the employee for hindering an investigation.

The inspector must have been horrified when he saw bodies stacked like cordwood, with fluids from decomposing bodies leaking onto the floor. This discovery led to an investigation that lasted many months. David's employees were vigorously interviewed by the police and threatened with prosecution for their complicity. Soon they were talking nonstop about all the illegal activities taking place. They admitted that one time they had crammed sixteen bodies into the Altadena Crematory furnace that was supposed to handle only one at a time. They fired it up and went to get something to eat. Once a body starts burning it's like a candle, as the fat melts and makes additional fuel. That's how the fire broke out, and it was no mere flare-up. It destroyed the structure, so it became necessary for David to move his facility to Hesperia. David was arrested on numerous criminal charges.

Enough time had elapsed between Tim's beating and Ron's attack that we never connected the two, so Ron couldn't believe it when a police detective named Dennis Diaz contacted him and gave him an account of how David Sconce had ordered both beatings.

As the trial proceeded, all the lurid facts came to light. A whole plethora of felony counts included mutilating bodies, commingling ashes, returning the wrong ashes to families, removing and selling human organs to medical research facilities, and removing gold fillings. All told, there were about twenty-eight felony counts against him, including some horrendous activities so outlandish that no laws governed them. Unfortunately, they offered David a plea bargain, which would reduce the charges to a much smaller number if he pled guilty to some lesser counts. The case was such a huge scandal that two books were published about the whole affair—*Chop Shop* by Kathy Braidhill and *A Family Business* by Ken Englade.

After David's conviction and imprisonment, even more shocking news came to light. Anyone who has seen documentaries or read articles on prison life is aware that incarcerated criminals often confess their crimes to fellow inmates. In some cases, these prisoners then pass the information on to the authorities for possible reductions of their own sentence.

This has happened so many times you would think that criminals would know better, but the lure to boast to others must be too great. While serving out his prison term, David admitted to a cellmate that he had murdered Tim Waters by putting oleander extract in his food. Tim ate out all the time and probably was poisoned in a restaurant when he left his table to use the restroom, providing David a chance to taint his meal.

The Ventura County Coroner's Office still had a vial of Tim's blood, because coroners often keep blood and tissue samples for years. In Tim's case, this had probably been done because the cause of death was questionable. After extensive analysis, this blood tested positive for oleander in a sufficient quantity to be a fatal dose. However, a problem arose in determining who might have had access to the samples and whether they were compromised. I'm sure the attorneys would have argued these facts out in court, so the only way to proceed was to disinter Tim from Grand View Cemetery. They performed a second autopsy and took new tissue samples, but Tim had been dead for about five years and the new samples had been degraded and diluted with formaldehyde. As a result, David was never charged with Tim's murder.

Other witnesses came forward and gave testimony that David had been planning to kill his grandparents so his parents would inherit the business sooner, with the knowledge that he would be next in succession when they retired or died. One of his competitors was also allegedly on his hit list, as was the prosecutor who tried the case against him. David's original plea bargain resulted in a prison sentence, but he would remain on probation for the rest of his life. After serving four years in prison, he moved to Arizona, where he started a counterfeit bus pass scheme. It wasn't long before he was back in jail.

David's parents received lesser charges, always claiming that they were unaware of their son's numerous illegal activities. Following this outrageous case, the mortuary hired a Hispanic gentleman named Henry Reade to become their new manager. They apparently realized that by this time there had been such an influx of Hispanic people moving to Southern California that this could only help their business. Henry continued using us for accommodation services and before long we became good friends. He ended up driving for me on many films where I was driving the hearse and he was in the limo. Now, twenty years later, he has opened his own mortuary in Fresno, California, and we remain good friends.

45

A Family Affair

The nature of the tasks performed by morticians, in concert with people's emotional states over the loss of a loved one, seems to impart a negative connotation about my profession in the minds of many people, consciously or not. A perfect example of this was when Kathy first introduced me to her father, Paul. Although he was friendly to me, he never asked me anything about my business once he knew what we did.

Paul had been an engineer in Yugoslavia, an occupation held in high esteem. In Los Angeles, he was forced to retire from his streetlight engineering job with the city when he turned 68. The city had a banquet in his honor, where he was recognized for having designed the most well-lit intersection in the United States at Wilshire and Westwood boulevards. He tried staying home for about a year, and it certainly didn't agree with him. When we would go to Kathy's parents' house for dinner, he would complain about his inability to find work.

Pierce Brothers Mortuary had a contractual agreement with a husband-and-wife team to get their death certificates signed, much as we had done for Utter-McKinley. I would often run into Mr. or Mrs. Hess at the health department while filing a DC for our own mortuary. During one chance meeting, she said that they were looking for some retired person who might be looking for work. I mentioned the offer to Paul and he was incensed, stating, "How could you believe that I would even consider such a job?"

Paul definitely didn't want the job, but my approach was "Try it, you'll like it." For about three weeks he got bombarded with my rationalizations, like "The DC office is only in the fleet garage and you will be out on the road 90 percent of the time," "You can catch up with current events, because every doctor's office has the latest magazines to read," or "You will never have to set foot in any of their branches," which wasn't exactly true.

I explained if he didn't like it he could quit with no hard feelings. He tried it for three days and then agreed to try it for two more weeks.

In less than one year he was making casual conversation about the business and would ask me questions like "Did you hear that Pierce Brothers just acquired two more units?" By the second year he was spending many of his lunch breaks in the embalming room at the Pierce Brothers' main branch, discussing religion with their embalmer, who was a Mormon. Now that we had something in common, he caught up on all the unasked questions from earlier years.

Fortunately, we were able to travel to Russia together in 1987, during the period of glasnost and perestroika. The Russians were embracing tourism, but there were a few times when things got hairy. When we arrived, one of their stone-faced customs officers in Moscow asked to see the magazine Kathy was holding. It was an issue of *Redbook*, a nonpolitical women's magazine, but probably not the best one to have brought. The officer said, "What is this *Redbook* and why are you bringing into our country?" She showed him the magazine and flipped through it so he could see that all the articles and ads were about the latest trends in women's fashions.

We experienced a few more instances that made us quite aware of where we were. Moscow was quite sophisticated compared to many other cities in the USSR. The vehicles used to transport dignitaries and politicians were called *Chaikas*, and they came in every shade of black. It was like stepping back in time, because they looked exactly like the last Packard Patrician cars built in the U.S. in the '60s. It made me wonder if the Russians had used old Packard blueprints to produce the car without having to invest any money in research and development. After all, the Russians had a long history of reverse engineering.

When three American B-29 bombers made emergency landings in Russia in 1944, the Soviets refused to return them to the United States. It must have been embarrassing when they became aware that their new bomber, the Tupolev Tu-4, had metal plates riveted in places where our air force had merely patched holes from shrapnel damage. Stalin's engineers had made him exact copies, just as he demanded.

One evening after attending an opera, as we entered our hotel in Moscow, Kathy turned to say good-night to her parents walking behind us. When the two guards at the front entrance heard her say "Spokoynoy nochi" to them, they grabbed her arms and started dragging her back down the stairs. This was an Intourist Hotel, which didn't allow locals to enter. I showed them our room key, but it didn't help. Paul stepped in and said to them in Russian, "Take your hands off my daughter, we're Americans."

We quickly learned about the desire of locals to get into the tourist-only gift shops, but even more so into the Intourist Hotels, which had the best food and entertainment. As we were about to enter our hotel in Saint Petersburg, we were even approached by two well-dressed young men in suits, who spoke English and asked us to enter the hotel with them. Paul declined and explained in Russian that doing so might get us into trouble.

Saint Petersburg, which was given back its original name after being called Petrograd and Leningrad, was unequivocally the most beautiful city we visited, and the Hermitage Museum was breathtaking. Large riverboats were used to transport tour groups beside some of the most architecturally beautiful structures in all Russia, including Catherine the Great's summer palace.

Another unpleasant experience occurred in Kiev and by this time my tolerance level was running out of steam. We were preparing to enter our rooms, which were just across the hall from each other. The maid had just finished cleaning Kathy's parents' room and was about to lock their door. Paul told her in Russian not to lock it because they were going right in. She shook her head no and continued to fumble with the large set of keys, so he repeated himself. She pointed at a switch in the doorjamb and, without saying a word, pointed to her ear and then down toward the basement, letting us know we were being monitored whenever someone entered or left the room. When we opened our own door we noticed a sensor there as well, so I reached up and toggled it rapidly a dozen times. Kathy said, "Are you out of your mind, do you want to get us arrested?" Fortunately, we weren't hauled off to a Soviet gulag.

Over the years, we took Paul and Vera on many vacations with us. They always had interesting stories to tell, which ran the gamut from life in Russia and Yugoslavia to their arrival in America. Paul also told me a funny joke about the Soviet philosophy of never wanting someone else to have something you didn't have. He said the Germans guards in World War II had to watch the American POWs every second, but if the Russian prisoners were being held in a large pit in the ground, the Germans wouldn't even have to post a guard because if one of them tried to climb out, the other Russians would pull him back down.

After Paul died, I tried to get Vera to write their story, but she said it was far too painful to recall those unhappy memories. I'm grateful that Paul took the time to relate these experiences to me, which must have been difficult for him as well.

46

Movies and TV Abound

After our name became synonymous with funeral vehicles throughout the film industry, the studios started asking us to appear in their shots as extras. We were never allowed to speak during filming, but they did compensate us for the use of our image on camera. At the end of the shooting day they would issue us a voucher, which entitled us to receive some additional compensation.

For an episode of *Moonlighting*, we provided a hearse and a limo at a church where there was a funeral scene. The filming took place in Toluca Lake, adjacent to North Hollywood, where the location manager had found a church with a New England flavor to it. Even the trees around the church were without leaves, as they would be on the East Coast in fall and winter. Cybill Shepherd and Bruce Willis were filmed arriving there by car. Bruce rubbed his hands together and blew into them, which was funny to see since it was quite warm that day.

Another episode was filmed in one of the chapels at Inglewood Park Cemetery. In the plot they accused a wife of having murdered her husband, just as his funeral service was about to begin. The widow ran outside to make her getaway and jumped into the hearse that still had her husband's casket in it. The chase went from the chapel all the way through the Century Drive-In Theater, where Kathy and I used to go when we were dating, and ended at a local baseball diamond where a game was in progress. The hearse went out of control and swerved, causing the rear door to fly open and the casket to be ejected. It slid across the field and then came to rest. Bruce had already jumped out of his car realizing she was cut off, so as the casket slid up and stopped at home plate, Bruce waved his hands in the familiar baseball gesture and shouted, "Safe!"

Until the late '80s, the most cars we ever provided for a movie were three or four. Then we received an order for ten limos for a miniseries called *Lady Mobster*, which starred Susan Lucci and covered two generations of the five Chicago crime families. It began with the head of each family arriving for a big meeting. We pulled up a long ramp and into a warehouse, driving five early '70s limos. A daytime shot stood out for me because one of the actors was Joseph Wiseman, who played the part of Dr. No in the first of the James Bond films.

We then waited until dark for the second-generation bosses to have their meeting in the same warehouse, supposedly a generation later. This time we used current model limos, but the scene was rendered more complicated by a rain machine and the darkness. It was interesting to see these scenes all shot on the same day but representing such a long time apart.

We also furnished a white hearse and three white limos for the filming of the TV movie *Elvis and Me*, based on Priscilla Presley's book by the same name. They wanted to re-create a funeral procession that looked exactly like the real one for Elvis. They showed me still shots of the actual white funeral cars and wanted me to duplicate them with the proper year and color. I called every mortuary in LA that had white cars of the proper year. These were firms we had been serving for years, so they were willing to rent me their cars for this memorable scene.

They used a house in Glendale that was supposed to be Graceland, where the studio personnel broke out their equipment and dyed the grass greener. As the procession pulled away from the house, we drove through Graceland gates that looked exactly like the real ones. We then drove to a city park in swanky San Marino that had a roadway and grassy areas that looked like the long drive from Elvis's house.

For years, moviemakers have enhanced their work by adding actual footage from historic events. Being aware of this technique didn't prepare me for what they had done in the Elvis miniseries. We had apparently matched his real funeral procession so well that they decided to merge this scene with actual color newsreel footage of the real funeral. It surprised me to see our procession going through town with hundreds of adoring fans waving and screaming.

Home of Peace Cemetery had a mausoleum where they filmed a scene for *Bonfire of the Vanities*, starring Tom Hanks and Melanie Griffith. After lunch I went looking for my friend Henry Reade, who was driving one of the three limos. They told me he was in the chapel playing the organ, so I headed over there. At the front of the chapel was a casket they had picked up from me the previous day. I recognized the body in the casket as being that of Alan King, but he wasn't moving a muscle or visibly breathing. I thought that maybe he was getting into the spirit of playing a corpse, but Henry told me it was actually a rubber replica of him. Even at just five feet away, it looked unbelievably lifelike—or should that be death like?

Rosedale Cemetery was used a great deal for location filming, and we were given instructions to report there quite often. One shoot was for a *Columbo* Movie of the Week episode, costarring Ian McShane. He told me that *Columbo* was so popular in Europe that the revenue from there alone paid for the show's production.

We got an order for a hearse to report to Rosedale Cemetery for a new series called *Over My Dead Body*. It starred Edward Woodward, who had previously appeared in the popular TV show *The Equalizer*. The report time was the usual 7 A.M., but there wasn't a soul there, so I parked the hearse in front of the grave they had opened the night before, just as I would on a real service. Quite a while later, they arrived with the casket and cemetery props they'd picked up from me the previous day.

The set decorator started yelling, "Who the hell parked this hearse here?" Not only was he rude, but only the two of us were standing there, so it was a pretty stupid question. He told me to get the damn thing out from in front of the grave so the prop and camera trucks could start unloading.

When filming finally began, they had not moved the hearse back in front of the grave. After about thirty minutes of filming, the director suddenly asked, "Was the hearse in the establishing shot? Where is the driver?" The establishing shot is the opening sequence, where they use a wide-angle lens to capture the entire graveside scene. In response, a couple of crew members pointed at me. After I explained the incident of getting yelled at, he seemed to realize it was a lost cause to reshoot the entire opening shot.

He then asked an assistant how many mourners there were for the graveside shot. When he was told that they had ordered only twelve, he became very upset. At this point he looked back at me and asked, "Has the studio paid for your body for the whole day?" and of course they had. Because I showed up in my usual black suit, he said, "Good, you're going to be a mourner," and paired me up with a young lady I had spoken with earlier. She was a pretty convincing actress because as we stood at the graveside, she was actually crying. As they filmed the service's conclusion, we walked away from the grave and I put my arm around her to console her, which seemed like the natural thing to do. At least this time they weren't yelling at me.

The most unnerving production I was ever involved in was an order for a hearse to report to Rosedale to be used in a music video. About 200 gang members were present, and the assistant director explained to me that this was an attempt to "bury the hatchet" between Los Angeles' two infamous rival gangs—the Crips and the Bloods. The rationale was that if both gangs participated in the same video, they might somehow lessen the bad blood between them.

You could feel the tension as the gang members walked alongside the hearse while we passed all the standing headstones. Repeatedly, a gang member would flash his gang sign, and each time that happened we had to stop and start all over again. This went on for over three hours. By that afternoon, tension had risen to the point where my instincts told me it was time for me to get my ass out of there.

Without a doubt, the most realistic cemetery scene I saw filmed was at the Westwood VA Cemetery for a movie called *Hard to Kill*, with Steven Seagal and his then wife Kelly LeBrock. They had limos, police cars, motorcycle officers, a military color guard, bugler, gun squad salutes, and bagpipes playing "Amazing Grace." The entire day of shooting probably cost about $50,000, and unfortunately it wasn't even used in the film. The only reference to the funeral in the film was a color photograph of the officer on a *USA Today* front page.

The extent to which studios sometimes go to create an authentic-looking cemetery is amazing, but it's costly to rent a working cemetery for a day, so when they don't have a big enough budget or the scene is short, they fake it. On one episode of *Doogie Howser, M.D.*, they set up a cemetery shot on a grassy San Fernando Valley parkway. Because all the scenes were close-ups, you couldn't even tell the difference.

Probably the strangest funeral scene I participated in was for a Virginia Madsen horror movie called *Candyman*. The villain was played by a tall, sinister-looking black man who had a large hook instead of one hand that he used to kill his victims. They instructed me to approach Madsen's casket at the conclusion of the graveside service and activate the lowering device, so that the casket would gradually descend into the grave that they paid the cemetery to open. The camera panned up to a knoll where about 100 nicely dressed African Americans were all in a line, two abreast. They slowly came down the hill and each dropped something into the grave as they passed by. They didn't talk to each other and appeared almost zombie-like.

For another movie, they shot two funeral scenes with the same hearse on the same day. It was a film with Laura Dern called *Afterburn*. They also used rain in one of the shots to make it appear like a different time of year. All the actors had to change their clothes, but they let me appear as the stereotypical black-suited funeral director. The most interesting thing about this film was that it was based on the true story of a fighter pilot who was killed when his jet crashed. After an extensive investigation, the Air Force claimed that it was caused by pilot error, but the pilot's wife doggedly sought proof from the military and defense contractor General Dynamics that mechanical failure in the F-16 caused the crash. As it turns out, the jet had an intermittent flaw that only showed up after a certain number of flight hours.

The longest I ever appeared on screen was in a Tim Robbins film called *The Player*. He and Greta Scacchi were leaving a graveside service and stopped to chat before they parted company, while I stood in the background next to my hearse. The director knew that this was my profession so after the shot he complimented me for looking convincingly bored while waiting.

When one of the studios began filming for a feature called *Chaplin*, starring Robert Downey Jr., the script called for an early '70s Cadillac limo. Charlie Chaplin had built a large Tudor-style studio on La Brea and Sunset. Many people only remember the property as being the home of Herb Alpert and the Tijuana Brass. Over the decades there were only slight changes, so the architecture remained the same. The limo was used to depict Chaplin's final visit to his studio just before his death.

While preparations were being made for the scene, I spoke with a uniformed motorcycle officer whose job was to direct traffic on La Brea during the filming. He was riding a fairly old black-and-white Kawasaki 750cc bike previously owned by a funeral escort. After I talked with him about my love for motorcycles and mentioned that my favorite model had been a 1956 British Triumph, he said, "What got you interested in antique bikes?" That kind of question really makes you think about your age, because the bike was only two years old when I was riding it.

Another interesting project was the filming of a Clint Eastwood movie, *In the Line of Fire*. Clint played an aging secret service agent trying to figure out who was plotting to kill the President. Our first shot was a motorcade of limos, motorcycles, and trucks with Secret Service agents watching closely to see if there were going to be any attempts on the president's life. The lead limo was an authentic Cadillac presidential limousine, with bulletproof doors and windows that they had located at a General Motors storage facility. The limo was scheduled for destruction, but the studio got GM to let them use it first.

They filmed our arrival at the Westin Bonaventure hotel multiple times. The motorcade would start a few blocks away, and many people on the street were watching to see what all the hoopla was about without realizing that it was just for a movie. My limo carried secret service agents and was immediately behind the president's limo. My next two limos carried military and dignitaries. It was hard to refrain from laughing as we approached the hotel because many people who were walking on the streets seemed to believe they were observing some official protocol. To make it even funnier, the man playing the president was waving at all the people, who thought he was someone really important.

The next scene was of the limos leaving after unloading their passengers. We were told to slowly pull away from the hotel, but what we weren't told was that a taxicab would come screeching up along the departing limos and that Clint was going to jump from the cab and run between my limo and the second limo. As a result, the second limo driver almost struck Clint. Although they reshot the scene, the assistant director told me later that he liked the first shot because of the shocked look on Clint's face when my second limo almost ran him down.

Because of my participation in so many productions, reading movie credits was always interesting and allowed me to see the names of the many people I worked with over the years. I have often thought that it would be nice to thank all the studios that supported our motion picture rental division. Aside from the major studios like Universal, Fox, Paramount, MGM, and CBS, the productions that had the most impact on our business were Steven Cannell and Spelling-Goldberg Productions because of their many weekly TV shows that often depicted funeral scenes.

47

What Makes You the Expert?

After renting vehicles and going on movie drives for several years, I added mortuary and cemetery prop rentals to our service. When independent out-of-town film producers would arrive in Los Angeles, they would often contact local studios for leads. Because I had become part of this small fraternity of brothers in the industry, they always recommended calling us for all funeral-related cars and props.

One prop rental we had was from a production company that didn't even call us. A film crew was set up under the Harbor Freeway, a few blocks from our mortuary. After approaching the scene, I noticed three men having difficulty with a cot that wouldn't collapse enough to fit into their coroner's wagon.

I approached them and said, "You know what your problem is?" Without getting up, the director turned around with a contemptuous look on his face and said, "No, what's my problem?" I informed him that they had an ambulance stretcher and what they needed was a mortuary cot. He stood up and asked, "So what makes you the expert?" I told him that we owned a mortuary just down the street and that we had the proper cot that they could rent. One of his people followed me to the mortuary to pick it up and had me demonstrate how to operate it.

Sometimes a studio would ask if they could send someone over to conduct research about a movie they were making. I would happily help them with information about anything to do with funerals, body preparation, burials, etc. On one such occasion, a studio asked if I could spend some time with three actors who had many questions about the funeral business. When they arrived, one face was very familiar to me. It was Christopher Atkins, who had been in *The Blue Lagoon* with Brooke Shields. He was preparing to star in a movie called *Mortuary Academy*, along with two other actors, one white and the other black. Their first questions were about embalming procedures, so we went to our embalming room. Under a sheet was a male body, which didn't seem to bother them.

Some of the actors' questions were quite technical, so I asked our embalmer, Jerry Hendricks, to provide additional details. The inevitable question was asked: "Does a body ever sit up on its own?" Jerry explained that it was physically impossible for a deceased person to do anything more than just twitch or gurgle. Jerry was standing next to the body as he explained things in great detail. He topped it all off by saying, "Believe me, if this corpse sat up right now, I would be the first one out the door." The young black actor hadn't spoken a single word up to this point. His eyes widened and he said in a hushed voice, "No, you wouldn't!"

Providing equipment and vehicles for film productions eventually led to the renting of our mortuary for many movies and TV shows, some of which included *Tucker's Witch*, *The A-Team*, *Riptide*, *Hunter*, *MacGyver*, *Hooperman*, and *L.A. Law*. On the *L.A. Law* shoot, one of the crew gave me his cap with the show's logo on it, a California license plate reading "LA LAW."

For an episode of *MacGyver*, they sent some workmen to create a fictitious funeral home sign. I told them that they didn't have to change the name because we preferred the exposure, so in the opening shot of the show, the entire screen was filled with our sign. As they pulled back from it, MacGyver walks in the front door to pay his respects to his deceased friend, who had actually faked his death to avoid a mob hit.

On John Ritter's detective show *Hooperman*, they were investigating some thefts from the reposing room of a local mortuary. They had a plainclothes officer in the casket shortly after the mortuary had closed for visitations, and on his wrist was an expensive Rolex watch. When the thief snuck into the chapel and started to remove the watch, the detective grabbed him. A short struggle ensued as other detectives came running out from the draped-off family room. As soon as the perpetrator was on the floor and being held down, Hooperman started reciting the Miranda rights. Another officer stopped Ritter and told him that it wasn't necessary to continue, because the perpetrator had had a heart attack and died.

In addition to big productions, we rented our equipment and facilities for student film projects. One recently graduated film director wanted to film scenes for a project called *Beverly Hills Body Snatchers*. He came to the mansion to discuss the possibility of renting the mortuary to film just enough to show some executives his work. Our going rate was $700 per day, which he said he couldn't afford. I agreed to let them film for three days at one-fourth our usual rental rate on his promise that if he was able to sell the idea, he would return and pay the full rate. About four months later, he called and said it was a go, so they filmed at the mortuary for a full week.

The film starred Vic Tayback and Frank Gorshin. It was never released in theaters, but it did come out on video and the director sent me a copy. It made me feel good to have helped this young man establish himself as a director. His name is Jonathan Mostow, and he has since directed *Terminator 3, Flight of Black Angel, Breakdown*, and *U-571*, and assisted in the writing of them as well.

In 1990, actor Jeff Daniels came in to do some research for a movie called *Arachnophobia*, about a very poisonous spider from South America that is accidentally transported to the United States in a makeshift coffin. Daniel's character is a doctor in a small town where people are mysteriously dying. His discovery is personally unnerving because of his arachnophobia, an extreme fear of spiders.

Shortly after his visit, I furnished them with some props, including a casket, lowering device, folding chairs, a cemetery canopy, and an Abbott & Hast conversion for the shoot. The studio transported everything to the small coastal town of Cambria, although it was called Canaima in the film, a veiled reference to the national park in Venezuela where some of the filming took place.

The studio that produced *Tales from the Crypt* for HBO asked me to supply them with a polished hardwood casket. They wanted the top of the casket to be flat, but hardwoods are always expensive woods with rounded lids. The opposite is called a flat top-casket, made of pine and covered with an inexpensive cloth material. After contacting about six casket companies, we found one that had exactly what the studio wanted. The bottom of the lid started out with a curve, which then flattened out near the top. The flat part was eighteen inches wide, just enough for someone to lie on.

The story is about a man who wants to fake his own death to collect on an insurance policy through his wife. However, she is having an affair with his brother, a mortician, so they hatch a plan of their own to kill him and collect the money for themselves. The wife, played by Teri Garr, has purchased a beautiful hardwood casket for his funeral and is about to bid him a fond farewell. At the end, she and her lover are alone in the crematorium. They are so turned on by having pulled off their plan that they start canoodling on top of the casket as it moves inexorably down the conveyor, toward the flaming furnace's open door.

The most props and cars we ever rented was for a Universal feature called *Death Becomes Her*, starring Bruce Willis, Goldie Hawn, and Meryl Streep. In the film, Willis plays an alcoholic plastic surgeon who lost his practice because of his drinking problem, so the only job he can get is doing cosmetology at a high-class funeral home modeled after Forest Lawn.

The studio rented a hearse, three limos, and everything that you would find in a mortuary, including caskets, urns, and a variety of embalming equipment, all of which required three large studio trucks to retrieve. The set decorator wanted everything we had, so he even got some older prep room equipment. When he called me the next day, something told me he was going to complain about the older equipment, but he surprised me by saying that everything was great and that he wanted even more prep room props, so I purchased another $500 worth of instruments for the embalming room shots.

For five afternoons straight, I would drop something else off because every day the set decorator was calling me for more items. On one visit, he took me to a stage and showed me the room they had built to represent the morgue. It had marble walls and floors and stainless-steel refrigerator doors, and was shaped like a giant octagon. He told me they had spent $60,000 to build it. Unfortunately, the morgue scene in the film was less than two minutes.

The studio rented the famous Doheny Mansion in Beverly Hills and we shot there for three days, the longest shoot in which we ever participated. In one scene, the hearse was parked under the portico of the mortuary with family members standing behind me as I was pushing the casket into it. Meanwhile, the funeral director was telling Bruce they had just picked up the body of a famous movie producer who died from a heart attack while in bed with a young starlet. Willis was asked to start working on him immediately and to take the smile off his face.

Film work was a very pleasant diversion from funeral work, even though there was often a common theme between my real-life funeral-related activities and the fictional film productions I participated in. People have often asked me if my line of work was depressing. Sometimes that was the case, but all things considered, it was certainly never dull. There were numerous times when humorous things would occur that would take the edge off, and it was interesting to see how often those types of moments were memorialized on film.

48

Downsizing

As cremation continued to take the spotlight, we were contacted by the producers of *60 Minutes*, who asked us for an on-camera interview. We agreed and Ron hosted Mike Wallace and his camera crew. Wallace was very cordial until he started asking questions about the rapidly rising popularity and acceptance of cremation. Ron was candid about this phenomenon and explained that we welcomed anyone who chose cremation over burial. At this point Wallace evoked his famous ambush statement, saying, "Oh, come on, Mr. Hast, this is hitting you in the wallet and you can't tell me you like what you see."

We were well aware of what was happening in the industry and had done some contingency planning to downsize, because there was no question that the writing was on the wall. We had purchased a small rectangular building in the Silver Lake area, halfway between Hollywood and downtown. It was only a one-story building with a flat roof, so it would take at least six months to remodel the building to become our new mortuary. While still maintaining the mansion, we continued renovating this building and had an architect draw up plans for the addition of a second story with a fancy mansard roof. Our plans also included the addition of a garage to the back of the building large enough to hold four cars and a walk-in refrigerator.

Our new mortuary was so small that we didn't even have a casket display room. Families would select a casket from a large color catalog, and some of the funeral directors who got wind of this thought we were nuts. One day, when Ron was speaking at a funeral convention (as he often did), a funeral director challenged him. He insisted that families not only wanted to see the casket they were purchasing, but they also wanted to touch it, see what the interior looked like, and compare it with other caskets. Ron asked the man where he got his caskets, and without thinking about it he said he purchased most of them from the Batesville

Casket catalog. Everyone started laughing, and the man realized he had just shot himself in the foot.

At about this time, a woman called and wanted to know if we would like to sell the small lot off Laurel Canyon that we had purchased when we were still in high school. She explained that her husband was a builder, and they had purchased the lot adjacent to ours. They wanted to buy our lot so they would have enough space to build a house. The lot we paid $200 for in 1956 was sold thirty years later for $20,000. Talk about inflation!

Our transition to the new mortuary threw a monkey wrench into my rental business. There was only a two-car garage at the new location, and nowhere to house my four funeral cars or all of the mortuary and cemetery props. A portion of the money from the Hollywood Hills land sale was used as a down payment for a small house in the Lincoln Heights area of Los Angeles. That property served as a place to store all the movie paraphernalia and cars, as well as provide living quarters for our trusty gofer and his family.

The Los Angeles Parent-Teacher Association (PTA) purchased our mansion to serve as their main facility. They paid us $1,100,000, which was great except that the government was going to take over a third of that in capital gains tax. I did a little research and discovered that we could defer the tax through a Starker 1031 Exchange. We took $500,000 and put down payments on three apartments in Hawthorne.

Hawthorne is about a mile from LAX and was the undisputed bedroom community for the aerospace industry, with many multimillion-dollar defense contractors like Northrop and TRW in the neighborhood. The apartments were all performing well until the collapse of the Soviet Union a few years later. The greater percentage of our renters worked in the aerospace industry, and many of them relocated when the contractors began to lay off employees. With the Cold War ending so suddenly, our vacancy factor tripled in six months and many low-income families became our new tenants. Soon, we had a couple of tenants who were arrested for dealing drugs from our apartments. The economy in the whole town nosedived, and the rents did the same. In the end, we lost nearly half a million dollars, but it was almost worth it to have witnessed the fall of the Soviet Union.

49

Living in La La Land

By our twentieth year of operating our boat the *Tribute* in Marina del Rey, we had become familiar with many of the area's famous boating enthusiasts, or more accurately, we had become familiar with their boats—even though the owners were occasionally present. We had seen Natalie Wood and Robert Wagner's *Splendour* and Robert Goulet's *Rogo*, and our slip was next to Ed McMahon's boat *Katherine*, named after his beautiful young wife, until he discovered that she was having an affair with another man. Her name was immediately removed from the back of his boat, which remained without a name for quite some time.

After some years in a side channel of Marina del Rey, we moved our boat to the main channel, just up from where the big yellow cigarette boat from *Baywatch* was tied up. The studio that filmed the show approached us about renting our boat for use on an episode. They were so pleased with the results that our boat became a regular on the show. The studio sent a photographer over to take extensive photos of the boat's interior, mostly in the bedroom. Eventually, they built an exact replica of it on the *Baywatch* set, so they could shoot scenes without being on the boat.

Our strangest boating situation occurred on one outing when we had about thirty boxes of ashes and no families present. At the three-mile marker, which was designated as the closest to shore you could legally scatter, we spotted a Coast Guard boat approaching in our direction. We continued dumping ashes overboard, which spread out in large white pools on the water when they are not wrapped in cloth, as was always the case when families were aboard. As the *Zodiac* got closer, we could see that the young men aboard were trainees. One of them announced over his bullhorn, very dramatically, "Prepare to be boarded!"

The person in charge stepped onto our boat, prepared for a possible confrontation with his weapon at the ready. He had a rude awakening when we told him that we were scattering cremated ashes, but he wasn't completely convinced until we picked up some of the empty boxes strewn all over the deck and had him read a few names of the crematories that had performed the service. Now, he still could have thought that we were smuggling cocaine by representing it as cremains and dumping them as the Coast Guard approached, but that would have required him to take a little taste to make sure. That's how Gil Grissom on *CSI* would have handled it.

Most businessmen would give anything to write off a beautiful boat on their tax return as we did. The IRS never challenged the way we filed our tax return with regard to the boat, which was listed as a "marine hearse." Ron and I personally went on 90 percent of all scatterings at sea, and we averaged two or three per week. When serving a family on our boat, Ron would pour the ashes onto a three-foot-square piece of powder blue satin, fold it up into a small pillow, place it in a wicker basket, and arrange some white carnations on top, which were then given to family members to place in the water as well. After that, we would turn around and slowly pass between the carnations that were still floating.

Since we closely controlled the parameters during committals at sea, we felt that the possibilities of something going wrong were remote. Having performed the procedure hundreds of times, we had it down pat, or so we thought. Unfortunately, there was always that wild card with the possibility that some family might interject something into the equation. Once,

Abbott & Hast's "marine hearse" *Tribute* scattered ashes off the Los Angeles coast and later in San Francisco Bay.

we picked up a family as usual at the Marina del Rey guest dock. As they boarded the boat, they showed us some white doves they had purchased and planned to release after the ashes were placed into the water. We felt that it wouldn't be fair to refuse them this final remembrance, so we agreed. As the blue satin wrapping started to unfold in the water, some of the family members released their hold on the doves. Since they appeared hesitant to take flight, the family members assisted by launching them into the air. The doves fluttered awkwardly and crash-landed into the sea. Apparently, the pet shop that sold them the doves had failed to mention that their wings had been clipped to prevent them from flying away.

Because of its problems, the rules pertaining to burial at sea had become very specific. Scattering of ashes at sea was quite popular, but whole body burials were very infrequent. Some naval officers choose this method and the Navy now has a complete protocol for the entire procedure, including who is eligible for this type of burial. One of the first sea burials to be conducted using this protocol was for John Carradine, the well-known father of actors Keith and David. I noticed that they banded the casket with metal straps so it wouldn't come open, and they also used a barrel saw drill to cut three-inch holes in a dozen or more places to make sure it would sink. David had lived just down the hill from us, and we saw him many times.

The Hollywood Hills had so many well-known people that we frequently saw many of them taking a walk in late afternoon on our way to dinner. They included Sally Kellerman; Susan Clark and her husband, football star Alex Karras; Anthony Perkins; and actor-director John Cassavetes and his wife, actress Gena Rowlands, to name a few.

The valley had many great restaurants like Jerry's Famous Deli in Studio City, where we would see the likes of Loni Anderson posing for tourists by her gold Mercedes or six-year-old Drew Barrymore eating a hot fudge sundae. Peter Falk seemed to prefer dining out at his friend's restaurant down the street called Art's Deli.

Kathy and I thoroughly enjoyed living in the Hollywood Hills, with all of its opportunities to observe the famous and infamous. Rob Lowe purchased the house next door to us and completely remodeled it. He also paved over the upper yard directly adjacent to ours to turn it into a half-court for basketball. His doorbell was hooked up to his phone so whenever someone would arrive, we could hear his phone ring. Then he would push a button that unlocked the front door and let the visitor in.

Along Nichols Canyon, each house was about twelve feet above its neighbor's. Our kitchen windows faced directly down into his kitchen, hallway, and dining room. One evening we witnessed Rob and his guest disappear toward his bedroom, but half an hour later he showed up naked in his kitchen and got a bottle of champagne out of the refrigerator. It appeared that he was celebrating his latest conquest by dancing a little jig, like the one Humphrey Bogart watched Walter Huston perform in *The Treasure of the Sierra Madre*.

Rob's scandal came during the 1988 Democratic National Convention after he videotaped himself having sex with a 16-year-old girl, who then took the tape from his room and showed her girlfriends. One of them told her mother about the tape, and the cat was out of the bag. In no time, the paparazzi set up shop in front of his house. Because of all the construction in progress there was still a Porta-Potty sitting alongside his driveway. I'm sure this was a blessing to the news media because when they *had to go*, they didn't have to go.

For a while, he almost became a hermit because he didn't want to set foot outside his house. Food was delivered from a deli in Beverly Hills or the local pizza parlor. About a week into the siege, Rob was sunning himself on a lounge chair in his yard as the paparazzi bided their time out front. Kathy saw him while watering plants in our patio and decided to tell him that if he wanted to he could climb over our common fence and exit through our driveway. When she called his name he almost jumped out of his shorts, thinking that someone had gotten into his yard. He explained that he had a car parked at the bottom of the canyon, so he could climb over his back fence and hike down to it.

50

Lost Love

Kathy was usually reluctant to talk to people about my profession, but I certainly wasn't, and she knew that. The thing that annoyed her the most was when I would discuss it with complete strangers. One year we took a three-week trip to Europe and she asked me to not talk about my line of work during the vacation, which was fine with me. I didn't want to annoy her.

When the tour group assembled in Rome, we met our fellow travelers. One man mentioned to me that he had worked for a mortuary, so naturally we had something in common to discuss. Later on, he mentioned to the whole group that we had both worked in the funeral business. Oh, no! Our group was fairly small and we became friendly quite quickly. By the time we had been on the road for a week, a number of people on the bus would holler, "Look, Allan, there's a cemetery," every time we passed one. It got to be such a joke that even Kathy couldn't help but laugh about it.

One terrible day, I discovered how emotionally devastated someone can be when they lose a loved one. On May 23, 1990, while I was returning from getting a DC signed, the office called on my cell phone. They notified me that Kathy had been taken to North Hollywood Medical Center from her gym, where she had been working out. Ron was waiting for me when I arrived at the hospital. Kathy was in intensive care, and they had no clear diagnosis at that time. When they told me she was on life support, it didn't seem possible, because Kathy was only 48.

The hospital determined that she had suffered a brain aneurism. I stayed at her side, leaving only for meals and sleep. They continued to monitor her condition for three more days but said that there was no brain activity. Many times in the past that diagnosis appeared on death certificates that I had gotten signed, listing the cause of death as CVA, or cerebral vascular accident. The doctors told me that without brain activity there was no possibility of recovery, but in desperate hope I had them run another series of brain scans, which all came back negative. The doctors said the only option was to disconnect her life support. It was like having a terrible nightmare from which I could not be awakened, and it was by far the hardest decision I would ever make.

It was impossible for me to stoically accept what fate had handed out, and I entered into a state of deep depression. My doctor had put me on a tranquilizer and my thinking was not clear, so Ron stepped in to make the necessary arrangements. For the first time in my life, I felt completely hopeless. My own men picked up Kathy, and our manager, Jerry, did the embalming.

I finally saw her the day before the visitation. The only thing that wasn't right was her makeup. I had watched Kathy apply her makeup for over thirty years and knew exactly how she liked it. After the mortuary closed for the evening I went home, gathered her cosmetics, and returned to the mortuary by myself to apply her makeup as she would have done. My hands were shaking and my heart felt like it was about to burst, but I really needed to do it right.

I felt suicidal and the only way I could function was with tranquilizers. I recalled Natalie Wood's funeral and how sad I felt for Robert Wagner losing the woman he loved. He appeared to be under sedation at the service and I could certainly understand why. I had no desire to continue living for another day without Kathy. If it weren't for my sons and their support, I'm sure I wouldn't have survived that terrible period in my life.

I called Ron the day after the funeral and asked him to call my real estate agent in Monterey to put our Pebble Beach summer home up for sale. The house had been our private hideaway and held many treasured memories. Since our boys were both in college, we would often leave them in LA and go to Pebble Beach, where we would spend time alone together. We would visit the many places we loved, free of work and time constraints. Sometimes, we would drive to a private beach near the house where Kim Novak lived. We had the key to a private gate where a trail led to the ocean. We would sit in silence there, mesmerized by the ocean and lost in our thoughts.

Life without Kathy was unbelievably difficult. I drank alcohol every night until I could finally fall asleep. After years of being in control of my own destiny, someone who could come up with a solution to any problem, I found myself at a total loss and wondered how I would ever get through without her. Kathy was four years younger than me, and most women outlive their husbands by ten to fifteen years, so I never expected to face her death. It has now been over twenty years since I lost the love of my life, and she is still in my thoughts every day.

51

Howard Hughes

One thing that seemed to help with the grief was to keep as busy as possible. I placed an ad in the paper offering to sponsor a new venture, and it didn't take long for someone to take me up on it. A man calling himself Chris Radford called and said he was an investigative journalist writing a book about Howard Hughes. After a number of phone conversations, we met and reached an agreement for me to help finance his research. He even started driving a limo for me on movies, which gave us an opportunity to discuss his findings during the long lulls between shots.

Chris recounted how he had been hired by a Hollywood ghostwriter to work on a manuscript about Howard Hughes. The client was actress Terry Moore, Hughes's former girlfriend, and the book was called *Howard Be Thy Name*. The ghostwriter was an alcoholic and wasn't up to the job, so he didn't tell anyone about Chris's involvement, and Terry Moore never knew that Chris was in possession of her manuscript. After Moore canceled the project, Chris was told to destroy the manuscript, but he kept it instead.

Some years later, he was moving to another apartment and came across the manuscript. His phone and TV service had already been shut off, so with nothing to do and all of his belongings packed in boxes, he decided to read the chapters he had not yet reviewed when he was told to stop working on the book. The more he read, the more interested he became, until he decided to research the insights revealed by Moore and publish a book about his findings.

Hughes's office was on Romaine Street, just east of La Brea. Chris pointed the building out to me as we were heading to my house one evening. He explained how they had developed an interesting system for receiving certain documents there by having someone lower a basket on a string from a second-floor window.

Moore, who had a close relative who was a Mormon, suggested that Hughes hire a member of that faith to be in charge of his security because they didn't drink or smoke, and they certainly didn't carouse with other women if they were married. He particularly liked the latter reason because he knew that illicit sex had been used for decades to blackmail someone into revealing closely guarded secrets. This was an important consideration since Hughes worked on secret government projects like the Glomar Explorer, an effort to raise a sunken Soviet submarine.

He took her advice and hired Frank "Bill" Gay to be in charge of security. As Hughes lost employees by attrition, Gay hired other Mormons, and soon some people started calling Hughes's closest aides the "Mormon Mafia." In 1972, after he sold the tool division of Hughes Tool Company, the Mormons renamed the remaining company to Summa Corporation.

When Hughes died in 1976, Moore claimed that she and Hughes had secretly married in 1949, but she had no documentation to prove it because Hughes had signed the marriage certificate with an assumed name and the skipper of a private yacht had allegedly performed the ceremony. The attorneys for the corporation did not recognize Moore as a legitimate heir, so she marched into the lawyers' offices with her own attorney and a copy of her manuscript. Repeatedly, she threatened to tell what she knew about them, but they only took notice when she did an interview with a small-town newspaper in Arkansas.

In a final showdown, she showed the article to the lawyers and claimed that she would be holding a news conference in a few days in which she would reveal everything about the Mormons' control over Hughes's estate. At that point they announced that an out-of-court settlement had been reached with her, which has been estimated at several million dollars. Terry did publish a book called *The Beauty and the Billionaire*, but there was no mention of the Mormon Mafia or any other scandalous material.

In his research, Chris had learned of Suzanne Finstad, a paralegal and author who worked on the Hughes estate for a prolonged period of time. She had apparently been privy to the Moore case and was present at every meeting with the attorneys. She had written a book in 1984 about all the legal proceedings entitled *Heir Not Apparent*. When we contacted her to do an interview, she claimed that she had been badly beaten after its publication and warned us not to pursue our investigations further, or we might suffer the same consequences. She refused to tell us anything more, other than that she was still in fear of her life.

A friend of mine told me about a man he knew named Peter Hurkos, who was a well-known psychic. Peter and his wife got a surprise visit to their home one evening by their friend John Meier, who had been employed by Hughes for many years. Meier had a suitcase with him and asked Peter to keep it for him. He told Peter that it contained a great deal of money and numerous documents. Meier explained that this suitcase was his insurance policy, in case there were any repercussions as a result of his terminating his employment with Hughes.

We tracked Meier to his home in Canada and phoned him, explaining, that we were planning to publish a book about Hughes. Surprisingly, he agreed to work with us on the story. Chris flew to Canada and spent two days there, and Meier was enthusiastic about helping us. When we tried to follow up with him, we got a recording that the line had been disconnected and there was no referral number. Meier apparently rethought his participation and decided that he didn't want anything to do with our project.

I found out that the harbormaster at Marina del Rey, Chase Ramsgate, had once worked for Howard Hughes in the Bahamas. He told me he would get meticulous notes from his boss every day, written on yellow legal pads, and he seemed to be willing to talk about his experiences while employed as a secretary. However, when asked for an interview with Chris for possible use in a book, he was no longer willing to discuss any of the details. It was very evident that he was fearful of having his name mentioned in any way.

At this point, Chris began to develop some noticeably paranoid behavior. Every time he left his apartment, he would watch his rearview mirror to see if anyone was following him. He was afraid that if the wrong people found out about the book, his life could be in danger.

When his car broke down, I provided him with an old station wagon. The rear window had become disconnected and fallen down inside the tailgate, which needed to be fixed right away to keep fumes from entering the car. In the meantime, we decided to go with a temporary patch, so the window was held up with clear plastic packing tape.

One day as he was leaving his apartment, Chris noticed a car that seemed to be following him. He proceeded to make a series of right-hand turns, and the suspicious car made the same turns. Soon, they had made a complete circle, which confirmed that he was being followed. In a complete panic, Chris sped up in an attempt to outrun the suspicious vehicle. Just as it seemed that he lost the car following him, a car pulled out from a parking lot and he T-boned it. Chris was only stunned, but the passengers in the other vehicle sustained some serious injuries.

They took Chris to jail and charged him with reckless driving and evading arrest. A detective with the Culver City Police Department contacted me by phone and wanted to know if Christopher DeHaas worked for me. It seemed fairly obvious that they were referring to Chris Radford, so I confirmed that he did. Shortly after that, Chris called me from the jail and told me the whole story. He explained that he couldn't trust anyone with his real name as a result of his paranoia.

The reason he was being charged with evading arrest was that a female Culver City police officer had spotted him speeding and went after him. After the accident, he told her that he was evading a suspicious vehicle and in his panic he didn't know that a police car had begun chasing him. Chris assured me that had he been aware of the police officer's presence, he would have stopped, but the police officer claimed that he had to know she was in pursuit because her lights and siren were on and that his tailgate window was open, which wasn't true.

I went to where the wagon was impounded and photographed the tailgate. One side of the window was still held up by the tape, while the other side had broken loose during the crash and was down inside the tailgate. A photo studio made me a life-size photo of the half-open and half-closed tailgate window. During his trial, Chris's attorney questioned me at great length, particularly about the photo enlargement, which she considered an important piece of evidence. Almost every question she asked me was objected to by the prosecutor, which the judge almost always sustained. They were absolutely determined to shut me up, so my only option was to answer quickly, before any objection was made so the jury could at least hear my statements.

The testimony given by the female police officer was very damaging to Chris. She insisted that the rear window had already been down, even though the photo clearly showed that it was not down until the impact. When questioned about the police report, she admitted that she hadn't written it. The defense attorney asked if it was her name on the police report and the officer said that it was, but her supervising officer had written the report and even signed her name. It was unimaginable that the judge allowed her testimony to continue after this admission.

I thought for sure the jury would find Chris not guilty, but after a short deliberation it did find him guilty and he was sentenced to three months in the county jail. Ironically, the trial may have been a death sentence for Chris, because some facts about his Howard Hughes investigation came out during his testimony and anyone could have passed along this information.

When Chris was released from jail, my friend Paul Nix agreed to let Chris move into a room in his house until other arrangements were worked out. During this time, Chris called me almost every night with updates on his research efforts, but then his calls abruptly stopped. Paul claimed to have no knowledge of his whereabouts and still had all of his belongings. Despite my efforts to locate him, he was nowhere to be found. It's now been almost two decades since he last contacted me, so it appears that he's dead. While his bizarre disappearance doesn't prove his conspiratorial concerns, it certainly does make me wonder.

During the last decade of his life, Howard Hughes migrated from Las Vegas to the New England area, then to the Caribbean and finally to Acapulco, Mexico, where he occupied the entire top floor of a resort hotel that had all its windows blacked out or covered with aluminum foil. Among other motivations, Hughes was able to avoid state income tax by not being domiciled in any one state for more than the maximum number of days permitted by law. Near the end of his life, Hughes had very little contact with anyone.

Because there was so much speculation about whether Hughes was dead or alive, an influential journalist named James Bacon contacted the Acapulco police department and requested that they conduct an investigation. As the police prepared to raid the place, a Hughes staff member got wind of it and invited them inside. It is doubtful the staff was aware the police would bring a Mexican doctor along, who performed a physical examination of Hughes and insisted he be hospitalized immediately. However, Hughes's keepers did not hospitalize him as the doctor had requested. As time passed, no one heard anything about his medical condition.

Finally, an EMS company was contacted in Florida to send an air ambulance to bring Hughes back to Texas. Chris had interviewed several people who witnessed the plane's arrival, which had landed in Acapulco but sat waiting on the tarmac for about five or six hours. Chris believed that Hughes was then on the verge of death, but his people certainly

didn't want the Mexican authorities stepping in to conduct an investigation. The people Chris had independently interviewed stated that they
had observed Hughes being wheeled out on a stretcher, but none of them
ever saw him move, implying that only his dead body was placed on the
airplane. At the insistence of his keepers, the pilot called in just after they
entered Brownsville, Texas, airspace and reported that Howard Hughes
had just died, which means he had officially died in the United States.

His body was immediately taken to Methodist Hospital, owned by the
Hughes Corporation. Normally, the local coroner's office would have
jurisdiction in any case of this kind, but the coroner was told that a team
of forensic pathologists would conduct the autopsy and would prepare
a full report with the cause of death. It had been reported that Hughes's
health had been compromised by kidney failure. In an effort to control
residual pain from his plane crashes, Hughes took codeine, but suffered
complications from its use.

Even more bizarre was that X-rays showed a number of broken hypodermic needles still in his arms. Hughes could have afforded the best
health care in the world, but apparently whoever had been giving him
injections was not very proficient. It is also possible that he was administering them himself as part of his self-imposed isolation.

The firm handling his estate ordered hundreds of certified copies of
his death certificate for the many people who needed them to legally
verify his death. In order for me to get a copy of the certificate, it should
have been a simple matter of contacting the health department in Harris
County, Texas, but this was not to be. Upon my request for this public
record, the health department refused to issue it to me, informing me that
Hughes's DC had been red-flagged for twenty-five years, so no one could
get a copy until 2001. That was contrary to everything I had come to
know in my years in the business.

After contacting the mortuary in Texas that handled Hughes's private
burial, I told the manager that our magazine was planning a series of
articles about famous people's funerals. At first he was hesitant, but he
remembered me from years before when I would drop off burial permits
at Utter-McKinley's main office, where he had been working at the time.
When offered the option of writing the article himself, he agreed. He
even confided in me that they had used a decoy hearse so the press would
follow it instead of the unmarked vehicle that was actually used to transport his body for burial.

I followed up with him awhile after we ran the article and asked him to send me a copy of Hughes's DC, which all mortuaries keep in their files. His demeanor completely changed. In our previous conversation he was quite friendly, but now he said, "Don't ever call me again. I have nothing more to say to you."

In 2001, when the twenty-five-year restriction had run out, I was finally able to get a copy of his DC.

Howard Hughes died in 1976, but his death certificate became public only in 2001.

52

My Russian Fascination

A couple of years after Kathy's death I had begun dating with no positive results. Then one afternoon while I was getting a DC signed, an older couple came in to the doctor's office with a beautiful young woman. As they took their seats, I noticed they were speaking Russian. I took several glances at the young lady, but every time she saw me looking at her my eyes went back to the magazine on my lap. Finally, I didn't look away, and to my surprise, neither did she.

Having been married for thirty years, I wasn't accustomed to chance encounters, but I retrieved a business card from my wallet and wrote my home number on the back. As I got up to introduce myself, the nurse came out and took her back to see the doctor, accompanied by the elderly gentleman. His wife remained seated, so I figured the next best thing was to go over and talk to her. I asked her if they were Russian, and she said that they were Polish but were speaking Russian for Olga's sake.

As we continued talking, I told her about my Russian wife and two sons. It turned out that they were not her parents but rather friends of her parents in Moscow, and that she was here on a visitor's visa. The lady agreed to inform Olga about my dinner invitation. To my surprise, the lady called that night and said Olga had accepted my invitation, so we started seeing each other on a regular basis.

When Olga had first arrived in the U.S., she never planned to become a permanent resident. When it was learned that she spoke Russian and had a college degree in electrical engineering, the Jet Propulsion Laboratory (JPL) in Pasadena employed her to tutor their engineers in the Russian language. An abundance of people in Southern California spoke Russian, but through her work supervising a power-generating plant in Russia, she was familiar with all the necessary scientific jargon, which the average Russian didn't know. The people she was tutoring already spoke some Russian so she didn't have to be fluent in English.

JPL knew that she was a foreign national, so they paid her off the books. Sometimes when I arrived, the lessons were just concluding, at which time a man would pay her cash. If JPL were to have hired a real Russian scientist familiar with all the scientific terminology, it would have been necessary for them to pay much more than the pocket change they were giving her.

After several months of dating, she told me her visa would be expiring soon and she would have to return to Russia. I asked her to marry me, but she declined because she said that she had a difficult disposition. I just kept discussing it with her and she finally agreed, but told me she didn't want a traditional religious ceremony, so I asked my friend Zeke to officiate for us. He was the Lutheran minister that I had pulled the prank on about blessing the rubber dummy in the casket. His church was in Santa Monica, and he performed our ceremony with Ron acting as my best man for the second time. As we were leaving the church, the first thing Olga wanted to do was to be taken to Westwood Village to see Marilyn Monroe's crypt, where there was a vase always filled with fresh flowers.

Olga was genuinely surprised about my knowledge of Russian customs and the language. One of my favorite Russian expressions translates to "Don't draw devils on a blackboard." That meant it was bad karma to dwell on negative thoughts. Olga had a short fuse and sometimes came

Olga at Marilyn Monroe's crypt in Westwood Village.

on strong, at which time I told her, "You should change your name to Katyusha," which was the dreaded Russian multiple rocket launcher. Those feared weapons produced an other-worldly screeching sound as they launched their munitions in rapid succession during World War II. On another occasion, she called me from her cell phone and was complaining loudly about something. I told her to stop acting like Ivan Grozny, which is Russian for "Ivan the Terrible," and she got a big laugh out of that.

During my attempt to help Olga get her green card, it became obvious that the Immigration and Naturalization Service (INS) had its head up its you-know-what. We submitted our forms and a copy of our marriage license, as well as photos from our wedding and honeymoon in Hawaii, but we didn't receive any correspondence in turn. Following numerous calls, it seemed the INS would not even let me speak to someone without an appointment, which I could only obtain through a written request. After I followed their instructions, they sent a letter to my house addressed to her maiden name, Olga Chernychova, which absolutely infuriated me. After all of the supporting documentation that was sent to them, they wouldn't even address the letter in her married name.

At our first meeting with the INS, the Korean interviewer spoke to us in broken English with a very heavy accent, which made it difficult to understand what he was saying. He finally got around to asking the question he seemed most curious about—our ages. I told him that I was 52 and Olga was 27, at which point he picked up his pen and jotted a note in Olga's file. What difference did our ages make if we chose to get married? When my mother and father were married, he was 42 and she was 17, and they were together for more than thirty years until his death. So it was exactly as that famous philosopher Hank Williams Jr. once sang, "It's just an old family tradition."

Even before we were married, it was clear that Olga had some serious health problems. We went from one specialist to another and they ran multiple tests with no conclusive results. The answer finally came one evening on *60 Minutes*, which started with a scene of Ed Bradley wearing a white radiation suit, proclaiming that he was speaking from the most dangerous place on earth. He said he was in Semipalatinsk, Kazakhstan, close to Mongolia. According to Bradley, the Russian government had been experimenting on the people of this area to see what the long-term effects of radiation would have on the human body. It wasn't long before they got their answer, as many babies were born with birth defects.

After the show ended I asked Olga if she had ever heard of Semipalatinsk. She responded that she knew exactly where it was, so I asked her how she knew. She said that she was born in Ust-Kamenogorsk, just forty miles away, adding that everyone there had been aware of the Soviet nuclear tests being conducted. Olga told me that her mother's doctor discovered that she was suffering from radiation exposure and told Olga's father that he should get her out of the area as soon as possible. That's why they moved to Moscow.

It turned out that Olga was right about her disposition because one day I returned home and was shocked to find that she had moved out and rented an apartment in North Hollywood. We continued to see each other and I paid all of her expenses, hoping she would reconsider her decision to live alone. I spent many nights at her apartment, which made it much the same as our living together. When her father arrived from Moscow for a visit, he slept on the couch in her living room. One night, while she was translating for her father, something came up that surprised us both. It was when she informed her father that he was slightly younger than me.

Losing Kathy made me realize the extent to which someone can give their heart and soul to another, but my feelings for Olga were never the same. In fact, my motivation was well exemplified in the lyrics of a Kenny Rogers song that begins, "Show me a bar with a good lookin' woman, then just get out of my way." It goes on to say, "Somethin's got a hold of me, it's cheap but it ain't free," and ends with a realistic picture of my frame of mind at the time: "Love or somethin' damn near like it's got a hold on me." Looking back on that fateful day I first saw Olga with her pure Russian beauty, I'm sure I had an immediate Pavlovian reaction. The funny thing is I don't remember drooling.

In retrospect, my thirty-year love affair with Kathy could have never been replaced by anyone on this earth, because my first taste of Russia still lingers in my heart and on my tongue.

Olga at 25.

53

Some Memories Never Die

It seems that the more time that passes since Marilyn Monroe's death, the more interest there is in her story. Whenever someone was conducting research for a book or documentary about her death, they usually contacted Westwood Village, which had my permission to give out my name and number. All these years later, reporters still contact me to ask questions or request a formal interview. The question that comes up most often is "Do you think she committed suicide or do you think she was murdered?" I have always felt that she was murdered, but we will probably never know.

An attorney in London, making a documentary about Marilyn for the BBC, contacted me for an interview. When he arrived in Los Angeles, he came to the mortuary and we talked for over an hour. At the end of the interview his last question was whether I thought she was murdered. I turned the tables and asked him the same question. He admitted that when he had originally been asked to investigate her death for this documentary, he considered it nothing more than a Hollywood fluff piece. He decided to take the assignment strictly for the money and a chance to do some traveling with all expenses paid, but said that now he was confident that she had been murdered and by what means. He had changed his opinion about the manner of death only after interviewing over eighty people.

He stated that it was possible that an overdose had been administered to her by means of a drug-laced enema. Now, the obvious question was, why wouldn't she have fought her attackers? Many in-depth interviews established the fact that she had a history of overmedicating herself with sleeping pills and chloral hydrate, the infamous Mickey Finn. Once she was in a drug-induced stupor she wouldn't have been able to fight back. The cause of death from barbiturate poisoning is actually asphyxiation because the drug causes the diaphragm's involuntary movement to cease, which halts respiration.

I remember seeing Dr. Noguchi's pathology report that noted a great deal of barbiturate residue in her intestines, which had become discolored and inflamed. A drug-laced enema would explain that condition. If she had taken the drug orally in a large enough dose to kill her, it would have killed her before it had time to reach her lower intestines. There should have been more barbiturate residue still in her stomach, and there wasn't, according to Noguchi. A documentary produced four decades after her death made a flawed attempt to address this question. The filmmakers took a beaker of water, added some powder and placed a rotating paddle into the liquid to stir it, but a person lying motionless on a bed has no such agitation. That wasn't a valid comparison by any standard.

In 2005, John Miner, who was key in our investigation, announced he also felt that Marilyn had been murdered. It took him over forty years to admit that, but he explained that he had sworn to certain parties he would never reveal his conclusion. There is no question that Marilyn's death and the subsequent investigation became the most politically motivated case in the twentieth century because of her well-known involvement with John and Robert Kennedy. Miner must have been under a great deal of pressure to keep quiet.

Milton Greene was one of the photographers who took many photos of Marilyn, but he had also been instrumental in helping her break her 1951 contract with Fox Studios. Milton convinced her that a star of her magnitude should be making much more than what her contract stipulated. Greene had entered her life at a time when she was especially vulnerable. When she finally won the legal battle, she started Marilyn Monroe Productions as its president, with Milton Greene as its vice president.

One of Greene's sons, Anthony, made a documentary about Marilyn called *Life After Death*. Anthony's office called and asked me to take part, which I did. Many years later I came upon an HBO program in progress and saw myself talking about Marilyn. It really caught me off-guard because they had never sent me a copy of the documentary, as they promised.

Before her death, Joe DiMaggio had purchased crypts at Westwood Village, one directly above the one for Marilyn and another kitty-corner to hers. When DiMaggio and Marilyn divorced in 1954, DiMaggio sold the two crypts to a friend of his, Richard Poncher. When Poncher lay dying in 1986 at age 81, he asked his wife, Elsie, for a final wish. He made her promise that she would put him facing down in the casket directly above Marilyn. So there lay Poncher for two and half decades, his wish fulfilled by his wife when she asked the funeral director to turn him over after everyone had exited the chapel. But while *Playboy* publisher Hugh Hefner secured an eternal space beside Marilyn in 1992 for $75,000, it seems that Poncher's eternal sleep may be disrupted. Elsie was trying to sell the crypt where her husband was entombed and planned to move him to the adjacent crypt intended for herself, which she doesn't need since her wish is to be cremated.

Interestingly, much of the fascination with Marilyn Monroe originates from abroad, as half of the calls that have come in over the years have been from other countries. In one such call, a German lady asked me to verify a Marilyn photograph. I knew before she even told me what photograph she was referring to. It was in Anthony Summers's book about Marilyn called *Goddess: The Secret Lives of Marilyn Monroe*. The picture was taken at the coroner's office of her lying on a morgue table. You can clearly see her swollen and wrinkled neck and the discoloration of her face that I remember well from the Westwood Village prep room. Amazingly, Theodore Curphey had instructed the coroner's office personnel that no photos of Marilyn were to be taken, presumably to avoid the possibility of the photo leaking out. However, the Los Angeles Police Department did take photos of her there as part of their investigation.

All coroners' offices have one or more people whose job is to document the dead with photos. In Thomas Noguchi's best-selling book *Coroner*, he expresses appreciation of his faithful forensic photographer Bill Lystrup, who had been one of our limo drivers for years before he went to work for the coroner's office. Photographs of the dead are never intended for distribution, but just like my experience at Westwood Village, there are often large monetary incentives offered to anyone who can procure such a photo for publication.

The only thing strange about the call from Germany was that this was many years after *Goddess* was published. The caller stated that they were going to use the photo in a German magazine called *TV-Movie*, but they couldn't use it unless someone who had seen her as she appeared in this photo could verify it. Even with my assurances that the photo was authentic, they wouldn't use it unless it was shown to me and acknowledged as being genuine. Two weeks later a gentleman arrived at the mortuary with the photo and got my confirmation.

The following month they called me again, saying the magazine had sold out in two days and caused a firestorm of controversy. Now they were requesting an extensive interview with a picture of me holding the photo in front of our mortuary. They offered me a fee of $500 because it was going to take the better part of a day. When it was over they sent me a check for something in the neighborhood of about $350, because that's what 500 deutsche marks converted to in U.S. dollars. Silly me for not remembering they had offered to pay me in a foreign currency.

Later, a representative of *Der Spiegel* magazine in Germany contacted me about an interview for their annual issue called *Spiegel Special*. He and his photographer accompanied me to cemeteries with celebrities' graves, like Holy Cross Cemetery, where Bing Crosby and Gary Cooper are buried. They seemed especially interested in being able to stand at the grave of Béla Lugosi, or Count Dracula, if you prefer. Afterward, we went to Forest Lawn to visit the mausoleum where Clark Gable and David O. Selznick are entombed.

I also did an interview for a Japanese magazine that photographed all of my Marilyn memorabilia, including her lock of hair, falsies, and the memorial folder from her funeral. One of our employees from the '60s named Drake Jasso, who knew I owned these items, called me up one day and wanted to know if I was interested in doing a deal with my memorabilia collection. Drake, now a vintage magazine dealer, had about forty copies of the first *Playboy* magazine, which featured Marilyn. Just being the number one issue made them extremely collectible, but Marilyn's appearance made them even more valuable. A man named Ed Pitts contacted him about buying a copy, but apparently he was not prepared to spend $5,000 for a pristine one.

During their conversation, Drake mentioned that his former employer had spent three days working on her funeral and that I had three or four rare items. Ed asked Drake if he would set up a meeting with the three of us to talk about a trade of some kind. He claimed that he had her original 1951 Fox contract, which was the first time she used the stage name Marilyn Monroe—derived from her mother's maiden name, Monroe—instead of Norma Jean Baker. This was a seven-year step-up contract that began her salary at $500 a week and each year thereafter bumped it up in increments of $250. By the fifth year of the contract, the studio was making millions from her films.

Drake called and said we could all meet at a restaurant in Studio City that was closed to the public for the day because of a book signing. In exchange for the contract, Ed wanted the lock of hair, the memorial folder, and $5,000 in cash. I didn't want to invest any cash in the trade, so I took Drake aside and asked if he would be willing to give him a primo copy of *Playboy* instead. When we made the offer, Ed agreed to the deal but then began expressing some concern about the authenticity of the lock of hair. I told him to call Westwood Village to confirm my presence throughout her preparation and service.

As he pondered his decision, a large crowd gathered to purchase books and have the author sign them. Since Ed had chosen our meeting place, Drake asked if he knew what book was being sold that day. Ed said that an award-winning *Time-Life* photographer, Leigh Wiener, had published a book on the thirtieth anniversary of Marilyn's death. He said the book had photos Leigh had taken at her home, the coroner's office, and the cemetery. "Well why didn't you say that in the first place?" Leigh's book would have to have some photos with Ron and me because we were both were pallbearers and also assigned tasks to perform concerning all aspects of the funeral. The probability of these events coinciding without my knowledge was absolutely stunning.

We asked a hostess to bring us a copy of the book, which was called *Marilyn: A Hollywood Farewell*. Sure enough, there were a number of photos that showed us both. The hostess overheard me pointing out our pictures and asked if she could tell Leigh. We were then introduced, and he asked me to sit down so we could talk. At least a dozen people were lined up to purchase his book, but he just kept talking to me in spite of them.

Leigh told me he would make me a couple of 8" x 10" glossies from his original negatives, because they would show more detail than the photographs in the book. He was also delighted when I purchased two copies at $90 each. He signed both but wrote a special dedication in one expressly for me. It read, "This is a special book for Allan L. Abbott. You are in this book. It is a pleasure to share this strange and sad experience with you— separated by so much time—I hope you find meaning and pleasure in truth from these photographs and words. My very best, Leigh A. Wiener, 14 November 1991."

About a week later, Leigh called to say that the photos were ready and gave me his address. Surprisingly, he lived only a mile from me just off Mulholland Drive. After receiving the photos, I asked him how he was planning to market his books. He told me that he had scheduled book signings at a number of major cities, but he could not attend them because he had just gotten out of the hospital and was too sick to travel. I asked him if he had made arrangements to have them sold in bookstores, and he said he had no interest in people pawing through a sample copy out of curiosity or tearing out a page. He explained that the book represented a high point in his career and was not an issue of money. Only 500 copies were printed, a quarter of which he had signed.

There was no question in my mind that funeral directors were the perfect customers for the book, because Marilyn's was the funeral of the century. I offered to market it through *Mortuary Management* if Leigh would allow me exclusive distribution rights. He was willing to consider my proposal, pending a review of our magazine. After I showed him several copies the next day, he agreed and my ad started the following month. The books sold briskly.

When my supply ran low, I made an unannounced stop at Leigh's house, which was on my way home. His wife, Joyce, answered the door and said Leigh was unavailable, but when he heard my voice he hollered, "Allan, is that you?" Leigh was on a massage table in his living room, receiving physical therapy. He had been fighting the government for years to get them to pay for his medical expenses.

Leigh was one of the photographers present at the Trinity atomic bomb test in Alamogordo, New Mexico, only seven miles from ground zero. Many people present at the test claimed they became sick due to their proximity to the radiation, and some had died prematurely. The doctors Leigh had consulted with stated that most of the people they had seen with this rare blood disease had been exposed to high levels of radiation. Three days after my stop at his house, Drake called me to say that he had seen Leigh's obituary in the newspaper that day. I called his wife to offer my condolences and found that the funeral service was going to be private, for family only.

After my supply of books was gone, I called Joyce to see if she would furnish the remaining copies to me. The IRS had paid her a visit, explaining that she would be required to hire an expert to appraise everything that Leigh's business owned, including all of his cameras, negatives, and published books. In light of this overwhelming task, she was no longer willing to sell me any more books. Sadly, our subscribers continued to write in for many months, requesting copies.

Before his death, I had asked Leigh how he had managed to photograph the interior of the coroner's office, since they had refused requests from all other photographers. He had gotten the name of the officer who had turned him down the first day, and asked if he could check back the following day to see if there was any possible way to document the event. The deputy told him that he would be off the following day but assured Leigh that the policy had no exceptions.

Leigh went out and purchased a bottle of very expensive Scotch whisky and went to the coroner's office the following day, asking to see his "friend of many years." He was told that it was his friend's day off, so he explained to the deputies on duty that he had just flown in from New York and brought this expensive Scotch to share with him because they hadn't seen each other for many years. Leigh told them he had to fly back to New York the next morning, but it would be a shame to have to leave without anyone enjoying a drink with him. He proposed drinking it in friendship with the two guards. After a few drinks and a lot of conversation, he asked if he could take their pictures in front of the refrigerator doors, one of which held Marilyn's body, as a personal keepsake. They agreed, and he got the shots for his book that no one else had been able to acquire. Leigh also said that he had taken a picture of Marilyn that day but that he would never allow it to be published.

At a much later time, I decided to give Joyce a call just to see how she was doing. What once was Leigh's home phone was answered by an unfamiliar voice on a message referring to the Wiener Group. The next day, Devik Wiener called and informed me that he was Leigh's son. He recognized my name and knew about my selling his dad's book, for which he now owned the rights. The timing was perfect because he had just been awarded his father's intellectual material in court, following a legal battle with his stepmother. He agreed for me to continue selling them again until they were all gone.

The only books available now are secondhand copies that change hands on eBay for hundreds of dollars. One mint-condition, signed copy was purchased for $1,200 by a young man in San Francisco. He called and asked if he could drive the two hours to my home to have me also sign his copy, which I did.

Drake and I shared ownership of the original 1951 Fox contract for years and eventually sold it, along with my other personal items from her funeral, to a well-established collector in Corona, California, who specialized in Marilyn memorabilia. He later consigned these items to an auction house in New York and everything went fast. A plastic envelope of five or six hairs fetched $2,000 each. In preparation for the sale of the falsies at the auction, someone had done a beautiful job of mounting them in a shadow box with a black lacquer frame and glass. A prospective buyer saw my signed letter of provenance on our company letterhead that was mounted inside the shadow box. He wanted me to authenticate the falsies because he was about to spend a great deal of money for them.

I examined a photo, but the falsies looked too perfectly round and I could not see the seam for the material stitched on the back. This led me to believe that they may not be the originals. I told him the photo was inconclusive, so he had the shadow box shipped to me for closer inspection. When it arrived I could see that matting covered the sides of

Marilyn Monroe shadow box, featuring the falsies she used to accentuate her figure.

the falsies, so I carefully raised an edge, revealing the ragged edges and stitching. That satisfied me that they were genuine.

The media buzz from the auction generated a number of newspaper articles. Immediately after that, a call came in from the show *Hard Copy* in New York. The first question the lady asked me was "Why would Marilyn Monroe have used falsies?" I explained that her makeup man, Whitey Snyder, had told me that at 36 she felt that her breasts were starting to show the effects of gravity and that wearing falsies between her bra and sweater produced the effect that she wanted because she enjoyed being provocative.

She then asked about me doing an on-camera interview. I had no interest in traveling to New York, but she said they would be happy to come to my home. She had prepared a number of questions but mostly wanted me to discuss Marilyn's reason for using falsies. My explanation was very clear, but not too explicit, only describing the definition created in her tight sweaters by wearing them. She asked the question again, with some slight nuances, and each time my response was that she wanted to give the impression that she wasn't wearing a bra.

As I walked her out to their van in my driveway, the interviewer even commented that I had not used the "N" word, as she put it. Here I was going to be on national television and she was trying to get me to say the word "nipples," but she wouldn't say the word herself, even in our private conversation. A sure sign of nipple-phobia.

More recently I received a call from a man named Mark Bellinghaus, a collector and avid Marilyn enthusiast. He informed me that the *Queen Mary* in Long Beach Harbor was having a showing of a large number of Marilyn's personal effects, and a woman named June DiMaggio had arranged with some shady promoters to sell alleged Marilyn memorabilia. She claimed that she was the niece of Joe DiMaggio, but, strangely, no one seemed to know who she was. Furthermore, she was never able to produce a single photograph of herself with Marilyn. Mark informed the media that the whole premise of her claims consisted of lies. None of them seemed interested in exposing this fraud, so he contacted me for further confirmation.

June claimed she drove in the car with Joe when he left the cemetery the day of the funeral, but a very clear photograph in Leigh's book shows Joe being driven away and no woman is in the car. The book also had dozens of other pictures taken that day and is a clear photographic record that June was never even at the funeral. She made preposterous claims that she cooked Marilyn dinner the night she died and that her mother was talking to Marilyn on the phone at the moment she was being murdered. After Mark started calling the newspapers and telling them this woman was a fake, some items were removed from the exhibit.

Drake called one day to inform me that the Marilyn shadow box was back on the market. We had both seen how such collectible items continued to rise in value, so we partnered together to acquire it. In 2012, on the 50th anniversary of Marilyn's death, we received a considerable offer for the box, which we turned down, knowing that it would be worth more to the right person. In 2011, Marilyn Monroe's estate took in over $70 million. Today, she is still one of the most recognized women in history.

54

Moving On

Living in LA made my involvement in so many different ventures possible. Many large cities have funeral livery companies, but only in LA, because of its proximity to Hollywood, could I have ventured into so many aspects of the entertainment industry, with celebrity limo drives and funeral car and prop rentals for movies and TV shows. And Los Angeles' proximity to the ocean enabled us to offer our *Tribute* scattering services to mortuaries throughout the country. The Los Angeles Harbor between San Pedro and Long Beach is the busiest harbor in the world, receiving 45 percent of all freight arriving in America. It was also the ideal place for me to ship containers of hearses to countries all over the world.

In spite of its many benefits, life in LA was no longer remotely as it was when I was growing up there. Crime had become rampant, traffic congestion was miserable, and the air quality was dreadful. After Mischa finished college, he moved into the Pebble Beach condo that I purchased after selling the house there. He had to get away from the smog that was causing great difficulty with his asthma. Once Greg graduated from college, I was planning for us to make the move to the Monterey Peninsula as well. That would be the fulfillment of my dream since visiting the area for the first time in 1953.

Now all that was needed was to talk Ron into selling the business. Ron wasn't keen on moving, and he told me repeatedly that there was nowhere else he would rather live. However, when I talked him into visiting Marin County, on the north end of the Golden Gate Bridge, he fell in love with the area and purchased a home in Tiburon.

After that, we directed our attention to things like finding a buyer for the mortuary and selling the movie cars and props as well as my funeral car exporting business. I sold all the props to three prop houses in LA. Meanwhile, one of our funeral counselors, Enoch Glascock, made an offer to buy the mortuary. After we worked out the deal, there were only two things left to do—sell my house and find a new home for *Mortuary Management*, which we would continue to publish. Enoch allowed Greg and me to rent the upstairs office at the mortuary where the magazine had been operating since we moved there.

Enoch was a shrewd businessman and had a dry sense of humor. He was always joking around. One day right after Halloween, Greg walked into the administrative area of the mortuary, where everyone sat in cubicles, to use the copy machine. As Enoch stood near Greg, he used the old line, "Didn't anyone tell you that you could take your mask off now?" After a moment of silence, Greg responded, "But it's Prince Charming, don't you like him?" Everyone listening to the exchange from behind their divider said, in unison, "Ooooh." Enoch was speechless, as he knew he had been out-joked.

As we tied up the loose ends of our business interests, the activities that had consumed every minute of my day were winding down rapidly. Enoch came upstairs one day and said he had just received a call from the media inquiring about whether or not we owned a Ziegler Transfer Case, a metal box the size of a casket with an airtight rubber seal. This inquiry was the result of a widely covered news item about the strange and inexplicable case of Gloria Ramirez, who died in the emergency ward of a hospital in Riverside and came to be known as the "toxic lady." While she was still being treated in the ER, a nurse fell ill after administering oxygen and drawing a blood sample from her. Shortly thereafter, other staff members, including a doctor, also complained of nausea and light-headedness. Some scientists started to speculate about a mysterious chemical reaction, but others wrote it off as some sort of mass hysteria.

Because of the speculation that harmful fumes emitted from the patient, officials placed her body in a Ziegler Transfer Case, about which the media wanted to learn more. They contacted Enoch for more information after they found out he had one, but he didn't want to do an on-camera interview, so he referred them to me. A news crew was sent over to film me with the Ziegler, demonstrating what the unit looks like and how it functions. Up to this point we had used it only to pick up decomps, but the military had used similar ones by the hundreds to ship its war dead back from Vietnam to Dover, Delaware.

Although the mystery of what happened was heavily contested, one of the doctors sued the hospital to clear her name of any responsibility. After many months, a scientist at the Lawrence Livermore National Laboratory arrived at a very plausible, albeit astounding, explanation. Livermore Labs postulated that Ramirez had been taking dimethyl sulfoxide (DMSO), a solvent sometimes used as a topical home remedy for pain. The idea was that through an unusual confluence of chemical reactions, this turned into DMSO4, a poisonous gas that was used as a chemical weapon in World War I.

DMSO turned into DMSO2 in Ramirez's system as a result of administrating oxygen to her. When blood from Ramirez was drawn, the relatively sudden and sharp drop in the temperature of her blood from body temperature to the cool air of the hospital could have created the lethal compound DMSO4. Her body temperature was too high to allow creation of the compound internally, but witnesses said when Ramirez's blood was drawn, they saw crystals in the syringe, and some scientists have stated that vapors from those crystals were the source of the mystery fumes.

With Enoch now in full operation of the mortuary, he hired some extra people to help him out. One of the people whom he hired as administrative assistant was a beautiful and good-natured girl named Ingrid, who had been sent to the United States by her parents in Guatemala to get an education. Greg would see her each day as they crossed paths at work. He was obviously smitten with her and took every opportunity to engage her in conversation.

One of her tasks was getting DCs signed, and one day Greg overheard her being instructed to drive all across the vast San Fernando Valley. He knew she wasn't familiar with many of these areas so when she was about to leave, he ran downstairs and offered to accompany her as her copilot. That was the fastest I ever saw him move.

After they became friends, he started to ask her out for the evenings. At first she was quite reluctant. She knew that as soon as our home was sold we would be moving to Monterey, 350 miles away, and that perhaps this was just a fling. Greg convinced her that he was serious, so they started seeing each other on a regular basis.

When we finally moved, everyone predicted that the long-distance relationship would end, but I knew full well that it wouldn't. As soon as we had moved into a temporary rental house, Greg got his own phone line and called her faithfully every few nights. After a great deal of searching, I found a home with a panoramic view of the bay in an area called New Monterey. On the other end of town is Old Monterey, the original capital of California, dating back to 1770. We also found an office for the magazine that was down the hill from my house, just two blocks from Cannery Row, immortalized in John Steinbeck's famous novel.

Greg and Ingrid dated for two years, which involved his making the six-hour drive down to Los Angeles once a month. After getting engaged, they decided to get married in her church near downtown LA, which was only half a block from the old Abbott & Hast colonial mansion. We had often seen the worshippers standing in front of the church on Sundays, so it seemed very fitting to return to where we were located for so many years.

55

Surviving Alaska

In 1996, shortly before Greg and Ingrid got married, we went to Anchorage for the first time to visit my brother and mother, who had moved there in the late '80s. Mischa had traveled to Anchorage a few times already, so when Greg and I made plans to visit, he prepared us a list of must-see places, including Denali National Park, the Alyeska Pipeline, and Matanuska Glacier. We spent two days at Denali photographing the scenery and wildlife, including Dall sheep, wolves, and grizzly bears. On the day of our departure, we had breakfast in the little town at the entrance of the park, checked our map, and planned our return schedule.

In order to see the oil pipeline and the glacier, we would be taking a different route back toward Anchorage. Not only was the route longer, we didn't know that the road from Denali to the pipeline became a gravel road full of potholes after the first eight miles. There was one town along the way where we could stop that afternoon and have some lunch, but the washboard effect of the road slowed our progress to only twenty-five miles per hour.

Several hours later we arrived at the Matanuska Valley and spotted a panoramic overlook, so we stopped to photograph a beautiful rainbow. It had just begun to drizzle. To avoid getting my head wet, I grabbed a plastic dry-cleaning bag from the backseat and tore off a corner to use as a cap. We didn't arrive at Matanuska Glacier until about 8 P.M., but since it was staying light until 10 P.M. at that time of year, we went for it.

The glacier is not a state park, since you have to cross private property to see it. We paid our toll at the gift shop and looked at a hand-drawn map of the trail in a glass showcase, showing the route from the parking lot to the glacier's face. They would not provide a copy for liability reasons. As we approached the glacier, we saw many people going to and from the face, so we followed the path.

In my studies of geology we learned how glaciers move slowly down a valley, gouging out large amounts of moraine, which can range in size from huge boulders to coarse gravel, so it wasn't surprising to see expansive fields of this debris on top and along the sides of the ice. Unlike the other people standing along the edge taking pictures, we climbed onto the glacier and worked our way up about a mile or more. We navigated around spires of ice that looked to be about ten feet high from the nearby highway, but were actually about thirty feet tall. We were both taking photographs and got carried away by the magnificent sights.

There was a beautiful bright blue ice cave, which must have been twenty feet from floor to the ceiling. The floor had massive blocks of ice that had broken off the ceiling and landed right where we were standing, so after a few photographs we moved right along. We followed along deep ravines cut by meltwater streams that fed into crystal-clear pools and even a small lake near the center of the glacier.

We were so engrossed in this fantasyland, neither of us comprehended how far we had climbed up the glacier. Before we knew it, the sky began to darken. As we began to work our way back, every route we attempted posed some kind of hazard that prevented us from continuing. There were giant fissures, huge slabs of steeply slanted ice, and mud pits made up of dense glacial silt. For every two steps forward, we took one back, trying to get around the dead ends.

As we struggled to find a route, there was a persistent and troubling realization that we were in over our heads. Neither of us was in a panic, but we both had an unrelenting feeling that this wasn't going to turn out well. My jacket was only a windbreaker, but since our hiking was generating sufficient heat, it didn't seem that cold while we climbed up. When it got dark, it grew much colder and it became difficult to see the many hazards that lay before us. We were wet from small streams we had crossed and mud we had sunk into knee-deep. Finally, we realized that we were putting ourselves into more danger by moving in the dark, so we resolved to spend the night on the glacier.

There was a flat patch of moraine on the ice where we decided to stay until first light. We sat back to back on a large rock, but in only a few minutes we were both shivering uncontrollably. The only way we could keep from freezing was going to be marching in a circle to keep warm. The worst feeling of cold was on my face, but then I remembered the plastic bag that had kept my head dry from the rain earlier that day, which was still in my pocket.

There was just enough moonlight to see rain clouds gathering overhead, which was extremely concerning. Getting wet from rain would certainly increase our chances of becoming hypothermic. I've heard it said that you get the feeling of sleepiness when you're about to freeze to death, but sleep was the last thing on our minds. We were in continuous pain from the effect that the cold had on our muscles as they tightened. I was expecting Greg to quote Oliver Hardy and say to me, "Well here's another fine mess you've gotten us into."

After the longest night of our lives, the first sign of light never looked so good. We were slowly able to make our way off the glacier and painstakingly navigate around the mud and pools of water until we reached a tree line. We walked through the dense forest until it crossed the road, which we followed back to the parking lot. When we reached the car we found some leftover orange juice, but after we had breathed freezing air all night, it burned in our throats.

We eventually came to a small town and stopped at a McDonald's. We hadn't eaten since 3 P.M. the previous day, so a burger sounded really good. When I placed my order, they told me that they didn't start making burgers until 11 A.M. I felt like Michael Douglas's character in *Falling Down*, who encountered a similar situation after having a very bad day. Fortunately for him, he had a gun that he'd taken from his would-be robbers and used it to persuade them to fill his order. I didn't have a gun, but one can always imagine the possibilities.

We found out that not long after we got stranded, a student in a mountaineering class lost his life there. While attempting to fill a container with water, he slipped into a crevasse that carried him down a hole (called a moulin) that drains water deep into the glacier. Clearly, glaciers are both stunning and deadly places. Even though we could have died that night, Greg and I agree that this was one of the most memorable experiences we have ever had.

Greg on Alaska's Matanuska Glacier, before it became a near-death trap.

56

Just Like Old Times

When we lived in the Hollywood Hills, it was a common sight to see a celebrity out on a stroll, but in Monterey that doesn't often happen. The most notable exception is actor/director Clint Eastwood, a prominent resident of the peninsula with business interests in Carmel. He became mayor of Carmel in 1986 on his promise to support small business interests, including bringing back ice cream cone sales. The city council had banned them because tourists would discard the cones carelessly. Clint kept his promises and served his term for just $200 per month—a mere fistful of dollars. The whole event was so notable that a local band by the name of the Medflys wrote a song called "Don't Mess With the Mayor," which included the title melody from Clint's spaghetti western *The Good, the Bad and the Ugly.*

One morning, when I was running some errands at our local Carmel shopping center, a man pulled up near me and got out of his gold Mercedes. He looked very familiar, but I wasn't sure who he was because of his gray hair and beard. If my suspicion was correct, I knew his voice would be the only positive giveaway. I asked if he knew the time and he responded in his perfect British accent, "Half past nine." My next question was "Are you Patrick?" He slowly said, "Yeees." Patrick McGoohan had always been one of my favorite actors. Kathy and I especially enjoyed his starring roll in *Secret Agent* in the '60s. When I mentioned that to him, his reaction was "My God, you must have been a child when that was on." I asked him if he was just visiting, but he told me that he lived in Carmel.

In 1998, Universal Studios called our former mortuary regarding props, so they were given my number in Monterey. Universal was preparing to do an annual episode of *Columbo*. It was going to be called *Ashes to Ashes,* and Patrick McGoohan was going to play a funeral home owner. They wanted all new caskets, urns, and as much prep room equipment that could be provided, plus a small two-body refrigerator and a rolling body-lifting mechanism.

I told the set decorator that all of my props had been sold and that he should check with the three major prop houses. He said that he had already called all of them, but he wanted everything new. After some quick calculations, I gave him the bad news, which was that everything would run about $20,000. I also informed him that Universal had been a little slow to pay and that this was going to require a lot of up-front payment. He then asked, "Do you still have access to all of this type of equipment?" and of course the answer was yes. Surprisingly, he said he would send me a check that day for $10,000 to start the process moving forward.

I wouldn't be present for the required setup of much of this equipment, but a good friend of mine, Brett Minor, who had worked in his parents' mortuary for years, said he would be happy to oversee the project at the studio. He operated his own Ferno equipment repair service and was one of the most knowledgeable technicians in the field. Another friend who is a licensed embalmer, Rueben Andreatta, also agreed to spend time there, showing the carpenters and set decorators how to build an authentic looking embalming room. In the process, he became the technical advisor for the show.

Over the next few weeks, the studio called and added numerous items to their ever-growing list of props. When they told me that they were going to have a scene in which ashes would be scattered from a helicopter, I warned them of the problems with scattering ashes in a windy environment and advised them to use dust-free cat litter, which looks almost identical to cremated remains. They also requested a photograph of a crematory retort and an official mortuary brochure. I called my friends at Mountain View Mortuary in Altadena, who provided the studio with a brochure that they reproduced exactly, except with a picture of Patrick and his mortuary's name.

Brett and Rueben set up everything as it arrived. Under Rueben's direction, their carpenters build a state-of-the-art embalming room on a sound stage. One evening, Brett asked me where they had obtained the cremation retort, which was something we didn't normally furnish. When I told him that it wasn't real, he said, "Of course it's real, it even has the firebricks in the interior." The furnace wasn't real, but it looked fantastic with all the lights, gauges, an electrically operated door, and simulated firebricks.

One night Rueben called and said that I had to come to LA and see Patrick's beautiful mortuary interior, including an office with a fireplace, a good-size chapel, a separate room housing the crematory furnace, and a prep room. The idea of returning to Los Angeles didn't appeal to me, but he was absolutely insistent because they had built "the embalming room to die for." Now, how could I refuse with a description like that? Sure enough, everything looked like the real McCoy. On a table in the hallway of the mortuary set was a stack of the brochures they had made. There were over a dozen of them, so I knew they wouldn't miss just one, which ended up in my pocket.

After participating in over 300 shoots, I had never asked anyone for an autograph. The studios paid me for my professional services, not for me to act like some starstruck fan. However, this rare opportunity seemed like an exception, particularly considering my retirement from the business, so I asked Patrick to sign the brochure, which he did, right under his photograph.

In the episode, Patrick kills a reporter, played by Rue McClanahan, who had accused him of stealing a diamond necklace from a wealthy woman's body. When it came time to place her body into the refrigerator, they used a stunt double for McClanahan. However, it was so upsetting to the stuntwoman to be in such a claustrophobic dark space that when they opened the door and let her out she threw up.

Following the production, Rueben took over the props to continue with the rental business. One day he called and asked if he could drive up to pay me a visit. When he arrived, he presented me with a script for the pilot on an upcoming HBO series called *Six Feet Under*. He was going to be furnishing all of the props for it. Although he had been a licensed embalmer for many years, he admitted that he didn't know much about running a mortuary, so the reason for showing me the script was to check it for technical accuracy. After the series began, they also contacted Greg to get some copies of *Mortuary Management* that they could use as props around the fictitious Fisher & Sons Funeral Home.

For quite a while, Rueben and I would have hour-long conversations about the business and many of my experiences. As many people had done before him, he kept telling me, "You've got to write a book." Writing is not my forte, and without a computer the thought of spending hundreds of hours compiling an autobiography, let alone trying to remember everything that happened over four decades, seemed daunting.

Nevertheless, many people continued to encourage me, so I started scribbling my recollections on paper. It was going to require a lot of assistance from Greg along the way, with his years of editing experience. When he started reading the details of my experiences, he told me that after having been involved in so many notable events, "You were like the Forrest Gump of the funeral industry."

57

Screwed by the Government

I decided to invest in some rental property in Monterey. Rather than going into debt, it seemed wiser to think of a way of raising some additional capital. After selling a valuable oil painting by Russian seascape artist Eugene Garin, the only other possession of great value remaining was my collection of ivory sperm whale teeth with beautiful scrimshaw. Kathy and I started our collection on a visit to Hawaii in the late '60s, when almost every shop was selling them. It was legal to do so because the Hawaiian Islands had been heavily involved in the whaling industry at the turn of the nineteenth century, and they considered this part of their heritage.

Seeking guidance on selling scrimshaw, I placed a call to the National Oceanic and Atmospheric Administration (NOAA). They said the only way you could legally buy or sell this type of ivory was from one private collector to another, which was always my intention. After Greg put a notice on the Internet, responses began coming in. I always made it a point to explain that these teeth were collected at a time and in a place that was legal.

One of the callers started out by saying he was calling me from "rainy Oregon," which sounded rather strange and was an unusual way to start a conversation. He stated that he was planning to visit a friend in Monterey and asked if it would be possible for him to drop by to see my collection. When he arrived, he asked permission to take pictures of the pieces for further consideration. We talked awhile, and he said he would call me when he decided what he wanted to purchase.

Within a week he contacted me to say that he wanted to purchase a certain tooth, adding that he would be back down to Monterey in a few weeks. The night before he was to arrive, he called and said that he couldn't get time off work, so he asked if his friend in Monterey could pick up the one he had chosen and pay me for it. Once the purchase was made, his friend asked me to mail it to him, which I did. Shortly after he received the tooth he called me again and said that he wanted an additional piece, which he would pick up personally.

When that day arrived there was a knock on my door, but instead of him, there was his friend, accompanied by two police officers. They served me with a search warrant and asked if there were any firearms in the house. None of this made sense until they confiscated all the pieces that he had photographed for the alleged offense of selling a whale's tooth across state lines, which turned out to be unlawful. It's too bad that when I first called, NOAA didn't inform me of that fact. It dawned on me that they asked about guns because some people would get so incensed by having this done to them that they would resort to violence.

It turns out that the caller was actually agent Thomas Gaffney with the NOAA. They informed me that my hearing had been scheduled in Oregon, even though the transaction took place in California. I was then told that a response had to be submitted within thirty days. In my entire life, I've never heard of a case where the federal government responded to anything within thirty days. The attorney I hired said that he would handle the paperwork expeditiously in order to appeal my case, but explained that he didn't think I would ever get the collection back because NOAA had a legal department with the capacity to outspend me until I gave up.

The only response we received was to inform me that my attorney's letter had arrived two days late so there would be no further appeal, although they failed to produce any evidence that the paperwork was in fact late. The judge who signed the search warrant told me she heard a conversation taped by the NOAA indicating there was probable cause, even though the recording was only the agent's end of the conversation.

I believe that NOAA was only acting in response to a series of lies from agent Gaffney. He had obviously manipulated the case to make a name for himself at the agency. At the time Gaffney purchased the whale's tooth I was unaware that it was illegal to mail it, and he was counting on this fact.

In criminal law, entrapment is when a law enforcement agent persuades a person to commit an offense the person would otherwise have been unlikely to commit. Possibly the highest-profile case involved auto executive John DeLorean, who was contacted by undercover federal agents and enticed into drug trafficking in an attempt to raise funds for his faltering car company. He successfully defended himself against the charges, showing that his involvement was a result of entrapment.

261

During the discovery process we received recordings of my conversations with the agent over the phone and in person that were made illegally, without my knowledge or permission. From what I was able to deduce, Gaffney had not recorded our initial conversation at all because he did not have a warrant. However, he knew that a tape of only his end of the conversation was legal and would help prove to a judge that there was probable cause, so he simply fabricated a new tape after the fact. When they provided my attorney with a copy, the immediate giveaway that this was a bogus tape was his opening line: "I'm calling you from su . . . rainy Oregon." It was obvious that he had almost said "sunny" and then quickly corrected himself. Amazingly, he didn't even start a new recording to correct his stupid blunder!

We also reviewed a copy of the tape made at my home. It had a continuous background noise that made it difficult to hear what was being said. The noise was a deliberate attempt to reduce the listener's ability to hear it clearly. Gaffney had created the interference by deliberately running his fingernail over the microphone's metal mesh. You could hear the sound of his fingernail running across the mike repeatedly, with a slight pause each time he lifted his finger and stroked it again.

According to my attorney, a grand jury indictment is never issued if the only thing they hear is the law enforcement's side of a taped conversation. However, the only way to pursue the case would have been to waste another $10,000 in attorney fees. To add insult to injury, NOAA's fine for mailing the original tooth was more than what they had they paid me for it. According to their own research, they determined the collection they confiscated from me was worth $80,000.

I also faced some dreadful dealings with the federal government in my efforts to get Olga's green card. After months of pestering them with letters, we finally got a second meeting, which was a disaster. At the conclusion, they told us that she would have to start her case all over again, with a medical report, fingerprints, photographs and a revocation of her work permit. This took place during a time when Congress had gone on the record stating that the INS was the worst-run division of the entire federal government.

During this second meeting, we were told that the setback had come about because of our failure to attend a previous meeting in Los Angeles. We were shown a dated copy of the notification, which had been mailed to my former home in Los Angeles, and told that it was our responsibility to have notified them of our change of address. Fortunately, I had my file containing every document regarding her case. My records included a certified mail return postcard showing that they had been notified of our change of address, which was signed and dated before the meeting notification letter was sent to the wrong address.

At a third meeting Olga informed them that we were no longer married, so they said she would have to start a case over again on her own. I urged her to file a Freedom of Information Act (FOIA) request for her entire INS file. I'm sure the government hates this law. After Olga had struggled with the problem for many years, her Russian friends were telling her that I must have had something to do with it. Shortly after the FOIA request was sent, she received a call telling her to come in for a meeting in LA. She was instructed to have me present, even though there was absolutely no provision for an appearance by someone who had no "status" in the case, since we were no longer married.

After I drove from Monterey the previous day, we appeared together before an interviewer. At the end of the interview the woman gave Olga her green card. I told her about Olga's suspicion that I was hindering her case. She looked at Olga and said that after having reviewed her file for an hour and a half, she had never seen more impassioned letters from a husband, let alone from an ex-husband. That made my whole trip worthwhile. Olga never did receive a copy of her INS file, but at least she had her resident status and eventually got her American citizenship.

58

An Odyssey to Remember

A recent opportunity to take a return trip to LA gave me a chance to reflect on some of our experiences there. I had received a call the week prior with a request to be interviewed about Marilyn Monroe. Having arrived in town a bit early, I took the opportunity to wander through Westwood Village Cemetery. I visited Natalie Wood's grave. To my amazement, it was decorated with arrangements of fresh flowers and a balloon. Someone had also placed a birthday card there, which was addressed to her in loving memory and was signed with only the name Tom. All these years later, she is still being remembered.

Judging from our half-century involvement in the funeral profession, I see how people's attitudes have broadened about death and funerals. In 2005, a book called *Celebrity Death Certificates* was sent to me. The creator, Mike Steen, knew me from about thirty-five years earlier, when he was working in the industry. Mike then produced two more books covering hundreds of other famous people's DCs.

Looking through these books, I was surprised to realize that we had provided the equipment for so many of the listed funerals. Most were for celebrities who had died during the mid-'60s and early '70s, like Marilyn Monroe, Clark Gable, Gary Cooper, Mario Lanza, Jack Warner, and Jimmy Durante. Others included Ernie Kovacs, Jeffrey Hunter, Jack Benny, Karen Carpenter, and Natalie Wood. The only celebrity whom we served directly at our mortuary was the swimming and film star Esther Williams, when her husband, Fernando Lamas, died and we handled the cremation. We also provided services for a musician killed in a car crash on Laurel Canyon Boulevard. Luther Vandross came in personally to make the funeral arrangements.

One night, just as it was time to turn off the TV, my compulsion to channel-surf won out. As I flipped through the channels, a familiar face stopped me in my tracks. On the screen was Carol Vitale, a former

Playboy Playmate turned broadcaster who had interviewed me several years earlier on her *Carol Vitale Show*. The instant she appeared on the screen she said, "The most interesting person I ever interviewed was Allan Abbott, the funeral director to the stars." Carol was talking to Joe Franklin, the famous East Coast interviewer who was familiar to me because his show was syndicated in Los Angeles. The improbability of turning to the channel at the exact second she made that statement was absolutely uncanny.

Looking back, I find it hard to believe that two friends could become involved in such a variety of unusual endeavors for half a century. Back in 1958, when we accepted the offer from Utter-McKinley to handle all their DC work, we were already similarly serving the three Jewish-owned mortuaries. They referred to my job as "schlepping" death certificates all over town on my motorcycle. That word wasn't in my vocabulary, but was an obvious reference to the tedious job of running from place to place. While I was watching a documentary about World War II recently, the narrator said the Germans were schlepping their large artillery pieces from one area to another. It was time to consult the dictionary to confirm the definition. It's a Yiddish word that was adopted by other languages, meaning to move things around, but the definition contained another, rather negative, connotation. The example given was a person who would carry around an umbrella on a sunny day. That's just great! Because of my willingness to risk life and limb in traffic daily, the inference was that only a total dork would do this. Now I'm really insulted.

We witnessed many major changes take place in the funeral industry over the half century since we began, the most significant of which were the trends toward cremation and cost reduction. It reached a point by the late '90s that cremation represented the vast majority of services in metropolitan areas, particularly on the West Coast. We saw the writing on the wall early and embraced cremation through our scattering services. Price consciousness became so commonplace that Costco and Walmart began selling caskets and urns through their websites, or small displays in their stores.

When funeral directors realized how much traditional burials were declining, many began to furnish beautiful and unique cremation urns that could be almost as expensive as caskets. A company called LifeGem even began offering to take a small portion of the cremated remains and turn them into a man-made diamond. Another enhancement in cremation included new methods of scattering in some very creative and unusual ways. One company offered to pack a portion of a hunter's ashes into shotgun shells so a loved one could blast them into the woods. Another company, named Celestis, began offering the launching of cremated remains into space. The company's maiden launch in April 1997 included ashes from *Star Trek*'s Gene Roddenberry, destined for Earth orbit.

In the movie *The Big Lebowski*, there is a very comical portrayal of two friends' efforts to keep their funeral costs down. When a good friend of Jeff Bridges and John Goodman dies, they decide to have him cremated. While they are seated in the arrangement office, the funeral director explains that the ashes must be placed in a "suitable receptacle" and that the urns they have in their display area range in price from a few hundred to a few thousand dollars. After Bridges and Goodman quickly head over to a grocery store, the next scene shows them leaving the mortuary with a five-pound coffee can that was emptied out to fill with their friend's ashes.

The characters then take a short trip to the coast, where they stand on a rocky cliff overlooking the ocean, preparing to scatter the cremains. These places are always windy, but there was no expectation on my part that they were going to portray this realistically. Goodman recites a fairly nonsensical eulogy about their friend, which irritates Bridges, standing several feet behind him. When Goodman finally pops the lid off the can and ejects the ashes, the wind picks them up, blowing them completely past him and hitting Bridges directly in the face. I busted out laughing so hard that tears were coming out of my eyes. For once they got it right.

By 2000, the industry had undergone major transitions and some of them began to have a significant impact on our publication business. The bread and butter of *Mortuary Management*'s revenue came from advertisers. In the '80s and '90s, the consolidators had all advertised aggressively, each enticing independent owners to sell to their conglomeration, while a bidding war often ensued that rose funeral home values to unrealistic levels. By the late '90s, it was clear that the earlier estimates of demographic explosion from Baby Boomer deaths were not translating into lucrative profits because of the transition to less expensive funeral choices.

Then a final straw broke the conglomerate's collective back. The Loewen Group of Canada, the second largest of the funeral companies, was sued after purchasing a family chain of businesses and allegedly violating its agreement with them to retain their services for pre-need funeral coverage. Loewen not only lost the suit but was hit with a massive punitive damages judgment. The funeral company stocks dropped into the single digits, which was a sad outcome for the sellers who had accepted mostly stock in exchange for their life's work in the family business. Loewen later went into bankruptcy and the various conglomerates' ads were never to be seen again.

Greg had been with Abbott & Hast Publications since the mid-'80s and had taken over management of the company in 1994. He had seen us through choppy waters before, but by 2005, changes in the industry and the economy brought many businesses some very thin margins. In 2007, Greg and Ron decided to move the company to Michigan, where our art director was located and where the cost of labor was much less. Since Greg and Ingrid intended to stay in Monterey, they discontinued their service with the publications and transitioned into property management, a field they had already been involved with on the side.

Ironically, the last issue of *Mortuary Management* that Greg worked on featured a fiftieth anniversary commemoration of our partnership in which Ron wrote a nice feature, complete with photos from our archives. In retrospect, our partnership worked because whatever needed to be done in our business, one of us was there to focus on that need. Without question, Ron would come up with brilliant ideas of how to better serve the funeral industry, whereas my ten-hour days were spent taking care of the myriad tasks that needed to be done. In fact, many of Ron's ideas caused me to do all the grunt work to bring them to fruition.

I informed Ron of my decision to write about our adventures together, but I didn't expect his response. In the years we have been friends and partners, we never found it necessary to sugar-coat anything we said to each other. In that vein, Ron's reply was "What makes you think that the public would have any interest in what you have to say?" Well, thanks for the vote of confidence, partner. But I figured the proof would be in the pudding. Sadly, Ron didn't see the day that our complete story was published. In August 2013, Ron died of heart-related complications. Nearly 200 friends, family members, fellow yachtsmen, and funeral directors attended a festive memorial service held for him at the Tiburon Yacht Club. There's no doubt that he will be missed by many.

You often hear the expression that "everything in life is timing." If this book had been written much earlier, it probably would not have been well received because of the nature of the subject matter. In order to tell the inside story it's often necessary to be quite graphic, something that the public is much more open to now, at least if television programming is a sign of the times. In the last decade, there have been numerous forensics shows, including *Crossing Jordan*, three versions of *CSI*, *Body of Evidence: From the Case Files of Dayle Hinman*, *North Mission Road*, and *Dr. G: Medical Examiner*, in addition to the Bill Kurtis investigative documentaries *American Justice* and *Cold Case Files*.

CSI has come very close to realistically duplicating some of the things occurring in actual cases. As this show grew in popularity, it was apparent they also grew bolder as to what they were willing to depict with special effects. The show has presented plausible stories in great detail, using special effects for lifelike recreations of people who had lost their lives in some unusual way. They have many detailed shots showing scenes that are a true representation of what we had witnessed over the years. The show's realism is further enhanced because the team uses the proper jargon in conjunction with postmortem examinations. My only question is, where did all these hot-looking babes running around the forensic lab come from, and where were they when I was making calls at the coroner's offices?

In 2007, Ron and Allan commemorated the fiftieth anniversary of their partnership.

You may have surmised from my soliloquies that music and movies have always been my personal opiate, so this might also be an appropriate time for another quote from my favorite film, *Blade Runner*. Rutger Hauer's character, Roy Batty, grabs Harrison Ford's wrist at the last second, saving him from falling off the roof of Los Angeles' Bradbury building. Ford's character, Rick Deckard, can't understand why Roy saved him. Deckard looks at Roy in wonderment because they had just been fighting each other to the death. But Roy was already programmed to die, and in his final moments, he explains, "I've seen things that you people wouldn't believe. Attack ships on fire off the shoulder of Orion. I've watched sea beams glitter in the dark, near the Tanhauser gate. All of these moments will be lost in time . . . like tears in rain." Now that I have committed so many of my memories to this book, there will be no tears lost in the rain from these blue eyes.

Fade to black . . . that's a wrap.

Index

Great Books on the Lighter and Practical Sides of Death

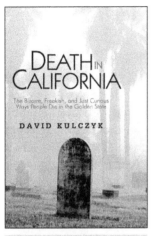

$15.95 ($17.95 Canada)

Death in California
The Bizarre, Freakish, and Just Curious Ways People Die in the Golden State
by David Kulczyk

Death in California chronicles 31 bizarre and grisly true stories, from a jet crashing into a Bay Area kitchen to the actor who discovered the absolutely dumbest way to light a cigarette. A grimly humorous history of hangings, murders, accidents, overdoses, suicides, and fatal stupidity, **Death in California** offers a bizarre, lighthearted, and cheerfully perverse glimpse into California's deadly past. Brutally funny, haunting, and poignant, this zany collection is delightfully weird and enthrallingly human.

$14.95 ($17.95 Canada)

Death for Beginners
Your No-Nonsense, Money-Saving Guide to Planning for the Inevitable
by Karen Jones

Too many Americans don't plan for death, costing their families thousands in unnecessary expenses and immeasurable grief and stress. Humorous, insightful, and relentlessly practical, **Death for Beginners** gives you the tools to quickly plan a funeral that will save your loved ones time, money and worry. Includes easy-to-follow worksheets to help you make smart decisions, checklists to help you do the right thing, clear information, and hundreds of helpful resources.

Hollywood Behind the Scenes
from Quill Driver Books

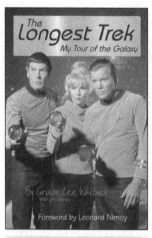

$14.95 ($16.95 Canada)

The Longest Trek
My Tour of the Galaxy
by Grace Lee Whitney

She opened for jazz great Billie Holliday, shared an upper berth with Marilyn Monroe in *Some Like it Hot*, and flirted with Jack Lemmon in *Irma La Douce*, but you know her as Starfleet Yeoman Janice Rand from *Star Trek*. The life of Grace Lee Whitney is a behind-the-scenes story of Hollywood, an untold story of the *Star Trek* world, but above all, it is a story of an awakening, the story of a woman who had to sink to the depths of self-destruction before she could rise to find her true self.

"Personal, moving and powerful ... this is a *Star Trek* book which will transform people's lives." —Leonard Nimoy

$16.95 ($17.95 Canada)

1939
The Making of Six Great Films from Hollywood's Greatest Year
by Charles F. Adams

The films and the culture of the greatest year in movie history are brilliantly explored in the film history **1939: The Making of Six Great Films from Hollywood's Greatest Year**. 1939 profiles the making of six of the most significant films of 1939: *Gone with the Wind, Stagecoach, Mr. Smith Goes to Washington, The Hound of the Baskervilles, The Adventures of Huckleberry Finn* and *The Wizard of Oz*, covering each film from the origins of the script to the finished film's debut and critical reception. *1939* is a book that no movie fan should miss.

Available from bookstores, online bookstores, and QuillDriverBooks.com, or by calling toll-free 1-800-345-4447.

The Wild Side of Life
from Quill Driver Books

$14.95 ($15.95 Canada)

400 Things Cops Know

Street-Smart Lessons from a Veteran Patrolman

by Adam Plantinga

400 Things Cops Know shows police work from the viewpoint of the regular cop on the beat—a profession that can range from rewarding to bizarre to terrifying in one eight-hour shift. Written by a veteran police sergeant, *400 Things Cops Know* takes you into a cop's life of danger, frustration, occasional triumph, and plenty of grindingly hard routine work. In a laconic, no-nonsense, dryly humorous style, Plantinga tells what he's learned from 13 years as a patrolman, from the everyday to the exotic. Sometimes heartbreaking, sometimes hilarious, this is an eye-opening revelation of life on the beat.

$14.95 ($16.95 Canada)

California Fruits, Flakes, and Nuts
True Tales of California Crazies, Crackpots, and Creeps
by David Kulczyk

From insane celebrities to wacky religious cults, if it's weird, it happens in California. A freewheeling catalog of misfits, eccentrics, creeps, criminals and failed dreamers, *California Fruits, Flakes, and Nuts* relates the hilarious and heartbreaking lives of 48 bizarre personalities who exemplify California's well-deserved reputation for nonconformity. It's a side-splitting, shocking, and salacious salute to the people who made California the strangest place on earth.

About the Authors

Allan Abbott grew up in Los Angeles. He entered the funeral business in 1957, delivering flowers to funerals. The funeral service accommodation company he founded with his high school friend, Ron Hast, grew into a full service funeral home. Allan pioneered many innovations in the funeral industry, including inventing the airtray to protect caskets transported by airlines, developing mini-hearses from modified station wagons and other hearse modifications, and offering some of the earliest services to scatter cremated remains by air and at sea. Abbott has participated in the funerals of numerous celebrities, including Marilyn Monroe, Natalie Wood, Clark Gable, Jack Benny, Gary Cooper, and Karen Carpenter. Allan's other business ventures have included providing limousine services for Hollywood celebrities, rentals of cars and mortuary props to movie and television productions, and publishing *Mortuary Management* magazine.

Greg Abbott served for over a decade as managing director of Abbott & Hast Publications, publisher of *Mortuary Management* monthly magazine and *Funeral Monitor* weekly newsletter. He joined the company as news editor while still in high school and gradually took on more responsibilities until he managed the business. In total, Greg spent twenty-two years with the company before changing careers when the business was relocated outside of California. He has a degree in computer science and

currently works in the property management field. His passions include artwork, writing, photography, and backpacking to remote locations with his wife. He is certified as a Wilderness First Responder and volunteers with the city of Monterey as an emergency responder.